**Please quote number and last date stamped
if you wish to renew by post or telephone**

In the Fast Lane

WEST INDIES TOUR 1981

N. N.

In the Fast Lane

WEST INDIES TOUR 1981

Geoff Boycott

ARTHUR BARKER LIMITED   LONDON
A subsidiary of Weidenfeld (Publishers) Limited

ALSO BY GEOFF BOYCOTT

Put to the Test
Opening Up

Published in Great Britain by
Arthur Barker Ltd
91 Clapham High Street
London SW4 7TA

ISBN 0 213 16808 1

Printed in Great Britain by
Butler & Tanner Ltd, Frome and London

Contents

Acknowledgements

The photographs in this book are reproduced by kind permission of the following:

Tony Becca (*Jamaica Daily News*): pages 143(b), 163(b), 177, 179, 189, 195.

Patrick Eagar: front and back endpapers, 55(a), 59, 63, 67, 89(a), 93(b), 101, 105, 107(a), 137(b), 201, 205.

Adrian Murrell (All-Sport Photographic Ltd): frontispiece, 11(b), 24-5, 31, 35, 38, 39(b), 46, 47, 55(b), 73(a), 81, 89(b), 93(a), 107(b), 110-11, 115, 119(b), 123, 124-5(b), 125, 135, 197.

David Rogers (Bob Thomas): 11(a), 39(a), 73(b), 103, 119(a), 124(a), 131, 137(a), 143(a), 145, 147, 151, 155, 158-9, 163(l&a), 165, 167, 173, 183.

AUTHOR'S NOTE

This account of the 1981 tour of the West Indies was not written with the advantage of hindsight, but as a daily record during the course of the tour. Its value therefore lies in the immediacy and accuracy with which those eventful months are recorded.

1

Absent Friends

The tour is only a matter of hours old, and the English players are still blinking in the Caribbean sunshine, but the wry thought occurs to me that reputations will almost certainly be destroyed in the next few months....

That is always the way, no matter how we try to bear in mind that the odds are heavily stacked against us, on account of the conditions and the formidable opposition. West Indies are the best side in the world, having half a dozen of the world's fastest bowlers to choose from and more Test-class batsmen than they need. They have proved it time and time again.

Everybody accepts that at the start of a tour, in fact it is pretty unanimous among the media that we are on a hiding to nothing. They wouldn't back us with Confederate money – and, from a strictly logical and realistic point of view, neither would I.

But it will be different by April, if England have lost Tests and the series. There will be no logic then, no reminders that West Indies are the best, no allowances made at all. People will look at the figures and use them to bury somebody's Test career; there will be the usual hue and cry and the realization, by those who are wise after the event, that of course so-and-so wasn't good enough and should never have been picked in the first place. Everybody will be an expert in retrospect.

Like everyone who has ever played or watched a cricket match I have my own views about the tour party – and I wouldn't have picked quite this squad. As I see it, there are at least three absentees who should have been on the plane with us – but I accept that that's a matter of opinion and that it is the selectors who make the decisions.

What is important to remember – in the sunshine and the relatively relaxed days before the tour really gets under way – is that, give or take an opinion or two, the players in the squad represent the best we have to offer in terms of potential and known performance.

Whatever happens during the series we could not have picked a squad which was obviously, indisputably better. And they will not become bad players between January and April.

So who would I have brought who isn't here? For a start, Phil Edmonds. The bowling needs balance and the squad includes three off-spinners but no slow left-armer; considering there are only two left-handers in the West Indies side, that doesn't make a lot of sense to me. West Indians are known to be the best leg-side batsmen in the world, so – unless the ball turns a lot – off-spinners are going to be negative at best. They will take wickets, because somebody is bound to, but I doubt very much whether they will take them cheaply or decisively.

I know the selectors were anxious to strengthen the batting as much as possible, and there was a doubt about Edmonds's fitness at the end of last season. But there was a big gap between then and the start of the tour; surely it should have been possible to devise a strenuous training programme for Edmonds and test his apparently suspect knee some time before we left? I seem to remember that others had to prove their fitness after being chosen. Perhaps Edmonds's relationships at Middlesex didn't help him. It is an open secret, for instance, that he doesn't get on with Mike Brearley and there is no doubt that Ian Botham leans heavily on Brearley for advice. A train of coincidences, maybe, but I reckon Edmonds was very unlucky not to be selected.

Bob Woolmer is another I would have included on the tour – simply because I reckon he's a very good player. He had an unhappy time with Packer's circus, chiefly because he broke a finger and had the devil's own job playing himself back into form and confidence. Then he was dropped by England after a couple of Test matches at home, and I feel he was discarded too soon. I don't know if his association with Packer went against him and I have no reason to believe it did; my views on Packer are well known, but all that is supposed to have been resolved, and if former Packer players are good enough for England they should be picked on merit.

The choice of Roland Butcher above Bill Athey was something of a surprise – and I'm not saying that because Bill is a Yorkshireman. It just seemed illogical. Athey played well in the one-day internationals, was picked for the Centenary Test, but was then suddenly left out of the tour. If Roland Butcher is a better player he should, presumably, have played ahead of Athey in the Centenary Test....

The selectors get a bit of stick and I reckon they don't always deserve it, but there are times when they lay themselves wide open, and this was one of them. Poor Bill Athey must still be wondering what on earth went wrong – and who could blame him? There are times when the selectors should put their reasons on the line, for the sake of the players and even for their own reputations. Nobody needs a public inquiry, but a bit of straightforward explanation would not go amiss, and players in Athey's situation are entitled to it.

It seems to me that Butcher got the vote partly because he has some familiarity with local conditions, partly because the captain prefers mid-order batsmen who can attack, and partly because, as a Barbadian, he could obviously help in public relations. There is some sense in that, provided always that the player concerned is good enough to demand consideration on merit.

Mike Procter is now available for England, having played for Gloucestershire for twelve years, and I can't think of a good reason for not picking him unless he declared himself unavailable. I talked to him about the situation at a function in London some months ago and he seemed keen enough then on the idea of playing for England. So much so, in fact, that I told Alec Bedser, the chairman of selectors, that it might be worthwhile considering him.

There would almost certainly have been political repercussions if England had picked a white South African. Politics wrecked a tour twelve years ago when South Africa refused to accept Basil d'Oliviera in the England party and no doubt everyone wanted to avoid another controversy which might have caused a turmoil in international cricket.

Ideally, politics and sport should not have to mix, but obviously they do. And if that is the case, there cannot be room for two kinds of racial discrimination. Was Procter left behind because it was politically safer that way? I really don't know, but it will be interesting to see if he is selected for the series against Australia in England. On ability he was obviously worth a place on the Caribbean tour; it is not as though we are exactly overburdened with all-rounders of his calibre.

I have already mentioned that Ian Botham sometimes seeks advice from Mike Brearley and I wonder just how disinterested that advice can be. I do not think anyone could manipulate Botham, but Mike is a shrewd string-puller, a clever politician. And bearing that in mind, I want to get the record straight on how much advice Botham seeks and receives from me.

Before we left England I was asked on TV if I would give Botham the benefit of my advice and my answer was simply that he never asked for it. That was a fact: it was not a dig at Botham. In fact he did ask my advice once – in a one-day international at Headingley when Bob Willis did not play – and it was given readily enough.

The fact that Botham did not seek my advice does not make me like or respect him less. I think Botham is a terrific lad and a great player; as far as I am concerned we get on like a house on fire, and although we are very different people I think that feeling is mutual. What does irritate me is when an interviewer asks whether or not I will give advice, which is a subtle way of suggesting I refuse to help captains out. That is absolute rubbish, and my annoyance at moments like those is directed at the interviewer and not in this case at Ian Botham.

One newspaper blew the story up into a suggestion that there was bad blood between the two of us, and the tour manager Alan Smith even checked with Botham to see what was going on. Botham told him there were no problems between us. It was doubly irritating because I had agreed to go on TV only when the manager asked me to do it as a personal favour. The interviewer said how grateful he was and then seemed to load a question to give a totally unfavourable impression of my attitude.

Ian Botham is a strong-minded individual who may consider that asking my advice is a sign of weakness. If he consults me in public the Press usually pick it out, which may not help. It is up to him, and I don't regard it as a snub or anything like that if he doesn't – but you can only offer advice where it is wanted. If Ian Botham wants my advice on any tour or during any England match he only has to ask.

9

2

Some Sunday...

Antigua is a fair representation of every Englishman's vision of paradise: swaying palm trees, a golden ribbon of beach adjoining our hotel complex, a sea as warm as bathwater and twice as clear.... It might have jumped straight out of a dozen travel brochures – and the Test and County Cricket Board gave us five days there at the start of the tour to acclimatize and get the feel of the Caribbean way of life. As a different generation of gladiators might have said, 'We who are about to die salute you.'

It wasn't all sun, sea and relaxation, of course, but the lads made the most of it while they could. David Gower watched the locals whizzing about on motorized speed-skis, tried one himself and would probably have learned to control it had we stayed on for six months or so; Peter Willey and Mike Gatting suddenly went sartorially berserk in multi-coloured caftans which made the locals look positively conservative; David Bairstow took to a red porkpie hat . . . and Graham Gooch tried underwater alcoholism.

Like several of the players, Gooch went out in a glass-bottomed boat to the beautiful coral reef which rings the island, and tried his hand at snorkelling. Unfortunately for him he swam alongside the boat, and the sight of his snorkel poking out of the water was too much of a temptation – down went a large rum punch and up came Gooch, not quite sure whether he was drowning or having the time of his life.

The fleet was in, in the shape of HMS *Intrepid*, and a few of the lads went aboard for a visit. Bairstow and Graham Stevenson returned, somewhat reluctantly, with tales of draught John Courage. Bruce Forsyth and several English golfers, who were on the island for a pro-am tournament, joined in a beach party, and there were times when business seemed a million miles away.

It never was, of course. We went through our physical training under Bernard Thomas and had nets at the local police ground, where conditions were adequate without being exceptionally good. And already there were ominous teething troubles, especially among the bowlers.

Botham developed a stomach upset and a temperature of 102 degrees which cut his bowling practice to a laughable three overs, Old was confined to bed for a day

Time to relax in Antigua – down to the sea in ships and all that.

The marine life was pretty interesting ... three local specimens, thinly disguised as Mike Gatting, Graham Gooch and John Emburey.

with a stomach disorder, Stevenson was troubled by sore legs and Willis seemed to find it hard to generate any real pace. Only Dilley looked quick in practice, knocking out my off stump to prove it and dining out on the fact for a couple of days. We were already looking at our quicker bowlers and wondering who would be fit enough to put in when it came to the crunch. And the West Indies Test selectors would soon have to sit down and decide which one of their pace attack to leave out.... It was an ironic thought, and one that might have been funny if it were not so ominous.

As well as the fastest bowlers in the world, West Indies also have the slowest lifestyle and that can be a bit maddening at times. Order tea for three o'clock, and it will arrive surely enough – but not necessarily on the right day.

They are still building the new double-decker stand at Antigua's Test ground and seemed perfectly happy that it would be finished on time. But not, one imagines, if they employed the same workman who was labouring gently on building a stand at the police ground. Somebody asked him mischievously if it would be ready for Sunday, and without batting an eyelid he replied, 'Sure man, sure. Perhaps not this Sunday, perhaps not next Sunday, but some Sunday, some Sunday....' You can't argue with that.

The flight from Antigua to Trinidad was by way of a sort of airborne milk train which stopped off at Barbados and St Lucia, took three and a half hours and I swear doubled back on itself at least once. The entry into St Lucia is spectacular if only because the runway pokes out into the sea and incoming flights have to bank unnervingly to approach it from the landward end.

The sea below was magnificently green-blue and so clear that as we banked we could see the bottom, and small ships looked as though they were suspended in mid-air. We made our turn, lost height rapidly and stopped – I am glad to say – about 150 yards from the wet end of the runway. A brief stopover and on to Trinidad.

The Hilton in Port-of-Spain must be one of the world's few major hotels which is built upside down. It is perched on a hillside overlooking the city and approached by a steep winding road which takes you to the reception area – the top floor. From there you take the life *down* to your room, and the nearer the ground you go, the higher the number of the floor. So if you are the third floor you are above somebody on the fourth floor. Still with me? To put it another way, if you want to reach the tennis courts beneath the hotel, you get into the lift at reception and go down to the twelfth floor. Simple really, once you escape the suspicion that you really should be playing tennis on the roof....

Beneath and in front of the hotel is the Savannah, a huge parkland area which houses among other things a zoo and a private cemetery. Since it has recently become part of a new one-way traffic system, it is probably the world's biggest traffic island, too.

We practised at the Fatima College ground, driving each day past the Roxy cinema which was showing *Phantasm*, with a lurid poster which claimed, 'If this one doesn't scare you, you're already dead.' It is a thought we may return to. The pitch was better than the one in Antigua with a more even bounce and we used bowlers in pairs from each end to give the maximum opportunity for match practice. Botham had shaken off a strained hamstring and was able to bowl, but he had still had very little in the way of practice and, frankly, his lack of preparation worries me. He is one of the few great players we have, and it's imperative he should be fit and sharp as quickly as possible.

3

Battle Lines

Alan Smith told us at the outset of the tour that, when he was called upon to give a speech, his theme, as tour manager, would be that we had come to the Caribbean to make friends. That might sound a bit trite, but it was sensible and fair enough. Only thing is – we wondered if anyone had mentioned it to Messrs Holding, Croft, Clarke, Garner, Marshall, Roberts. . . . Perhaps if we made friends off the field they could be persuaded to make a few *on* it!

It was absolutely essential to face facts as they were and not kid ourselves with any fanciful ideas. It was going to be tough, really tough, and if we forgot that for a moment we were heading for trouble. That is why I was not too impressed with the theory that the West Indies players would be tired after a tour in Pakistan, the arduous culmination of eighteen months' solid Test cricket.

Soon after our arrival, news began filtering through of their performances in island matches. Holding was supposed to have a shoulder injury, yet he took five wickets for Jamaica against Trinidad; Garner was said to have lost some twenty-five pounds in weight during the Pakistan tour, but he took five wickets for Barbados on the day we arrived; Roberts and Clarke took six wickets each.

Viv Richards made 168 not out against Trinidad and followed that with 106 against Jamaica, Haynes made 160 for Barbados, and Lloyd and Kallicharran, arriving late from the tour, both made centuries. In fact, practically all the Test players made a lot of runs or took wickets in the Shell Shield matches – and that didn't look like post-tour tiredness to me. It sounded as though they were fit and rarin' to go.

West Indies do not have a good record at home against England, and Ian Botham frequently used that as point in our favour. Fair enough, we needed all the reassurances we could get. But the fact is that West Indies have never had a side as professional and ruthless as this one; we simply can't kid ourselves that they are Calypso cricketers who would buckle under pressure. That might have been the case once – Tony Greig had that in mind when he made his infamous remarks about 'grovelling', and the West Indies captain Clive Lloyd had conceded his side used to lack some professional steel.

But they have learned a lot, playing Packer cricket and in the day-to-day competitiveness of English county cricket. They know how to buckle down and graft when they have to, and it is sheer pie in the sky to imagine they will fold mentally at the first sign of trouble. West Indies now have professional hardness to go with their amazing natural ability, and in that respect the history books are no longer relevant.

Botham's attitude and influence is reflected in the choice of players like Butcher, Gatting and Gower – attacking mid-order batsmen who could snatch us a win, he believes, by taking the fight to the West Indies. It's a fine battle-cry, an heroic attitude if you like – but then so was the charge of the Light Brigade.

We are like two armies squaring up for a series of battles. West Indies have a massive advantage in heavy armour and artillery; we have experience and subtlety. We should be thinking in terms of outflanking and outmanoeuvring them, not smashing into them headlong; we must use tactics and think out our strategy rather than go over the top and hope for the best. That is the unromantic reality of the situation.

So how can we go about beating them, which is my aim as much as anybody else's? Well, my experience on two previous Caribbean tours might give a clue. And let's dismiss straight away the element of luck: we will need it and it just might run for us, but we cannot rely on it, so it cannot be part of our plans.

In 1968 the West Indies were basically a better side than we were, but in Test after Test we frustrated them, we gritted it through when they knew they should have been beating us, we refused to be bowled out. In the fourth Test in Trinidad Garby Sobers declared and left us no more than a championship total to chase in terms of time and runs. And that was an act of pure frustration, the error of a man and a side who had been driven to distraction. We won the match by batting as purposefully as we had throughout the series – a victory for the right strategy, extended over a whole series, against a side who on paper should have had the series sewn up.

We were the underdogs again in 1974, and on that tour West Indies screwed themselves up not through frustration but through over-confidence. They had beaten us by an innings in the last Test in England – goodbye Illingworth – and they beat us by an innings in the first Test of the tour in Trinidad. Not surprisingly, perhaps, they had a pretty low opinion of us and reckoned it was going to be easy.

That series saw the emergence of Lawrence Rowe, who seemed to score a million runs every time he took a bat in his hands. In fact they batted in so much depth that their two greatest players, Sobers and Kanhai, hardly ever got to the wicket. And yet they still couldn't quite polish us off.

Dennis Amiss scored a double hundred in the second Test in Jamaica and we hung on by the skin of our teeth when logically they should have beaten us with a day to spare. In Barbados, when we should have lost again, Keith Fletcher made a century in the second innings – so after three Tests we should have been three down but had lost only one. And it was significant that determined batting rather than flamboyant attack had saved us twice.

15

We earned an honourable draw in Guyana, then went to Trinidad which is usually a result pitch. And when they came under pressure for the first time – in conditions which we could exploit – Sobers and Kanhai didn't look like batsmen. They had scarcely been to the wicket, and in a low-scoring match, with men round the bat, their lack of sharpness told. They paid the price for the complacency and over-confidence bred by the belief – no, the certain knowledge – that they should have won three Tests handsomely.

So I reckon we have to frustrate West Indies or make them over-confident – and you can't exactly plan to fill the opposition with confidence. . . . So it's clear to me that our strategy on this tour should be to frustrate.

That means we have to be prepared to bat and bat and bat again. As I said at one of our first team meetings before leaving England, our trouble is that we get out with dismal regularity on the first day, and from then on it is no contest – we are fighting just to save a Test. OK, we may get out to aggressive strokes, but I don't call that positive cricket; it's like making three flashy moves at chess, losing your queen and spending the rest of the game desperately trying to save the king from checkmate.

On a pitch of normal Test-match quality we must set our stall out to bat for at least a day and a half and make 300 to 350 in the process. We have to accept we will not score as quickly as West Indies for two important reasons – the quality of their bowling and the poverty of their over rate. They have a battery of world-class bowlers delivering no more than twelve overs an hour, and even the best batsmen in the world are not going to smash the ball about in those circumstances. That is reality.

It is not an exciting philosophy, of course, and it doesn't sound as appealing to the media as the gung-ho attitude, with talk about positive cricket and taking the fight to the enemy. Like a boxing match, the pre-fight publicity may promise a nose-to-nose confrontation with both men slugging it out, but the guy who gets knocked out in the first round has got his strategy wrong somewhere.

I am not being defeatist, just realistic. Of course we must be ready to take advantage of any situation in the Test matches; if we do get on top we must rub it in because I doubt whether we will get too many opportunities. But I am sure that our basic strategy should be cautious and down-to-earth because we are basically not equipped to play West Indies at their own game. That is the truth as I see it, and if it is unpalatable compared to notions of going over the top with a swagger-stick, well, the truth often is.

We were discussing the best way to face bouncers in the series and Graham Stevenson, pretty typically, came up with his own wry formula. 'Flat on your face, mate, and preferably at square-leg. . . .' As realism goes, it provoked a grim sort of laughter.

4

Food for Thought

Malcolm Marshall didn't take long to announce himself in the first match of the tour against a young President's XI. Three deliveries, in fact, and then the sort of bowling performance to remind us what we were up against in the Tests. It certainly was food for thought.

The ground at Pointe-a-Pierre is about thirty-five miles from Port-of-Spain, which meant an early start and a tiring journey through the cane fields, usually on the end of a line of traffic with every driver playing a private calypso on his horn. The match was partly sponsored by Texaco and was played at their ground, which is ringed by palm trees on one side and the futuristic oil refinery on the other. Now we know what money smells like. . . .

We desperately needed a good pitch for our first match, and it didn't look too promising. Heavy rain had penetrated the covers, and the pitch was damp at one end and scarred along its length; it was clear that the side winning the toss would put the opposition in – and they did.

Graham Stevenson was due to play, but one look at the pitch insisted we would be better off with an extra spinner and fortunately Geoff Miller had travelled with us as twelfth man. He had to send back to the hotel for his batting gear – and the quicker the better because it looked as though it might be wanted pretty smartly! The President's XI included Marshall and Hartley Alleyne, a fast bowler who would probably get into most Test sides, so we knew we would have our hands full; Kenny Barrington reckoned 150 wouldn't be a bad first innings score.

Even that looked a long, long way off after the first over. Marshall's first delivery reared off a length, his second rapped Rose on the fingers and his third was pushed into the hands of silly-mid-on. The ball took a piece out of the pitch each time, three ominous black circles in the straw-coloured surface. We feared the worst.

As it turned out it wasn't too bad. The pitch dried quickly under a hot sun and within an hour the extravagant lift had disappeared; it was the sort of pitch you could bat on with care – and David Gower surprised a lot of people with his deliberate, down-to-earth approach. For a difficult first hour he was the soul of discretion; I outscored him quite comfortably, and even that didn't seem to worry him in the least!

He went on to make 187, and his innings was hailed in some quarters as the emergence of a new, cool-headed Gower with a massive sense of responsibility and a less dashing approach. But that was to overlook the fact that he was dropped six times – the first when he had made only 16 – and the chances were the direct result of his old habits of flashing impetuously outside the off stump.

That proved to me, big score or not, that David Gower hasn't changed his spots yet. Many people want him to curb his shots and settle at the crease, but I don't think he will ever change, basically because he doesn't want to. He has built a reputation and won Test caps by playing the way he wants, and I don't think anyone will change him fundamentally. Why should they? As long as he keeps producing the goods – and that's the important thing – there is no reason for me or anybody else to put him down.

Gower will have moments of great elation and times of near despair. There are times watching from the other end when you feel he is almost trying to get out, determined to play every colourful shot in the book. He seems to have a sort of self-destructive element in his make-up – and there was little in his innings at Pointe-a-Pierre, long and valuable though it was, to alter that impression.

A drastically changed David Gower? Well, you don't get dropped six times playing safety shots. Gower may yet play an innings to prove that he can be restrained and totally controlled over a long period, but this wasn't it.

That is not necessarily a criticism, and it might be that Gower was playing to a plan of his own. This being his first knock of the tour, he might have set out purposefully to explore his strokes and accept the mistakes which refresh one's memory after four months away from competitive cricket. That is important because certain aspects of your game become habit and are done automatically; after a long lay-off it is easy to become rusty and you have to remind yourself of the possibilities and the pitfalls in every shot. So perhaps this innings was all part of Gower's long-term plan to get back in the groove; either way, the time spent in the middle can have done him no harm at all.

Mike Gatting played beautifully for his 94 in the first innings, even allowing for the fact that the spinners were very tired and a bit wayward by the time he got in. He swept, pulled and drove very fluently right off the middle of the bat: the best shots of the day in many respects. But it was noticeable that he didn't exactly take the quicker bowlers to pieces; when they came on it was a very different game.

Roland Butcher was under a lot of pressure, albeit rather different from the pressures which most of the team face. Everybody wanted him to do well, not least the West Indian crowd who greeted him as something of a returning hero. They wanted Butcher to succeed and England to lose. He timed the ball beautifully and it's an extraordinary fact that although he has lived and played in England for most of his life, he still has that unmistakable West Indian feel about his batting, something totally basic to his style and attitude. We took bets in the dressing-room on how long it would be before he hit the off-spinner over the top – and sure enough he soon unleashed a huge six. Very calypso.

18

Botham, being Botham, had to try and go one better. We knew as soon as he went in that he would try to hit the ball higher, harder and further than Butcher – and he soon produced one amazing shot which bore out our theory. It was supposed to go over wide long-on, and had he connected properly, there is no doubt that it would have cleared the boundary, the fence and the storage tanks ... but he got an inside edge instead and it whistled through mid-wicket for four before any of the fielders moved! (Botham said later that he was looking to hit the ball over extra cover, which proves at least that he has an imagination.)

The young West Indies' most impressive bowler apart from Marshall was a strikingly tall and angular off-spinner called Roger Harper. He was only seventeen, still at school doing A-levels in maths and physics, and he clearly has a potentially bright future in the game. His control was generally sound and his exceptional height – he stood around 6 ft 3 ins – meant he could bounce the ball awkwardly. That, plus some thoughtful variation and the ability to spin the ball hard, makes him a player we are bound to hear more of in the future. He is from Guyana, so, perhaps not surprisingly, there is an obvious Lance Gibbs influence in his action.

I was also quite impressed with Alston Daniel, a promising youngster from Tobago who bowled 'chinamen' with a great deal of control. He was very nervous, so much so that it took him a long time to pluck up the courage to slip in a wrong 'un, but he could be well pleased with his performance in his first big match under scrutiny.

We scored 330 for two off 106 overs on the first day but it was strikingly significant that very few of our runs came off the quick bowlers. Marshall finished with one for 21 off 14 overs, Alleyne with none for 43 off 19, so we did not exactly paralyse them – and that is an omen as far as the Test series is concerned.

Marshall is probably the best of the West Indies Test bowlers in terms of accuracy and variation. He went round the wicket against me for a couple of overs but then reverted to an orthodox attack – chiefly, I suspect, because that is the way he prefers to bowl. It might be different in the Tests when he is bowling under different orders and the object of the exercise is to hit the batsman as much as the wickets!

Multiply Marshall by three or four, and you have an idea of what we are up against in Test cricket. He conceded 1·5 runs an over at Point-a-Pierre, and if West Indies bowl around twelve overs an hour in the Tests we can expect something like seventy-two overs in the day. That means we should score just over 100!

It was also interesting to see how ill-at-ease the young West Indians were against our spinners. They seemed to play the quicker bowlers with ease but lacked any conviction or confidence under pressure against the turning ball. Thelston Paine of Barbados came with a high reputation, but struggled desperately against the spinners until Bairstow made a superb stumping when Paine got a ball which turned and bounced.

The only two who really looked impressive against the spinners were Alleyne and Jeff Dujon. Alleyne probably thought it was his birthday since he doesn't get much of a chance to bat for Barbados, and Dujon was the one player who looked to get down the pitch against the off-spinners, get outside the line of the ball and whip it on the leg side. He made an unbeaten 105 with the help of some missed catches, and while he was in the scoreboard fairly rattled along. We often looked a very modest attack.

Our fielding suffered, too, perhaps because, apart from his stumping of Paine, Bairstow had an unhappy day behind the stumps. The wicket-keeper is at the centre of the wheel, and Bairstow can be quite an inspiration, cajoling and encouraging fielders, but he missed two stumpings and became very deflated. His dejection communicated itself to the fielders, catches went down and we often approached the ball timidly on a rough outfield so that singles became twos. It was a ragged sort of performance.

I was very concerned with the impact – or lack of it – made by Chris Old. On slower, less responsive pitches he looks as though he might provide cannon-fodder for the likes of Richards and Greenidge; I can see them plonking a foot down the pitch and smashing him back over his head. We discussed it and I suggested he cut his pace and try to bowl a Bob Appleyard type of cutter, making the odd delivery go straight on with his natural outswinging action. Old agreed he would have to do something if he was to have a real role on the tour and I know he began to practise off-cutters in the nets. His problem is not a condemnation of Old, who is one of the finest seam bowlers in England; it's just a consequence of the particular conditions we can expect to face in the West Indies.

Graham Dilley has the extra pace, but the pitch was slow and he bowled well within himself. He didn't pull up any trees, but it was early days and I reserved my judgement on how he would fare; he is learning all the time.

Harper got me out for 87 in both innings, but I felt I played the spinners very comfortably. In the first innings he beat me with one that bounced, hit the inside of my right arm and scuttled on to the stumps like a rabbit bolting for home; in the second innings I felt I made an elementary error in my thinking.

I was striking the ball cleanly and hard, but the spinners dropped their fields deeper and I kept hitting good shots straight at the fielders instead of finding the gaps. I felt runs were bound to come and I didn't alter my game, which was a mistake because I became frustrated despite myself.

What I should have done in those circumstances, when shot after shot went straight to fielders, was to go down the pitch and play to mid-on or mid-off for singles; or I might have altered my guard to leg stump and given myself more room – I normally take middle stump to the off-spinner. Either way, I should have done something different instead of constantly playing the ball to the fielders.

In the end I tried to hit Harper over the top, lifted my head a bit and got an inside edge on to the stumps via a pad. Coincidentally, 87 is the unlucky number in Australia – just as 111 is regarded with suspicion by the English – because it is 13 from a century. I don't believe in superstitions like that – and I suppose I proved it twice in this match!

Marshall tells us that the ball will seam in the West Indies when the clouds fill in, and he proved that with a really professional spell during which he dismissed Rose and Bairstow in four deliveries. Rose made runs in his second innings but never really looked in; he seemed over-anxious to have a go at anything well up or short outside the off stump, but, most important, he spent time at the wicket – which is vital at this stage of the tour.

We batted to lunch on the last day and left the West Indies side four hours to get 372. I don't think either side expected to win at that stage – in fact Botham stressed the need to keep concentrating even if it got a bit tedious for the rest of the day – but I suspect the young President's side were still anxious to impress the selectors. They didn't harbour any thoughts of losing, but in no time they were four or five wickets down and the pressure was on them.

Miller and Willey bowled well and interestingly enough to English-type field placings. West Indians tend to have five men on the off-side when spinners are on; we bowl straighter with men in bat-pad positions and only three men on the off-side. Miller asked me at the nets if I thought he should alter his field placings for West Indian conditions, and I advised him to try the way he knew best first. He could always experiment if it didn't work out. We got a couple of batsmen out because they were trying to hit through the 'vacant' off side, and they slowly collapsed under pressure.

It was interesting to see the improvement in Peter Willey's bowling in the second innings, largely because he altered his grip and concentrated his action on getting more height and bounce, which is the West Indian way.

We won by 190 runs, and Miller picked up the man of the match award, which wasn't bad going for a player who arrived at the ground four days earlier expecting to serve a few drinks and then put his feet up....

5

Down on the Farm

'Another day in bloody paradise' read the slogan on one of the islands' more popular T-shirts. And after three frustrating days on St Vincent we knew exactly what it meant. The plans so carefully laid on paper to prepare us for the first one-day international of the tour slowly began to disintegrate.

For a start, the nets at the compact little ground, bordered by the airstrip on one side and the sea on the other, were hopeless as far as batting practice was concerned. We played on an old pitch on the square, one which had obviously been watered because it was wet and there had been no rain to speak of just before we arrived. Rose tried his luck and was repeatedly hit on the hands by balls which lifted awkwardly; nobody else risked it.

The following day the pitch had dried but the bounce was still unpredictable: one delivery kept low and the next lifted from worn patches. Rose was the guinea pig again but gave it up as a bad job; Gower came out of the net after a few knocks; nobody stayed in long because the ball was always likely to stand up, even with the bowlers at half pace. The players were angry and disappointed because we needed meaningful practice on good surfaces and against quick bowling – and there simply wasn't any chance of that.

I was not picked to play in the scheduled four-day match against Windward Islands, and there was some thought of packing me off to Trinidad in search of a proper net. It's not too bad for bowlers because they can get loose and find a rhythm on almost any surface, but everyone was very frustrated.

To make matters worse, if anything could, it rained. Not just a drop or a shower but three clammy inches in forty-eight hours, teeming out of a slate-grey sky through a mist which obliterated islands clearly visible a few hours before. Whatever happened to the sun-kissed Caribbean? And the fact is that there's an awful lot more to do at home than there is on St Vincent when it rains.

Trapped in the hotel watching the weather, with relatively little opportunity of getting out, no television worth watching, no theatre, no decent cinema ... the lads were bored to tears. Everybody seemed to stalk round the hotel with a book under his arm, the card sharps played until they couldn't face another hand, and the Scrabblers ran out of words. The evenings became a mournful drink at the bar, dinner and then early to bed with yet another book. We felt terribly stale.

When the weather brightened for a while a group of us played hard-court tennis – Rose, Butcher, Downton, Emburey, Gooch and myself – and some of the lads visited the picturesque Young Island for sightseeing and snorkelling. We were fortunate in that our hotel was superbly sited on the bay and very well run; the food was good and the staff couldn't do enough for us. In any other circumstances it might have been idyllic, with the beautiful white yachts bobbing on the sea and the green-topped islands in the distance, but we felt like prisoners, fretting because we knew we were wasting precious time.

The weather finally relented, and our management wisely asked the Windward Islands to scrap the four-day match altogether and play a couple of limited-overs matches. The first one was delayed by overnight rain and played over only forty overs a side, but that was better than nothing – and two one-day matches would give us an opportunity to involve more players.

Windwards do not have any real quick bowlers, but poor Rose collected his second disaster of the tour. He was out for one to a delivery from Winston Davis which left him late – probably the best ball of the day and just the sort of delivery Rose was hoping to avoid in his present form. The left-arm seamer Joseph Jack tested Butcher with a few short-pitched deliveries, and he played them with characteristic pulls and hooks in a nice innings.

Botham, of course, made his mark. Not just by playing well for 31, but by getting out to the sort of delayed-action decision which had the boys in the pavilion falling about. He went down the pitch to thump the off-spinner Stanley Hinds, missed and was stumped despite a floundering attempt to regain his ground.

Botham took a sidelong glance at the square-leg umpire, who had already given him out but was now standing with his hands by his side. So Botham picked up the bails, considerately helped the wicket-keeper to set the stumps again and was innocently preparing to resume his innings when the umpire galloped up and told him he had to go. Hysterics in the England dressing-room!

Paul Downton almost finished up in hospital after his first innings of the tour. Playing forward to a short-pitched delivery which bounced alarmingly, he saw it late and lost his balance and his helmet in an undignified scramble to get out of the way. An unnerving sort of start, but Downton just brushed himself down and played a sensible, competent little innings, hitting the ball through the gaps well. He finished with 23 not out and might have made more had the pitch and the outfield been quicker.

We finished with 166 for nine and won by 16 runs after a professional performance in the field, despite obvious signs of rustiness. Willis's first delivery floated towards Gower at point and Dilley let a head-high full-toss slip out early on, but they both settled into a sound if unspectacular groove backed by good field placing and some polished fielding considering some of the players had been out of competitive action for so long.

England practice, West Indies style: a pause at St Vincent for Geoff Miller, Chris Old, David Bairstow, Kenny Barrington and myself, plus a few bowlers and fielders.

Stevenson spent his first day in the field and began to look even redder than usual; Dilley said his legs felt like lead but still ran in really well. England's biggest jolt was the loss of Willis, who twisted his left knee – the one which gave him so much trouble in Australia in 1974-5 – and had to leave the field as a precaution after bowling only seven overs. All this with the first one-day international only four days away. . . .

Windwards started well and looked for a while as though they were going to win with quite a few wickets in hand; at least, I think they thought so themselves. But they had neither the mental make-up nor the expertise to pace themselves to have a real chance of victory; they lost momentum and wickets and suddenly wanted eight an over to win. Faced with our limited-overs experience, that was well beyond them.

The predicament which we faced on that weekend – with practice facilities, inevitable strains and even the weather going against us – underlined my belief that we had got our selection pattern wrong early on the tour. It is difficult to foresee every problem which might crop up, and that convinces me even more that those players most likely to play in the Tests should have played in the first match at Pointe-a-Pierre.

It is all very well saying that every player must be given a chance and that all opportunities are equal. But it is a simple fact that in any tour party, some are more equal than others – and the nucleus of the Test side must be given match preference in order to get fit and sharp.

Instead we had a situation where the scheduled four-day match was abandoned and where Gooch, Willis and Emburey – all certainties for the first Test if fit – were playing their first matches of the tour, three days before facing the full West Indies side. It does not make sense to me and we would at least have cut our losses had they played in the first game.

That is not a new philosophy as far as I am concerned, for I put it forward in Australia on the last two winter tours and was overruled, then as now, by our management policy. The best-laid plans on paper can be ruined by events on tour and although it gives me no pleasure to say I told you so – well, I did.

I desperately needed a hit, bad weather or not, so I fixed up a bit of practice on the day before the forty-over match. And anyone who saw it would have been totally convinced that the English are a bit mad. . . .

The pitch was a slab of concrete in a field adjoining the airstrip, the stumps were an old car tyre propped on a couple of wooden planks, the bowlers – perhaps not quite as incongruous as the rest of the set-up – were Ken Barrington and A. C. Smith. The fielders, most of them at least, were straight out of *Animal Farm*. A group of rather bored-looking cows patrolled mid-wicket, backed up by a distinctly unwelcoming rubbish tip; half a dozen pigs waited for the late-cut at third-man; cover and fine-leg were left to the tethered goats. Dotted between them were half a dozen local schoolgirls. . . .

I went back the following day with Old, Bairstow and Miller but somehow it

wasn't the same. The pigs had wandered off and the cows had strayed into the deep
– convinced, probably, that it wasn't much fun fielding for this Boycott feller. But
the goats turned up as usual, pressed into service by the fact that they were tethered
at mid-on and mid-off. The lads weren't all that keen on fielding, either, perhaps
because when they plunged a hand into the outfield they were never quite sure
what they would come up with!

Graham Stevenson and Peter Willey joined the expedition next day, and although
the surroundings were incongruous – putting it mildly – the concrete surface
certainly offered better batting practice than the nets. Poor Dilley had tried to bowl
off a normal run and at a decent pace in them and the captain had given him a flea
in his ear! But it would have been easy for somebody to get hurt.

Our outfielders turned up as usual, including the biggest black pig you have ever
seen. The cows weren't up to much as fielders go and developed a habit of moving
behind the bowler's arm, much to the annoyance of Stevenson. 'Sit *down*,' he
bellowed. 'Where the 'ell do you think you are – Bradford?'

The local kids raced about the field and into the undergrowth after the ball and
a couple of them helped out as bowlers. It's quite extraordinary how naturally they
play, even at a very young age. One turned out to be a leg-spinner and bowled quite
well – which was a feat considering he was wearing patent leather high-heeled
boots!

It would have been a great laugh had it not been for the fact that this was
supposed to be practice for facing the fastest bowlers in the world. I cannot imagine
any touring team being subjected to this sort of nonsense, certainly not in England;
there would be hell to pay. We made the best of a bad job, but it was laughable
preparation.

The second one-day match provided useful practice, even though the opposition
was not top class. At least it got players involved again – and the fact that we lost
the toss meant we had an opportunity to chase a total.

The pitch was so low and slow that bowlers were able to keep the scoring down
simply by bowling straight and a full length. It is almost impossible to strike the
ball with really effective power in those circumstances, and the batsman has either
to wait for a loose delivery or have a slog.

The Windwards' left-hander Lancelot John made 58 out of their total of 183, not
because he was a particularly good player but because our bowlers tried to bowl at
his off stump and inadvertently gave him room to play shots. Had they gone round
the wicket and bowled straight I doubt he would have scored nearly as many. But
we bowled professionally and although they had wickets in hand Windwards never
dominated or looked like making a really big score; their inability to force the pace
led to quite a few hair-raising moments between the wickets and if we had hit the
stumps from the field we would have cleaned them up cheaply.

Gooch was given the opportunity to have a bowl, which was important since he
may be our safety valve in the bigger matches. It paid off, and he was not only

named Man of the Match but Best Bowler too. It's not often he picks up a couple of awards like that.

From a purely professional viewpoint I was impressed by how quickly their bowlers had learned from ours. They soon did away with slips and bowled very straight to negative field placings, which was the right way but not necessarily the one they would naturally adopt. It took us quite a while to gain our momentum because we could only force straight half-volleys or yorkers to mid-on and mid-off, and had their second-string bowlers been better, it would have been a much tighter game.

Gooch is a very powerful player who hits the ball formidably hard from the middle of the bat, but even he was thumping shots which only trickled to fielders. He finally tried to hit the leg-spinner over mid-off – a shot which calls for a very good pitch – and was caught. A victim of his own desire to push the score along quickly.

Willey was sent in for a hit and played well, Stevenson did the same after I told him to have a look at the bowling before he tried to thump the leather off the ball. Because he is such a fine hitter, people expect Stevenson to clatter the bowling from the start and I think he sometimes feels he has a responsibility to respond, but it is not always possible. Like everybody else, there are times when he needs to take stock of the bowling before he lets himself go, and if he would bear that in mind I reckon he would have fewer failures, because he has such a good eye. I like batting with Stevo because I think I help calm him down.

We won comfortably enough, even though there was a bit of a tremor when we lost Rose and then Gower. Windwards obviously felt they had a chance then, but we had strong batsmen to come and I felt established and able to pick off the ones and twos. That's important because it keeps the score moving, and even five an over isn't out of reach. The danger is that you get two new batsmen at the crease, for then the target can creep away from you.

Another big point in our favour was that the lads coming in were quick between the wickets, so they could run my singles as well as belting the ball about themselves. The field was constantly on the move and when you have nine men switching position it's practically impossible to get them all in the right place at the right time.

I finished with 85 and was pleased with the way I played. Not having the power of some of the other players, on slow pitches I have to look for ones and twos and I felt I was moving with good rhythm.

Brian Rose was over-anxious, trying to whack the ball too hard, and got out for three. He was no doubt seen as our number three in the Tests and the selectors have a problem now. Do they give him another chance in the four-day match in Trinidad or perhaps cut their losses and let his likely replacement have a go?

6

Angles and Tangles

The entire population of St Vincent, give or take a Vincentian or two, could be housed in Wembley stadium. The first one-day international was their Cup Final, Horse of the Year Show and World Heavyweight Championship fight rolled into one – the biggest sporting event in their history – and I reckon everyone on the island turned up for the match.

At least, it seemed that way. They were queuing outside the ground long before the gates opened, long colourful snakes of spectators jostling for position, falling over their picnic lunches and deafening everyone with their inevitable transistor radios. The ground, flanked by the single airstrip on one side and threatening to tip into the sea on the other, was surrounded by a twelve-foot breezeblock wall with rusting strands of barbed wire and broken glass on the top, but that seemed to be designed to keep spectators in rather than out. Long before the first delivery, the crowd became impatient and began spilling over the wall, much to the amusement of their mates inside and the chagrin of the local police who made a token attempt to stem the flow and then quietly turned a blind eye.

The stands were full, the grassed areas were full, the rooftops and walls were dotted with figures risking a fate far more painful than mere prosecution. A ship had anchored in the bay, close enough to look as though it was in the car park, and two figures scaled the mast, from where they enjoyed a free view all day long. The island declared a public holiday for the match – if you can't beat 'em, join 'em – and the local water board workers also went on strike, which simply meant the locals had nothing to put in their rum except ice and more rum. Quite an atmosphere.

I felt we had a really good chance of winning, not least because Viv Richards went down with sinus trouble and was unavailable to West Indies. Viv was the vital factor in our one-day matches against West Indies in Australia the previous winter and obviously has a big psychological affect on both sides: we never underestimate his incredible ability and it was quite possible that without him West Indies would feel apprehensive. World-class players can dominate their own team as much as the opposition.

Gordon Greenidge was not selected either, and it seemed that their absence, plus a low, slow pitch, must work strongly in our favour. If we could get them in first I felt they, as men in form, would be thinking in terms of 200 plus - and we suspected it would be a low-scoring game on this pitch. Just the opportunity to frustrate them.

There was some speculation about the make-up of their fast-bowling attack, but I knew Clive Lloyd would keep faith with the quartet who had seen him through so many Test matches. Sure enough they plumped for Holding, Roberts, Croft and Garner - a pretty straightforward choice considering that Clarke had been suspended by the West Indies Board after a report on his brick-throwing incident in Pakistan.

Had he been available, Lloyd's choice might have been that much more difficult, so to some extent his suspension for a fortnight was something of a blessing. A cynical thought, perhaps, and it was good to see that the world champions had accepted their responsibility to set standards. No doubt Clarke was provoked, but there is always provocation for players on the boundary these days.

The pitch was the same one on which we had played the two one-day matches against Windwards, except that it had been watered to bind it together. There was a bit of damp in it, and when Ian Botham asked what I thought I had no hesitation in agreeing that we should put them in. We did - and it couldn't have worked out better.

Just as we suspected, West Indies played like men who have scored quite a few runs recently - and with an extravagant disregard for the state of the pitch and the ability of our bowlers to use it. They played right from the start as though they had been in for a fortnight, batsman after batsman getting out going for good-pitch shots. Bacchus tried to pull Old and holed out tamely to Stevenson at mid-on, Lloyd tried to hit Stevenson on the up and was snapped up by Willey at backward point, Kallicharran yorked himself attacking Emburey, and even Haynes got himself out after a sparkling start.

He was in great form, charging Old and belting him straight 'over the top' as though he was an off-spinner, but like the rest he was determined to play his shots come what may, and when he charged Stevenson, Emburey took a good catch at square-leg. All their in-form batsmen wanted to smash the ball around, just as we had hoped.

The pitch turned and I was surprised that West Indies slavishly used their left-handers, Kallicharran, Lloyd and Gomes, at numbers four, five and six. It was a thoughtless tactic against our off-spinners, and Gomes, for instance, never looked like making a run; he could have been out half a dozen times before Willey put him out of his misery. A bit of thought would surely have persuaded Lloyd to split his left-handers up, but we weren't complaining.

West Indies were baled out to a great extent by Mattis, who batted at three and made 62 before I ran him out to finish their innings. He played very well - correct, composed and steady, even when others were flinging their wickets away, and very straight against the off-spinners - just as he had when we first saw him at Pointe-a-

Picturesque and packed, the St Vincent ground during the one-day international.

Climbing room only for some of the thousands who filled the St Vincent ground.

Pierre. The fact that he was making his international debut and was anxious to establish himself probably helped his mental approach, but in any event West Indies would have been in hopeless trouble without him. As it was, a total of 127 was even lower than we had hoped. We were delighted.

All the bowlers had bowled well, even if Botham had a spell where he tried to blast West Indies out and lost much of his accuracy. A damp pitch and a streaky four by Haynes early in his innings were like a red rag to 'Both': he tried to dig some deliveries in short, and out here every batsman hooks.

Just before we went out I spoke to David Bairstow, still a bit apprehensive after a rusty start to the tour, still dwelling to some extent on three missed stumpings in previous matches. Bairstow is nobody's fool, he doesn't need telling when he makes mistakes behind the stumps – and he had worked really hard on his game after those early slips.

When practice pitches were too bad for us to use, because the ball turned and jumped, Bairstow would go out with the spinners and face delivery after delivery. Kenny Barrington batted, playing some and deliberately missing others on both sides of the bat, while Bairstow concentrated and sweated and strained to get it right. But he was still a bit unsure of himself before West Indies went in to bat.

'Everybody has strong points and weaknesses,' I told him, 'and it's too easy to dwell on mistakes. You may not be a wicket-keeper in the classic mould but you have qualities which others will never have. You take brilliant catches standing back, you lift and inspire the team, you have character and the sort of acknowledged ability which makes you England's first-choice wicket-keeper. And don't you forget it!

'For sixteen years there has been somebody trying to take my place in the England team. No doubt they will succeed in the end; I have always been aware that I am under pressure. But popular or not, I have kept my place on the strength of performance – and if you perform well Downton or anyone else will have to wait. Be positive and believe in yourself, otherwise you will start to doubt your own ability, and that is the beginning of the end.'

Bairstow kept wicket expertly, made a great leg-side stumping to dismiss Roberts off Gooch and then batted sensibly. I was proud of him. And of Stevenson, who was assured of his place after Dilley went down with a stomach upset shortly before the match and bowled a very fine line and length. Old bowled beautifully, in fact all our bowlers did just what was expected of them; our performance in the field was top class.

But then we had to bat. Gooch expressed what we were all thinking when he said the first ten overs of the new ball would be vital; if we could battle through that we would win, because the target was only two an over plus a few here and there – and they would have to find ten overs from somebody besides their front-line bowlers. OK, but we knew it wasn't going to be easy – and by the eighth over we were in a mess.

Colin Croft did the damage. Big, splay-footed and angular, he bowled from so wide of the stumps that it was almost impossible to master the angle of his deliveries. Lloyd brought him on after Holding had bowled only one over and it was a master stroke – one that Lloyd was to repeat with monotonous success all afternoon. I was deceived by the angle of delivery as I tried to run Croft down to third-man; Willey and Butcher both had to play at deliveries in defence of their off stump and were caught behind. Croft sometimes rolled his fingers over the ball and bowled cutters which makes the ball hold up and slightly slower off the pitch – and it was that combination of angle and cutter which had Butcher playing wide and too early.

Gooch was a victim of our lack of cricket in that he fell for an old ploy from Roberts, one which he would have spotted instantly had he had more opportunity to practice and get himself in a really sharp frame of mind. Roberts bowled him a short one and Gooch pulled it violently; the next one was wide and well pitched up and Gooch flashed and missed. A two-card trick if ever there was one, but practice is about mental agility as well as form and we had barely seen any fast bowlers. Roberts tried the same tactic shortly afterwards and Gooch 'nicked' it to first slip.

The match was won and lost then, with England 15 for four and with only three recognized batsmen in Botham, Gower and Gatting to come. The locals went wild, of course, and I suspect even West Indies were surprised by the sudden about-turn in the game; they must surely have expected to lose it from a total of 127. 'You beaten by pace like fire, man!' jeered the spectators near the pavilion, but nothing, ironically enough, could have been further from the truth.

We lost those early wickets not to sheer speed or intimidation – Roberts dug a couple in short but soon settled down – but to shrewd, professional bowling by a man who delivered the ball from a puzzling angle, pitched it up and let it do its own damage. Those who thought Croft did not have the vision to bowl like that were confusing a cricket brain with an academic brain; he knew what he was about.

Botham and Gower tried to re-establish the innings and the fact was that if they played really well we could still pull it out of the fire, especially since West Indies had to find ten overs from a less formidable bowler and we could surely knock him around a bit more freely. In a low-scoring match that could be crucial.

But Lloyd read the situation perfectly. Instead of using Gomes, as we expected, he plumped for ten overs of off-spin from Kallicharran, and on that pitch neither batsman could get on top of him. Kalli bowled into the off-stump rough to Gower, who could not time it or hit it through, and tied down Botham by bowling at his pads and employing a strong leg-side field. We kept expecting our batsmen to get after Kalli but he never let them and Botham should have been stumped on 22 when he made a desperate attempt to lift the pace.

The more Gower tried to attack Kalli the more frustrated he became. I could see the signs, and expected him to get out before he did. He was getting tense, trying to hit the ball harder and harder. This is understandable, but self-defeating in those circumstances, and he was getting nowhere fast. It is important to relax, to concentrate on timing the ball and to be content to push it into the gaps for ones and twos – easier said than done – and Gower finally holed out to cover.

They had done a fine job, a stand of 65 in 26 overs, which left us a target of 48 off 16 overs and meant we were still in the game. But every time Croft picked up the ball, things went wrong for us.

Gatting was deceived by the angle and yorked himself working across the line towards mid-wicket; Croft changed ends and Bairstow again trying to hit towards mid-wicket was bowled off stump by a cutter. Botham's fine innings had kept us in with a shout, even though we were always trying to catch up after that early collapse, but when he had made 60 he tried to run Croft down to third-man and was caught behind. Fourteen to win in five overs doesn't sound much of a target, but West Indies had their tails up, all our recognized batsmen had gone, and we knew it was still a hell of a job with two new batsmen at the crease.

Emburey and Stevenson put on nine priceless runs and we needed just five to do it, with two wickets to fall, when Emburey, trying to run the ball down to third-man, which is a typical one-day shot, was bowled off stump by Holding. Stevenson had stood up straight and played the fast bowlers well; while he is in there is always the chance of a sudden, match-winning explosion.

But Old is not the best player of fast bowling in the world, and Lloyd tossed the ball to Holding. The crowd went mad. They obviously thought Lloyd had gone that way, too, since Croft had taken six wickets and was pacing about like Albert Pierrepoint on a good day. But Holding is their fastest bowler and will always bowl quick and straight; Old's only hope is to play straight down the line of middle stump. A prayer might help.

Holding whistled one through Old's guard and on to his off stump, and West Indies had won by two runs ... I expect they could hear the din in Cuba.

Looking back, it was incredible how every move that Clive Lloyd made paid off. He brought on Croft early and wrecked the start of our innings; he used Kallicharran instead of Gomes and conceded only 25 runs when we desperately needed more; and every time he made a bowling change later in the innings he took a wicket. The magic touch was really on him that day.

Botham played a fine innings and almost won it for us, but his dismissal strengthened my view that, especially in low-scoring matches charged with tension, it is vital to have at least one batsman who sees it through to the end. Some people don't go along with the need for a sheet-anchor role, but I am sure that if Botham had been there at the death, having battled through as many overs as he did, we would have won. With one end sealed by an established batsman, life is twice as hard for bowlers who can't afford to give a single away.

It was a great game for spectators and I doubt the little island of St Vincent will ever forget it. But who said West Indies would crumble if things went against them? Seems to me that you have to get everything just right if you are going to beat them; anything less than one hundred per cent is not enough. We gave a ninety-nine per cent performance, which is no bad achievement considering our lack of preparation. And one per cent cost us the game.

The unmistakable Ian Botham hits a defiant 60 – in vain – at St Vincent.

7

Pinpricks

The England cricket team left the ground at St Vincent in a couple of minibuses, wrapped round each other like sardines, struggling for an inch of leg room, sitting on top of each other and bits of kit, looking rather like refugees. Inch by inch through a traffic jam which had built up for an hour and would take another hour to clear – just the way the West Indies Test sides leave Lord's. . . .

We were due to attend a function at the Prime Minister's residence soon after close of play, and we naturally pointed out to the authorities at the ground that we would need some sort of help to get through the traffic. Of course it would be all right . . . of course they would make special arrangements . . . of course we had no need to worry, it was all taken care of . . . and there we sat, cooped up and cantankerous, while the pedestrians strolled past the windows and the minutes ticked agonizingly away.

That, I'm afraid, was no more than typical of the tour so far, another of the upsets and inconveniences which might seem petty taken in isolation but which gathered like mosquito bites into a rash of frustration. Our physical preparation was hamstrung to a demoralizing extent by the weather, which was bad luck, but our mental state was badly affected by the lack of organization we met time and time again.

It was a serious problem, not one we would want to use as an excuse, but a real source of annoyance which I consider no touring team should be asked to tolerate. Our reputations and even careers are on the line when we tour, and I think we are entitled to expect an eye for detail in the organization.

That is not a criticism of the management we had on tour, Alan Smith and Kenny Barrington. They faced the problems at every hotel and every ground, wrestled with them and sometimes went blue in the face trying to impress on the locals just what we needed, why we needed it and – often just as important – why we needed it quickly. Try to get a telephone call out of Trinidad with anything like urgency, and you have some idea of the meaning of the word frustration.

If they were at fault in anything I suggest it was that they were too understanding and too polite. I know diplomacy is an important part of their job and they have a lot of masters to answer to, but there comes a time when a flat refusal to accept second best on behalf of the England team is more important than anything else. Demanding management is not necessarily bad management, and there were times, unfortunate perhaps but unavoidable, when it was necessary to be downright rude to get a point over.

The pinpricks, on and off the field, began from the moment we arrived. We accepted them with a joke and good grace in Antigua because we acknowledged that a special attempt had been made by the Board at home to give us extra time to acclimatize. The first few days were a bonus and we were glad of them.

But even there the arrangements were not up to much. The food at the hotel, for instance, was hopelessly inadequate and very dull. A five-year-old child might have been satisfied by the portions we were offered but the players went hungry and prowled off in search of something to supplement the diet at the local beach bars. We were offered a set menu, and our allowances did not run to the expensive *à la carte* alternative; I reckon I got through more chocolate bars than I faced deliveries in Antigua.

The first time we arrived in Trinidad, we discovered that not enough rooms had been booked for us at the Hilton and there was a hassle there – just the thing after a long day of travelling – before it was sorted out. Then we were told that the net facilities at Queen's Park Oval were no good and had to practise on a local ground. And here again, there was a total absence of local bowlers to help us out.

That is very important on any tour, and in many countries is provided by the hosts. Instead we had to rely on our own resources, which meant that our best bowlers bowled against our best batsmen – and the others had more or less to make do among themselves. Non-specialist batsmen never faced our top bowlers and consequently never batted against pace, and that was no sort of preparation for the Test series we faced. Local quick bowlers or even medium-pacers would have provided us with useful practice, but were not available.

The weather played havoc with the early part of the tour and nobody could be blamed for that. But the nets that we were offered were uniformly poor, so that batsmen who weren't in some sort of form never got the chance to improve. Brian Rose was a perfect example of the problem; he desperately needed a bat in his hand to improve his touch and get his mental attitude right, yet he constantly went into the nets first, found they were no good and gave it up with a sigh of resignation. Rose will be judged like the rest of us on his performances on this tour but what kind of preparation is this for an England player?

The whole sorry business reached a head in St Vincent, where we were reduced to batting in a cow pasture a couple of days before the first international. The nets there were wet when we arrived and hopelessly uneven when they dried out – so some of us trailed over to our concrete slab and had a knock simply because there was nothing better. I do not need to ask what would be the reaction of the West Indians, the Australians or any touring team if they were faced with a similar situation in England. I imagine the tour would soon be in a state of crisis.

If net and fielding practices were running smoothly, other annoyances might not

Opposite page: The Colonel in his familiar parade dress. Ken Barrington at the nets, always ready with advice, encouragement and a couple of overs of unfathomable leg-breaks. . . .

Left: Well I . . . er . . . yes . . . but perhaps no. Anyway, don't quote me. Alan Smith wrestles with another problem.

Below: Bending over backwards for fitness – Bernard Thomas puts David Bairstow through a familiar stretching routine in Trinidad.

be quite as irksome as they became. But we were constantly faced with pinpricks to which I believe no international team on tour should be subjected. Our meal allowance in Trinidad, for instance, was thirty dollars for lunch (about £5.50), which is cutting it really fine at Hilton prices. I had fruit platter, a steak, cheesecake and a fruit juice, and that came to fifty-five dollars (£9·90), which brands me, I suppose, as a real glutton! The evening-meal allowance just about covered the set menu, so hard luck anybody who didn't like what was served up.

It might sound unnecessarily petty to complain about the size of meal allowances, hotel rooms not being ready, transport to and from grounds being late or inadequate, and I can understand the public view that cricketers have a good life and should be prepared to put up with some inconveniences.

Sitting through an English winter, perhaps reading about the sunshine (when there was some) and the romance of the Caribbean islands, it may be difficult to understand the annoyances and frustration we felt at times. It is better than going down the pit and none of us should forget that. But we are professionals who are here to do a professional job and who are judged by the way we do it – and it is that fact that makes me feel that certain standards should be maintained on our behalf.

As I see it we are aware that our jobs are on the line – we would not be decent professionals if we imagined otherwise – and the point of preparation on a Test tour is that it should encourage players to eat, sleep and think cricket to the point where they can justifiably feel they are prepared. When I go to bed at night I want to feel that I couldn't do any more than I have to get myself in the right form and frame of mind for the job in hand, and I'm sure the rest of the players are the same. The value of proper preparation is important psychologically as well as physically.

So everything possible must be done to allow players to concentrate on cricket – and that's not easy when arrangements go wrong, when we kick our heels waiting for transport, when food and laundry arrangements are hit and miss. It builds up a sense of frustration which threatens to distract us from the task in hand.

And that frustration tells. After a few weeks on tour, and with the first Test still to come, we are still not 'thinking cricket' as a team, we are still bedevilled by annoyances which sometimes threaten the spirit within the party. As a senior player who has seen most of it before, I sometimes pass on the complaints of the players to the management. I do it forcibly because that's how the players feel. And not unnaturally, the management often feel it is a criticism of *them*; they are working hard to get things moving smoothly, and they are annoyed at the suggestion that they are dragging their feet. No such suggestion is intended, but it doesn't make for smooth relationships; we all feel the pressures.

Our travelling arrangements out of St Vincent were changed at the last minute, which was a bind for the management and a real annoyance to the players, who had to get up, bleary-eyed, at six o'clock in the morning to report early to the airport. Can't blame the management for that, can't blame the players, yet we are all caught up again in the feeling that it's just one unnecessary problem after another.

And when we arrived in Trinidad, the transport which had been laid on for us had no knowledge of the new flight time and arrived over an hour late. So we lounged around the airport, picked a spot on the floor of the reception area where we could, and suffered another dismal spell of killing time and wishing the whole damned tour would get a move on.

I think what we should probably have done was to commandeer a few taxis, reach the hotel as quickly as possible and send the bill to whoever had made transport arrangements which – through no fault of ours – had let us down again. I cannot see the England soccer team putting up with second-class status, so why should the England cricket team?

It is not really a matter of who is at fault, though the lessons we re-learn on every tour should surely be put to good use. It is a matter of taking whatever action is necessary on the spot to make things easier for the players with a formidable job to do. We are not malcontents, we are professionals representing our country – and with the first Test round the corner the odds are stacked heavily against us.

8

Trinidad Teaser

Brian Rose secured his place in the first Test as soon as he was picked in the side to play Trinidad at Queen's Park Oval. He made only 11, as it turned out, in a match ruined by rain and relatively inconsequential as far as our Test preparations were concerned, but the fact that he was in the side at all indicated that the selectors had decided to stick with him at number three. Gatting was overlooked, and I reckon they will leave him out of the Test side, too. It is asking too much of him to step into a Test team with so little match practice.

We wanted more runs from Rose, just as we needed Miller and Willey to have a long knock since they have had so little batting in the middle. Neither pulled up any trees, but neither was totally disappointing either: Miller played the spinners very competently before he was run out, freakishly, backing up, and Willey looked solid in making 28. He is known to be a better player of pace than spin, so the Trinidad match wasn't exactly his cup of tea.

Batting was a grafting sort of occupation and the pitch was so slow that it was relatively easy to read the West Indies' Test off-spinner Nanan and the left-arm wrist spinner Daniel we first met at Pointe-a-Pierre. The most interesting bowler by far was Harold Joseph, a twenty-four-year-old right-arm spinner who had made an immediate impact in his four Shell Shield matches before we faced him. It didn't take long to see why.

Joseph is a sort of cross between Johnny Gleeson and a conventional leg-spinner; he bowls from a slight stoop and then skims the ball on to you quite quickly, so there is little opportunity to get down the pitch to him. He disguises a variety of deliveries with bewildering expertise – leg-spinners turn out to be off-spinners, and off-spinners suddenly go the wrong way! They talk about 'reading' spinners, by watching the bowler's hand, but reading Joseph was like missing out every other page ... one right, miss one; one right, miss one. It was quite an experience.

Gooch took his first over and said, 'I'm playing this feller as an off-spinner.' Next over a delivery pitched middle and went past Gooch's off stump! His eyes rolled and his face looked a picture. Off-spinner indeed! For the next few overs we picked up a single where we could and laughed at each other as we passed: I've got away from the Mystery Man, now you have a go!

Joseph bowls off his middle finger and was always ready to turn his wrist over and bowl a googly or top-spinner. Every so often he threw up a high, slow one which looked like an off-spinner and turned out to be a legger which turned quite considerably. . . . Lots of variety, and if you could pick every delivery with absolute certainty you're a better man than I am. Even after we had been in for a while we needed all our experience to see us through, reading some and playing others off the pitch.

Trinidad breeds spinners, of course, because of the nature of their pitches. They look like rolled earth strips, which is basically what they are – just mud which is watered and rolled repetitively, then left to dry. They often look like cement which has cured too quickly, full of cracks which gradually widen until you can stick a fingertip in them. They play lower and slower as time goes on, and the odd delivery shoots along the ground.

It is Ramadhin's isle, but it has produced other fine and distinctive spinners, including Willy Rodriguez, a leg-spinner who could go from moderate to brilliant on his day and who delivered the ball so quickly he would often tear a groin muscle, the sort of injury medium-pacers suffer in England. Inshan Ali, the left-arm wrist spinner, has taken lots of wickets on his own Trinidad surfaces – and now comes Harold Joseph. I was not surprised, as some said they were, when he was left out of the West Indies Test side, because he was in his first Shell Shield season; but I was not surprised, either, when he took five wickets in the match against us.

I decided very early on that I was going to treat him as a leg-spinner, the way I did Gleeson. That was clearly the more dangerous of his deliveries and playing for it would cut out the greatest danger; if it turned the other way there was always the chance of getting a pad on it or trapping it between bat and pad. You might get away with it.

He finally got me out with a very good delivery, bowled from wide of the crease and given plenty of air, which drew me forward, pitched middle and leg and hit the top of middle and off. But I felt I had played quite well for 70; I was not unhappy with my performance that day, or my form in general.

Somebody suggested in the dressing-room that I looked very tired when I got out; perhaps they were hinting that exhaustion begins at 40! I've thought about that, but I really don't see my age makes that much difference, even out here where the sun is high by 9.30 a.m. and the heat is searing throughout the day. It is taxing batting for several hours, sweaty and exhausting, and it will probably be worse in the Test match, when we will need the helmets and chest-pads which we discarded for the Trinidad game. But I reckon tiredness played a big part in Gooch's dismissal and he's not quite forty yet. . . .

Gooch batted for three hours and forty minutes for his 117, a long and typically powerful innings containing three sixes and eight fours. One shot probably summed up the elemental power of Gooch's game – when Nanan put long-on back and Gooch promptly cleared him for a huge six. That might normally be a very unintelligent shot – when there's a man back it's usually best to push into the gaps and bring him in before letting loose again – but Gooch has the power to play shots like that with confidence once he has established himself. He can mis-hit and still clear mid-off or mid-on.

It was also good to see Gower get runs and spend time in the middle. He made 77 in two hundred minutes, and although I didn't think Joseph bowled quite so well against left-handers, it was obviously a morale-booster for David who now feels in decent form. He is going to need all his self-confidence soon.

Frankly, our bowling against the Trinidad side depressed me. Once Dilley and Botham expended a few overs with the new ball we looked a very straight-up-and-down attack, and no matter how we tried it was impossible to introduce much variation. The selectors who picked the squad should have been at the match: then they would have seen how difficult it is, even against a non-Test side, when you have three off-spinners and are saddled with a lack of variety.

You can change faces, you can switch ends, you can bowl over or round the wicket. But that is the limit to your options when you do not have a left-arm spinner. An off-spinner is an off-spinner is an off-spinner, and the ball turns the same way to the same field; Murray and Cuffy were taking a run a ball much as they liked, and there seemed precious little we could do about it; this was very dispiriting, with the Test just round the corner.

Botham seemed to let things drift and although I appreciate his predicament I can't help thinking that, as captain, he was a party to the decision to bring three off-spinners and therefore helped to create the problem himself. It is not that Emburey, Miller and Willey are bad bowlers – we have no better off-spinners in our game – but the stereotyped nature of our attack when they are on worries me and cannot help them much either.

It was important to make something happen rather than just wait on events and I suggested to Botham that he vary his field for the spinners, with two men for the drive, a deep long-on and deep mid-wicket. We did it, and it kept the batsmen quiet for a while; Murray tried to hit his way out and was lucky to drop between Stevenson and Rose on the boundary. Usually we are so predictable, so English.

Our spinners did need extended practice, and from that point of view the match was useful. Miller bowled pretty well and was the most impressive of our spinners again in this match; Emburey struggled, and I reckoned that was because he was bowling too slow through the air.

I suggested he watched how Nanan went about an over. He takes his time between deliveries, is meticulous about the placing of his field, adjusts and readjusts it if necessary until a batsman begins to wonder if he will ever actually get round to letting the ball go. But when he does he bowls it quicker than an English spinner would, pushing it through just sharply enough to make it difficult for a batsman to use his feet to get down the pitch to him.

Emburey's natural inclination is to hurry between deliveries and bowl the ball slowly, and even on a turning pitch they will attack him if he does that. I stressed that it was vital he compose himself between each delivery and check his field – it's easy for the most experienced fielder to wander in the heat – and if that niggled the batsman, so much the better. Think more slowly and bowl a little quicker; there need hardly be any drop in the over rate, and Emburey would be a better bowler for it in West Indian conditions.

Trinidad's reply to our total of 355 was to make 392 for eight. If the match had gone the distance they might have gone on even further and, who knows, we could have lost! It was a sobering thought, especially since England regard Port-of-Spain as the sort of pitch where our spinners might get us a result against West Indies.

There was an incident during the match, which I know got a lot of Press publicity at home, when Dilley and Botham seemed to disagree about who was going to bowl the next over. Dilley was about to start an over when there was an exchange of words and Botham called Stevenson up from third-man to take over.

I don't know the details of what went on and, frankly, I don't care. There will always be frictions between players on the field, brief moments of tension or bad temper. It has happened to me, it has happened to others who attract less publicity than I do, and I'm sure it will always crop up. The players forget it as quickly as it happens and get on with the job.

What does worry me is that Botham and Dilley don't seem to be hitting it off so far on tour. I have watched from a distance and it appears that there is something wrong between them, a trace of abrasiveness. And that, if it is true, must be a bad thing from everyone's point of view, not least since Dilley is the fastest bowler we have and we are going to need him fit and strong and in the best possible frame of mind.

Botham the captain seems very different from Botham the player who made such a remarkable reputation in such a short time. He has other responsibilities now, of course, but it is noticeable that he doesn't spend as much time bowling in the nets or throwing himself into the warm-up exercises. Some of the players comment on it.

What makes Botham what he is, is hard work, a tremendous pride in his physical presence, an appetite for hard going. When he slacked before, he was made to toe the line and took a great pride in showing that he could bowl longer and work harder than anyone else; nobody in his right mind could fail to admire him and respect his ability.

Botham may now feel that he has to save himself for the Test matches, if so he is doing himself a disservice. History shows that quick bowlers need hard preparation; they cannot simply turn it on, however much they may want to, if they don't build up to rhythm and peak fitness. For his own sake as much as England's, I hope Botham the captain does not neglect the disciplines that make him such a tremendous player.

Traditionally, England have a team dinner on the evening before every Test match. Home and abroad it's much the same, except that in England regulation dress is

When it rains in the Caribbean, it rains! Not much chance of an early start at Port-of-Spain.

Right: Hat trick by Ian Botham during his brief disagreement with Graham Dilley at Queen's Park Oval.

Opposite page: Four all the way, as Graham Gooch hits out with typical power during his century against Trinidad.

team blazer and tie; out here the requirement is Casually Smart. The food is good – often the best we have on tour – which usually brings on some comment about condemned men and hearty meals, but most important is the traditional opportunity to sit down together and talk through the opposition, what we expect from them and from ourselves. There are domestic details, too: what time the transport leaves, what we should wear, and so on. I have sat through these dinners dozens of times, and much of what is said is repetitive, a resumé of what we have discussed at previous dinners brought up to date in the light of new experiences. Many of the points made have been made numerous times before and will no doubt be made to a different audience many times in the future, but that does not matter. It is important to remind ourselves of some of the basic philosophies of Test cricket, and in any case there are always newcomers who may not have played in Test matches or not faced this particular opposition. The younger players usually listen and try to take it all in without saying too much; the older hands throw out a caution here, a suggestion or a reminder there.

There was a time when we used to have dinner and then sit down to talk, but that sometimes meant that it was quite late before we started our discussion, and even later before we finished. A couple of years ago I suggested that we had our discussion first and then ate dinner so that those who like to go to bed early before a Test could slip away. That's the way it's done now, and the meeting in Trinidad was pretty typical of what goes on.

Botham reminded us that we would have to field for long periods under a hot sun; we were bound to get sweaty and wet with perspiration, but that, he counselled, was not the same thing as being tired. We must beware of getting into a tired frame of mind.

Whoever was closest should always encourage the bowler, talk to him and help to keep him going. The non-players too had a big responsibility to the side; they could do a lot without bowling a ball or facing a delivery.

It is easy to think of the non-players in a Test match as dogsbodies, and there is a danger that they will look on themselves that way, but it is a foolish sort of attitude. Non-players have a fair bit to do and a lot to contribute. They can help out as bowlers, organize fielding practice and make themselves available immediately if any player wants a particular work-out, catching practice and so on. They can organize things at lunch and tea intervals, take away wet clothing to be dried, for example, and generally help, so that the players can relax. It's surprising how short the tea interval seems when you have been in the field all day; given a cup of tea and the chance to put your feet up you could happily sit back for an hour, but no sooner do you sit down, it seems, than the captain is rousting you out again. Non-players can help a lot, not just in having things ready but in encouraging players and geeing them up. Whatever's going on, the dressing-room should not be like a morgue, said Botham; he was looking for total participation from everybody in the party and cheerful participation at that.

As a matter of organization, three of the non-players could leave the ground after morning practice but two should always stay to share the job of twelfth man. When we were fielding, a third should be on call at any time.

Botham reminded everybody that umpires are only human, and that any show of aggression or dissent towards them could only rebound badly. Talk to them reasonably and politely; if you get their backs up it will be the worse for the side, he said. And Alan Smith interjected that West Indian umpires like to maintain a sense of dignity which was fair enough; there was no excuse for challenging that and it wouldn't do an atom of good.

Botham said he felt there had been something of a lack of communication, which might be his fault, and stressed that he was open to constructive comments on or off the field. If you make a suggestion and I still do my own thing, sort it out in the dressing-room afterwards, he said. He also urged on everyone that we should 'bubble' in the field; West Indies are poor runners between the wickets, a lot of betting goes on and they tend to panic if they don't score, so our fielding should aim to put them under strain. They're under more pressure at home than abroad, he said.

Willis chipped in to remind those four players who had not been named in the twelve that a lot could happen before the match started next day and they must work on the assumption that they might actually have to play. He stressed the importance of taking catches – one mistake could cost 100 runs against this batting line-up – and said it was important we kept our composure, even if things went against us. If West Indies got a lot of runs, for instance, they should never see the captain and bowlers getting fractious on the field. Don't let the wheel come off. . . .

No one knows better than Kenny Barrington what batting for a long time in a Test match is all about. If you got in, book in for bed and breakfast, said Barrington. You have to stay there and remember that they get just as tired as you do. If you start to feel jaded play for the end of each session as it comes, take a breather and start again. If one man gets out, another often follows quickly; that's the way it is in Test cricket.

Barrington also encouraged the spinners to try something new; he felt they had been too stereotyped during the match against Trinidad. Why not bowl on the off side with a deep point or deep extra, why not bowl a bit quicker at times? Illingworth and Titmus always used to mix their deliveries to make the batsman think and work. And it's an old principle out here that bowlers set their fields in such a way as to try and force batsmen to play across the line. Worth thinking about.

Gooch said we should be careful to put our best fielders in the most effective positions against individual batsmen and urged Botham to run in really aggressively with the new ball, bearing in mind that we had only one genuinely quick bowler in Dilley. Butcher pointed out that when the West Indies' bowlers tired they often brought on Garner to block it up for a while. Try and push him around for singles, that annoys him almost as much as being thumped for four, said Butcher.

Richards scores around forty per cent of the West Indies' runs, so naturally we gave some thought specifically to him. Willis ventured the fairly revolutionary theory that we should take out some slips early in his innings and prevent him instead from galloping away; we could even give him a single to keep him away from the strike and frustrate him. Botham wasn't too keen on that idea: what if he got a nick early on and we'd taken a couple of slips and gulley away? How would we feel then? Well, he hasn't nicked one yet, rejoined Willis. It was an interesting thought, and one we eventually acted on.

Rose ought to know a bit about Richards, and he reckoned he tends to get out to the off-spinner early in his innings. He tries so hard to work everything on to the leg side that he is known to get a leading edge. Interesting. And Gatting made a good point that Essex have got Richards out in the championship – Botham confirmed it – by having a man at short mid-wicket and orthodox mid-wicket because Richards hits a lot in the air through there. Another point well worth bearing in mind.

I have a little habit which I always recommend to batsmen in Test matches: look at the scoreboard and add two wickets to the score; that's a cautionary view of what your position really is. It's a strange fact, but if you lose one wicket in Test cricket another usually follows very quickly: 120 for two might look OK, but pretend it's 120 for four – not so clever. Add a couple of wickets every time, and it will guard against over-confidence because it goes without saying that you never give your wicket away in a Test match.

I told the batsmen to keep talking to each other, helping, watching from the non-striker's end. If your partner looks as though he's doing something which might get him out, tell him and do it straight away. Don't wait until he's out and then say at tea: I thought that might happen! You can see a great deal from the non-striker's end and your help may be vital – remember you have only one friend in the middle, and he's at the other end. Eleven other guys are determined to get you out, and the umpires aren't exactly on your side. . . . Their job is to be impartial.

Concentrate as hard at the non-striker's end as you do when you're facing. That helps your partner, as we've said, but it also keeps you sharp mentally. Batsmen get tired during a long day, their concentration wavers and that's when run-outs occur. Be guarded against it.

And I always tell non-striking batsmen to watch the fielder behind the square-leg umpire, either catching or saving the single. That's a blind area for the man facing; once he gets down he cannot see if that fielder moves so it's vital his partner watches out for him.

'Watch each other, back up, shout for everything and watch the man behind square' – that's the sort of thing Gooch and I say to each other as a matter of habit at the start of every innings. But then we've played in a few Test matches together; we should have developed some good habits. What comes naturally to us may be a bit of a revelation to younger players and the pre-Test discussion is a good time to drop these pieces of advice.

There are always administrative details to be passed on. Alan Smith tells us there will be a presentation before the match starts – just for the eleven players involved;

no need to wear blazers. Dress to and from the ground is cream England shirts and long white trousers; no shorts or T-shirts; white England tracksuit bottoms acceptable.

Barrington outlines the travel arrangements: everybody leaves for the ground 8.30 a.m. first day; after that two shuttles, the first for batsmen who want a net and the non-players to help them, the second for everybody else. The management have made arrangements for plenty of cheese and ice cream to be available at lunch. Some players, like Botham, like a substantial lunch, others, like me, make do with a hunk of cheese and biscuits. The ice cream is important: it gives instant energy without lying heavy on the stomach and the bowlers especially get through a lot of it.

Important points, suggestions, things to discuss, minor details: all part of the ritual which takes place on the night before every Test match. After the discussions and the meal some players like to go to bed especially early, others prefer to have a quiet drink and mull over the points which have been made for the next day. . . .

'Four taxis at 8.30 please. . . .'
The phone rang at the team dinner and Geoff Miller answered it.

'Call for you, Colonel, from Battoo Brothers. . . .' Ken Barrington, the long-suffering assistant team manager, wondered vaguely what the newest problem could be with the team's transport arrangements.

'Hello, hello. Mr Barrington? Battoo Brothers here,' said a voice rather more music-hall Pakistani than West Indian. 'I am afraid we are having problems with the taxis for the morning. A lot of people have arrived in Trinidad and our cars are going to the airport to pick them up. But we can spare you one taxi at 6.45 a.m. . . .'

Barrington put down the receiver with a sigh. 'Gawd help us. We want four taxis at 8.30 a.m. and they say we can have one at 6.45. Don't know what the 'ell it's coming to. One ruddy problem after another. What good's one ruddy taxi at that time?'

The first caller seemed to have been afflicted with a fit of giggles, the second rings five minutes later. 'Call for you again, Colonel; Battoo Brothers. . . .'

'Hello, Mr Barrington. Yes, we have some good news. We have now available two taxis for you in the morning. The only thing is that they have been involved in a collision.'

Barrington puts his hand over the mouthpiece. 'What do you make of that? Two taxis and they're ruddy well running into each other! What a palaver.' And into the phone: 'Yes, thank you for your help. Do the best you can. . . .'

The Colonel is used to problems and half expects them every time the phone rings. Perhaps that's why he does not notice that most of the team are purple-faced with suppressed laughter, that the rest seem acutely aware that something is going on without quite knowing what, and that Messrs Dilley, Bairstow and Gower seem to be absent from the room in relays.

The phone rings again. 'Mr Barrington? Yes, it is us again. You will be pleased to hear that we have found an eighteen-seater minibus to transport the team tomorrow. There is a minor problem though because we are short of spares. For a start, we are in need of a steering wheel.'

'Stone me,' says Barrington, as the phone clicks dead again. 'Ruddy bus 'ere with no steering wheel! Fancy having a bus with no steering wheel. How the 'ell are we supposed to get away in that. I dunno, one problem after another. . . .'

And the phone rings again. 'If that's for me I'm not in. Buses without steering wheels; what next?' says Barrington.

'Mr Barrington? Good news. We have the steering wheel' – 'Thank Gawd for that,' intones the Colonel – 'but I am afraid the bus has just crashed into the two taxis we found for you. . . .'

The Colonel begins to relay the message to the team when a light dawns in his eye. 'Wait a minute, wait a minute – this ruddy feller from Battoo Brothers has a Yorkshire accent! Where's Bairstow. . .? The Colonel, bless him, has made another of his million contributions to team morale. . . .

9

Heads You Lose

The first bottle of our West Indies tour sailed from the concrete stand on the far side of the ground from the pavilion at 1.55 p.m. on Friday 13 February. Black Friday they call it out here, and nobody in the England camp is going to argue with that.

The bottle had scarcely stopped rolling along the bumpy, deserted outfield before it was followed by a dozen others, then twenty, then a barrowload of cans came raining down from the second tier of the three-tier stand occupied – not coincidentally – by the strongest supporters of Deryck Murray's right to a place in the first Test match. Deryck was left out in favour of David Murray of Barbados, their favourite snubbed as far as many of the locals were concerned, and that fact scarred a day which the West Indian cricket authorities will want to forget.

We arrived at the ground to find the groundstaff working feverishly to make the pitch playable. An area some seven or eight yards square and about ten yards from the stumps at the far end was a quagmire, and the groundstaff were desperately raking out mud and trying to fill the shallow recess with fresh earth. And, far more ominously, the pitch itself was pocked with damp patches.

There were about ten of them, each the size of a saucer, covering an area just short of a quick bowler's length from the pavilion end. Any fast bowler bowling short and round the wicket must hit them – and when I looked, at about 9.30 a.m., it was possible to drive a finger into them to the depth of a fingernail. There was no way we could play on that and neither captain even considered a start on time.

The wet area beyond the stumps had been wet when we played the match against Trinidad, and didn't look as though it had been covered against the rain which fell quite heavily the day before. The official word on the pitch was that rain had got under the covers, which is not uncommon but seemed strange at the time. And as the delay lengthened, the plot thickened.

It was not until early afternoon – and after a group of English journalists pressed for a full statement – that the West Indies Board president Jeff Stollmeyer admitted that the pitch had been sabotaged during the night. Somebody had slashed the covers, apparently with a cutlass of all things, and dug holes in the pitch, the same holes which the groundstaff had tried to fill with earth, then rolled and watered in the hope that the hot sun would dry them out quickly. It wasn't quite the same as the version we had been given earlier in the day....

The Board's apparent reluctance to give us the full story – and our manager Alan Smith was kept as much in the dark as anybody – became more understandable as the facts unfolded. They reflected absolutely no credit on the Board or the administration of the Queen's Park ground.

We gradually learned that the club had received anonymous threats to prevent the Test going ahead because Deryck Murray had been left out. They had arranged for a security guard to police the ground and for searchlights to be installed, precisely to prevent any damage to the pitch. But the night before the Test the lights failed and the security guard failed to show up!

'Apparently the security demanded was not in evidence and the lights did not work,' said Stollmeyer. And that just about sums up the running battle against all kinds of shortcomings which we have had to put up with since the tour started. My own view is that if the West Indies Board can't ensure efficiency and co-operation from the people who actually stage the Test matches, there can be no hope of getting proper facilities for net practice and so on; and that, to me, is unacceptable.

The groundstaff finished their work as far as they could, dashed on with the covers when a heavy shower threatened at 1.15 p.m. and then opened the pitch to the sunshine and stood around waiting for a decision on the start. One of them stretched out and fell asleep next to the pitch; perhaps he was the security man who went missing the night before! Botham and Lloyd went out with their vice-captains to have a look, greeted with a roar of jeers and boos from a crowd who had been kept in ignorance of what was actually causing the delay. Like cricket crowds anywhere in the world, they resented the apparent lack of action, when all they saw was the pitch bathed in sunlight, no work in progress, and no indication from the public address system as to why the match was being held up so long.

What was needed was a simple announcement plainly stating the facts, even if it reflected poorly on the competence of the authorities. The same sort of statement was needed at Lord's during the Centenary Test in 1980. In my view that is the proper and best way to deflect criticism – a simple exercise in public relations.

Behind the scenes there was plenty going on. It was like a beehive, with repeated conferences between the Board and the ground authorities, the umpires, our manager and West Indies' manager Steve Camacho, and the two captains. Lloyd and Botham were adamant that the pitch was unfit, and did not want to run the risk of turning the Test into a lottery by starting just to spare somebody else's blushes.

But the umpires were under pressure – as the sole judges of playing conditions – to get the match under way. The administrators knew, as all administrators do, that once there was play to watch the crowd would settle and the circumstances might be quickly forgotten. No consideration, of course, for the player who might get hit between the eyes....

At 1.45 p.m. the umpires announced that once the toss had been made, the Test would start. Both captains were incensed, and the managers checked the playing

Queen's Park Oval, Port-of-Spain, Trinidad, one of the most beautiful grounds in the world –
when the sun shines.

Disgruntled Deryck Murray fans protest at his omission from the first Test match. Spelling is
obviously not their strong point. . . .

conditions to find out exactly what the regulations were, but it was clear that the umpires were in charge. It was a far cry from 1975, I recalled, when Ian Chappell flatly refused to play on after the Test pitch at Headingley was vandalized, but perhaps the regulations have been changed since then.

Apart from an occasional report that inspections were due, no announcement had been made to the crowd for the best part of three hours, and naturally they were frustrated and restless. It is easy to talk about volatile West Indian crowds, but in these circumstances who can blame them? Even the members at Lord's, after all, faced with similar frustrations in the Centenary Test, didn't exactly sit tight and think of England. They were angry, the players were angry and nobody seemed inclined to come up with the facts; then, as now, a bit of old-fashioned honesty might have sweetened the crowd's mood which was increasingly hostile.

When Botham and Lloyd finally went out to toss, the beer cans and debris from the concrete stand already littered the outfield and they were met with a storm of jeers and catcalls. Fruit was hurled at them as they walked towards the middle, oranges bouncing crazily along the parched outfield and they paused as if uncertain whether to go on. Botham won the toss and put West Indies in to bat.

We could not be sure what the reaction of the crowd would be once we actually got into the middle, and Alan Smith and Botham cautioned us to keep cool. If a bottle does actually come over near where you are fielding, don't over-react, just walk slowly to the captain and tell him. . . . 'What?' said Emburey, 'walk? If you see me running like hell in your direction you'll know what's happened.' Amen to that.

The situation was still very uncertain because Clive Lloyd had a theory that the bottles were thrown not simply out of frustration but in another attempt to prevent the match starting. Since they came from the stand where a large, pro-Deryck Murray poster was fixed to the wire fence, it seemed a plausible enough idea. As it turned out, there was no more crowd trouble.

West Indies total of 144 for no wicket at the end of the day was trouble enough, as far as we were concerned – and I'm afraid to some extent we inflicted it on ourselves.

Botham was obviously delighted to win the toss, just as Clive Lloyd would have been, and he and Bob Willis didn't have much hesitation in deciding we should put them in. There was obviously a big psychological advantage in that, since all the players had been sitting around wondering just how the pitch would play and – from a batsman's point of view at least – fearing the worst. But the thinking either stopped short at that or went horribly wrong on the field.

In the West Indies, where the pitches are rolled mud which gets lower, slower and takes spin as the match wears on, you would normally expect to bat first on winning the toss. Especially England, who have spinners who might be able to use the natural conditions later in the game with West Indies batting last.

Obviously it was the wet patches which were abnormal. They were still damp, despite a few hours of sunshine on them, and this could perhaps be exploited by a fast bowler going round the wicket from the pavilion end. Having won the toss, it was something we had to try.

But we didn't! I was absolutely amazed to see Dilley, bowling from the pavilion end, go over the wicket and totally ignore the line which would have made use of any devil in the pitch. In fact the first time he went round the wicket was in his ninth over, and then only for the last delivery.

So two teams had sat for a large part of the day, each reluctant to play because of the damp patches on the pitch. We had been lucky enough to win the toss and grasp a big psychological advantage – and here we were letting it slip away minute by minute. The sun was fiercely hot, and our so-called advantage was literally drying up before our eyes, yet Dilley made no real attempt to use it by going round the wicket. I could hardly believe it.

Botham and Old both bowled from the pavilion end but neither has the real pace to exploit the damp area, even from over the wicket. Botham might just have done it bowling at his fastest but, to me, Dilley was obviously the man to use – and I cannot imagine why Botham did not tell him to go round the wicket. It might have been, of course, that there was nothing much in the pitch, damp patch or not, but we surely needed to find out. If we weren't going to try that, or if we believed it wasn't worth trying, what was the point of putting them in?

You could argue that it was a defensive measure to prevent them bowling first and perhaps using the dampened pitch against us. OK – but that accepts there was probably something there to use and I felt we made no effort at all to exploit it. I do not want to labour the point, but I really thought this was bad tactics.

So why didn't I run across and tell Botham where I thought he was wrong? Well, every captain has to be his own man, and Botham is no exception. He obviously has his theories about the game and its tactics and his judgement is backed by the fact that he is England's captain. If everybody who disagreed with his tactics trotted across and told him, it would be chaos – and I doubt very much that Botham would thank them for it! I have to accept that Botham knows what he is doing, but his strategy on this occasion made no sense to me.

Haynes and Greenidge never looked in serious trouble, though Dilley bowled very well and made Haynes play and miss a couple of times. He and Botham sometimes drew Haynes forward and made him play at wide deliveries and he slapped his thigh in annoyance with himself. But in typically West Indian fashion he hooks and pulls anything coming through thigh-high from just short of a length, and the score mounted with ominous certainty.

The only time Greenidge looked faintly in trouble was when he played back to full-length deliveries from Emburey. He should have been forward, and I guess he knew it, but there were dispiriting periods that afternoon when we looked like a county attack – and not a very good one at that. As a batsman watching from the boundary, it hurt.

It seemed then that we had no hope of bowling West Indies out unless there was help and movement from the pitch. Apart from Dilley, who can be genuinely quick, we have a very English attack, geared to English conditions, with little room for variation.

That is not a criticism of the players concerned, it is a reflection on the make-up of the tour party. And it is one to which I'm afraid we will have to return from time to time. I hope I am wrong, that the players themselves prove me wrong, but the evidence on the first Test day was already gloomy.

Second Day

West Indies must have been licking their lips and wondering if the scoreboard had enough noughts to accommodate their score.... Judging by the way Greenidge and Haynes had played the day before, they were entitled to feel supremely confident. We knew we would have to bowl exceptionally well, field aggressively and, most important, try to out-think and outwit their batsmen. And even on a day when we missed a couple of catches, things went very much our way.

Dilley set the standard right from the start. He bowled beautifully, at genuine pace and with immaculate line and length, which was vitally important on this pitch. We put a man deep to stifle Haynes's favourite hook and pull, so when Dilley dropped short Haynes had to block deliveries he would normally have seized on; there was little for him to score off, and he fretted.

Emburey gave nothing away at the other end. He bowled very straight at both batsmen, with three men on the leg side in front of square saving the single, and one out, so they could not hit him over the top with safety. The odd delivery turned, so neither batsman could find room to hit him on the off side; it was tight and intelligent bowling, and although we didn't exactly look like running through them, they certainly did not get the galloping start which they wanted and we feared.

Emburey's use of a short-leg and silly-point should have paid off when Haynes was on 75. He got a bat-pad which squirted off quite quickly considering the slowness of the pitch and scuttled between Gooch's legs at silly-point. Haynes was well and truly out then for all he knew about it.

Botham in turn bowled tightly rather than explosively, using only two slips and concentrating on line and length, which was good to see. West Indies had expected to gallop on and were suddenly reduced to walking pace; the frustration told when Greenidge tried to hit Emburey over the top and gave a catch to mid-on. Greenidge was furious with himself as he walked off – there had been a big score for the taking if he had buckled down and he knew it.

Haynes didn't look any happier. He didn't seem to be able to get to Botham's end and was obviously uncomfortable against Emburey's wicket-to-wicket attack; in fact his only real scoring ploy against him was to skip out of line and dab the ball into the third-man area for twos and threes – hardly Haynes's game. I sensed that Haynes was becoming desperate to reach his century before lunch. He was in the nineties and clearly did not relish the thought of sitting through the break with only a few runs needed – and on 96 he went down the pitch to try and drive Emburey on the leg side. Emburey flung himself to his right, dropped his right arm and

The happy hooker Desmond
Haynes at work.

Concentration and class from
John Emburey, surely the best
off-spinner in the world today.

snapped up a brilliant catch with his knuckles on the pitch. West Indies 203 for two.

Mattis made his Test debut like a man walking into a fielders' convention. We crowded him with as many men as we could get near the bat without actually standing on each other, including a slip, two short-legs and a man close on the off side. The third delivery from Emburey was slow and just short of a length; he got behind it and followed it as it turned, pushing it straight into the hands of Miller at backward-short-leg. A duck on his Test debut – there are a few illustrious batsmen who have gone that way. Mattis was probably mortified, and Brian Rose was miffed too. He had fielded at short-leg all morning without the whiff of a catch, then Miller takes over and one drops into his hands like a ripe plum. 'There ain't no justice,' said Rose.

Richards, the Man himself, swaggered in with that characteristic roll of the hips and an air of slightly bored confidence. He dominates the field just by walking on to it, and there is absolutely no doubt that he plans to dominate the bowling as well. An uncommon dominator at that!

We had discussed Richards at our team meeting because he is obviously the key to West Indies' batting. Opinions on how best to handle him varied but it seemed that in the past we had pressured him early on in the hope that he would make a mistake – and that rarely seemed to happen. He is so confident and so powerful that his mistakes usually whistle off to the boundary leaving us with a moral victory, which is not much consolation.

Bob Willis felt strongly that we should try another tack and attempt to frustrate Richards, employ mainly defensive fields against him and attack his vanity by not allowing him to score quickly. He loves to hit boundaries and see the scoreboard rolling against his name, and it doesn't take much to get him into his long stride.

Having decided on that approach, Botham bowled superbly. His length was perfect, he bowled an immaculate line a few inches outside the off stump, and he made Richards wait and work unfamiliarly hard. It was one of the most intelligent pieces of bowling I have seen from Botham – the perfect exploitation of situation and pitch – and Richards, even Richards, felt himself hamstrung.

Emburey bowled splendidly, too, employing a deep mid-wicket and a man in the box for the drive. If Richards hit in the air through mid-wicket, which he is usually happy to do, the man in the box might catch it; and if he got it through he would only get a single to deep mid-wicket. So it was a risky shot for little return, and Richards seemed to know it. He was unusually fretful.

One slog off Emburey fell over Botham's head in the box and went for a single; he swept Emburey off the stumps and the ball missed leg stump by a whisker; he tried to drive Botham through the covers, was made to reach for it and got an inside edge past leg stump for a single; and then he attempted to square-cut Botham and missed completely. All that before he had a dozen runs on the board ... and although he pulled a good-length ball off Botham for four and straight drove him for another, Richards looked human. You may have to read that again, but it's true.

At lunch West Indies were 204 for three, which meant we had conceded 59 runs and taken three wickets in the morning session – a fine piece of work by any standards, and especially when you consider the situation at the start of play. We were entitled to feel pleased with ourselves.

Richards took ten off Emburey's first over after lunch, and it was clear that he was determined to throw off the shackles. He was out to play his usual dominating game. But when Miller bowled one just short of a length, Richards flicked it into Gower's stomach at square-leg. A strangely indecisive shot for him, as if he had decided to pull and then simply followed the ball round as it turned – but that's the danger when any batsman decides he will attack every ball as a matter of policy. With Richards gone for 29 and West Indies on 215 for four, the complexion of the match had changed dramatically.

Lloyd was under pressure from the crowd as soon as he showed his face. He was jeered and booed to the wicket by a large section of the crowd, who obviously could not forgive the omission of Deryck Murray. It was a sad reception for a fine player.

Gomes had struggled desperately without looking like getting any runs. Towards the end of the match against Trinidad our spinners reckoned they had him worked out; they bowled round the wicket and very straight to him, with a man in the box very straight on the on side, an unusual placing but obviously very effective. The longer his innings lasted the more uncomfortable he looked.

After seventy-five overs, Botham had to decide whether to take the new ball, even though the spinners were doing their work well. He took it after eighty-seven overs, which was sensible enough since the new ball usually gets wickets and West Indies had two relatively new batsmen at the crease; Dilley and Old shared it because Botham himself had bowled a seventy-minute spell before lunch, which is no joke in this heat.

Old bowled his customary nagging line and length, Dilley bowled with real verve and fire. Lloyd found him a real handful, especially when Dilley went round the wicket – Lloyd was hit on the glove, lollipopped a catch between Dilley and cover off a leading edge, ducked and was hit in the middle of the back for four leg-byes.

The fact that Lloyd was hopping around a bit made me think of the problems we faced when we batted. Dilley was hostile, no doubt about that; multiply him by three and throw in the giant Garner for good measure, and there was no way we were going to have a picnic. Old's medium pace was punished from time to time, but our batsmen would get no such relief against their attack. It also struck me how advantageous sheer power is to a batsman in these circumstances. When Dilley over-pitched, Lloyd thumped him for four; when he bowled slightly wide, Lloyd went on to the back foot and belted him for another. They were great shots built on Lloyd's power; Gomes or even I would have probably played the same strokes for two because we don't have the sheer power of a Lloyd, a Richards, a Botham or a Gooch.

When he had laboured through eighty-two long minutes for five, Gomes pushed through a delivery from Old and gave Downton his first victim in Test cricket. It was quite inevitable because Gomes had become totally static, completely bogged

61

down. He does not knock or cuff the ball for singles, he hits it firmly and pretty straight, so unless he got a wild one to attack, he was always going to struggle against bowlers in the right mood. Gomes had not scored for an hour before he was out, and his total inertia had made his dismissal just a matter of time.

Equally to be expected was the reception which David Murray received, a swell of boos and catcalls which, even if he did expect them, were no more right or acceptable for that. We thought we had him when he had scored only two and Gower swooped to take a magnificent diving left-handed catch at short-square-leg off Old. It certainly looked to me from mid-off that it had come off bat and pad, but umpire Sang Hue remained inscrutable.

The players had gathered to congratulate Gower before they realized the umpire had given not out, and their disappointment must have communicated itself to the crowd. But we were all aware that there was no point in questioning or challenging umpires' decisions; it happens sometimes in the heat of the moment, but there's no future in it.

Murray scratched around for runs until the last over before tea, when he cut and on-drove Old for boundaries that must have helped his confidence. These boundaries also suggested to me that Old was very tired – he had not done too much bowling in the middle before the Test and I was surprised when Botham kept him on after tea. 'You're quicker than me,' Old shouted across at one stage. 'Only when I'm fresh, pal,' I replied. . . . Botham eventually had to put himself on.

He bowled round the wicket to Lloyd into the bowler's footmarks. The ball kept low, the odd delivery squatted or slowed up; faced with a deep-set field Lloyd was forced to try and hit the ball harder and harder. He played and missed a few times, obviously finding difficulty in timing the ball on the slow pitch, which kept us interested.

Emburey switched to the pavilion end and bowled in sunglasses after tea, not because he fancies himself as cricket's answer to King Farouk but because the glare off the pitch was troubling him as the sun sank lower. He found bowling from that end easier because a breeze drifted the ball away and he could spin it back – a formidable combination for any spinner to exploit. Lloyd tried hard to get after him, but Emburey continued to bowl superbly, beat him on both sides of the bat and had him dropped on 57 when Lloyd swept him to Willey at deep-square-leg.

It was still a tight, cat-and-mouse game in which we were trying to think the opposition out, as we had been all day. Miller's field to Lloyd was a good example of that. He bowled round the wicket into the footmarks outside Lloyd's off stump and employed an orthodox left-arm spinner's field: mid-on, straight mid-wicket and a man for the sweep on the leg side; slip, man on the drive, four men in the covers (two seven or eight yards deeper than usual) and a mid-off almost on the boundary.

The point was that Lloyd was being forced to hit the ball hard off the front foot on a slow pitch if he was going to make runs. He might produce a magnificent shot, of course, or a bowler might ease the pressure a bit by dropping one short, but

Clive Lloyd's cat-and-mouse contest with John Emburey finally ends: bowled middle stump for 64.

generally Lloyd had to hit very firmly – and then the likelihood was he would get a single to deep-mid-off. It niggled him and he should have been out on 59 when Gower dropped him off Miller at short-extra-cover; five runs later he tried to hit a full-length delivery through mid-wicket and was bowled middle stump by Emburey.

Murray had made most of his runs when Old was tired after tea, working him through the leg side even when he bowled straight or on the off stump. Against the spinners he did not look at all comfortable, especially with a man close on either side of the bat. Murray tried all sorts of possible solutions: when he played from the crease he was rapped on the the pads; when he went down the pitch he had to use his pads again. It was indicative of his frustration that he began to try and hit over the top – once for four, once when the ball dropped just over Botham, and a third time when Botham sprinted back from mid-wicket and took a very well-judged catch. Hitting over the top is a hazardous occupation on a pitch of uncertain bounce.

Roberts and Holding finished the day with a flourish, both hitting sixes off the spinners, and West Indies were 365 for seven at the close. A very fine day for our bowlers, but, although I do not want to make any carping criticism, we conceded 86 runs in the last session and that was too many.

Old tired and gave away some relatively cheap runs, and both spinners suddenly determined to toss the ball up in an attempt to buy the tail-enders' wickets, which I think was bad policy. They had bowled magnificently all day – none better than Emburey – and they were bound to be jaded, but throwing the ball up to the likes of Roberts and Holding was no sort of answer. Perhaps they wanted to finish them off, to add a tidy end to a good day, but that mattered less than keeping the grip they had worked so hard to forge.

If tail-enders want to attack – as theirs usually do – they should be obliged to hit good deliveries, not offered cannon-fodder. We should have kept it really tight and gone at them fresh on Monday morning. The 30 or so unnecessary runs we conceded then would take some getting back against their attack.

It was noticeable that the crowd for the second day was low, around ten thousand, which is nothing for Port-of-Spain on the Saturday of a Test match. Considering that West Indies are in bad financial trouble and Sunday had been designated as rest day to avoid clashing with the annual steel-band contest – which meant the loss of another potentially good weekend gate – the authorities must have been worried. Local opinion was that thousands of would-be spectators had stayed away because they could not afford it: they were spending their cash on costumes for the Carnival and on rum and fun at the dozens of pre-Carnival events. That may well have been so – Carnival is probably the one thing that would take precedence over cricket in Trinidad – in which case it shows how badly this Test match was scheduled.

Third Day
Ian Botham suddenly put the first Test in his own, inimitable perspective. 'On that wicket we would struggle to get a result in ten days,' he told the Press. 'If we lose

64

now, a few heads will roll. . . .' As statements go, it was sharply reminiscent of another England captain who aimed to make West Indies grovel!

It was, of course, typically Botham - the first man out of the trenches, waving his swagger-stick and advancing into a hail of bullets - and to that extent it is easy to forgive his lurid language, even if it might return to haunt him.

What was ominous was that it reflected Botham's judgement of the situation; the England captain was suggesting that a draw was more or less a piece of cake. It certainly did not look that way to me and I have played at Port-of-Spain eight times, including four Test matches. Before you can exercise judgement you have to have knowledge and Botham's experience is somewhat limited; he cannot help that, but he should probably bear it in mind.

Botham's view that we should save the match easily was presumably coloured by what he had seen in the match so far; he read - or mis-read - the pitch in terms of English conditions, and was deceived by the fact that it seemed already low and slow. You have to judge the possibilities not in terms of how we bowled against West Indies but what they had to throw against us; it is almost literally a different game.

I am coming round to the view that the ace in their pack of quick bowlers is Joel Garner. If they feel they are running into trouble, West Indies can always bring on giant Joel and there is no way you can get after him - nobody ever has. So one end is sealed as far as free scoring is concerned, batsmen feel they are under pressure, and it only needs one of their three faster men to come off. It may be Croft one day, Holding the next, Roberts another ... either way you are in trouble. In a way, it might be easier if they had four genuinely fast bowlers; they might tickle your ribs and make life generally difficult but there is always the chance of runs. Batting against Garner is pure frustration, and I sometimes think the West Indian crowds, happy to think in terms of sheer pace, underestimate the big man's value.

West Indies resumed on 365 for seven and suddenly piled on 61 runs in forty-three minutes, largely because Roberts reminded us that he started life as a batsman and is formidably, punishingly strong. He murdered us.

Emburey was blasted for six by Holding, had to spread his field and inevitably conceded ones and twos so Botham had to take him off. Botham himself got Holding out in typical Botham fashion. After Holding tried to slog him, Botham ran in steadily went wide of the crease in the last two strides and fired in a yorker aimed at middle stump. The angle of delivery fooled Holding, who assumed it was going wide of leg stump and tried to turn it; he was lbw, and I have seen Botham get many tail-enders out the same way. Garner and Croft hung around; Roberts suddenly exploded.

He heaved Botham to wide long-off for four, a sighter for a six over long-on next ball. Then he took a couple and another six over mid-wicket! Botham intelligently decided to bowl a slower one but he dropped it too short and Roberts had time to step back and flat-bat it over long-on for another six. Four, six, two, six, six and then a leg-bye. Quite an over.

Lloyd declared when Roberts reached 50, and I don't quite know why. It would have made more sense to keep going, especially with Roberts in that frame of mind; every run could be important on a slow pitch if they hoped to make us follow on, and leaving us thirty minutes to lunch would have made just as much sense as the fifty-five minutes we faced. Still, 426 for nine was formidable enough.

Looking at the bowling analyses, it struck me how misleading figures can sometimes be. Graham Dilley bowled twenty-eight overs without taking a wicket, so I suppose in the most literal sense he was a failure. Yet he had bowled superbly throughout the innings without any luck; his performance gave everybody a lift and, wickets or no wickets, he had already had a very fine game.

We had a mountain to climb but Gooch went galloping through the foothills at a tremendous pace. In no time at all he was in double figures and I had faced only one ball, but I felt in very good form, driving Roberts through the covers for four and taking boundaries off Holding when he went round the wicket. I know when I am playing well, and everything felt just right.

Gooch was dropped on 15, a simple chance which Mattis at second slip should have held without any bother. Again, it was Croft's line which caused the problem; the ball was delivered from wide of the crease and Gooch had to play at it.

By lunch we were 45 without loss off 11 overs, and it was clear that the West Indies would not stand for that sort of scoring rate for long. Sure enough, they brought on Garner – and persisted with Croft because he was economical and always likely to take a wicket. He did.

Croft bowled me a bouncer, then bowled the next delivery wide – around half-volley length – and like a fool I drove at it. A thick edge to Richards at third slip and I was out for 30 – and very annoyed with myself. I should have given myself more time to readjust after lunch, a couple of overs playing carefully, but I felt in such good form that I wanted to get after them. What I forgot was that one mistake can put you back in the pavilion, where the best form in the world is no use to you. I should have known that.

I felt sorry for Brian Rose. He looked like a man out of form – just what we feared after a disappointing start to the tour – and there's no way you can face the best pace attack in the world in those circumstances. It's hard enough to play county cricket when you are out of form: against West Indies it is impossible. He braved it for an uncomfortable hour and then fell to a bat-pad catch by Haynes diving forward at short-square-leg. I wouldn't have fancied his situation, and I have played in a few more Test matches than he has. . . .

The next hour was a heart-stopping exercise in pure survival, and how Gooch and Gower came through it is anybody's guess. West Indies played it shrewdly. They had made their big effort for quick wickets and now they set out to stifle, employing fields which cut runs to a trickle and screwing down the pressure. Croft maintained a line outside the off stump, varied his pace and used cutters intelligently; both batsmen played and missed with unnerving regularity and the heat was really on.

High, wide and fearfully difficult to combat — Colin Croft shows his unusual angle of delivery against Graham Gooch.

Below: Brian Rose on the way out, caught by Haynes off Garner for 10 in the first Test.

Gooch almost pushed a delivery from Garner to short-leg, was turned round by Croft as he aimed to play to mid-on and missed, played and missed again. Gower edged Garner through the slips for four, survived an appeal for caught behind, played and missed again. Hard, hard work for them and very bad for our fingernails in the dressing-room.

It was interesting to see where Haynes and Garner fielded for Croft's bowling while we were under this sort of intense pressure. Garner stood at a position between short-extra-cover and silly-mid-off, and Haynes at short-square-leg, about five or six yards from the bat. Both were obviously looking for a catch from a delivery which popped – it was an unusual ploy.

Three deliveries in mid-afternoon indicated to me just how hard the lads were having to struggle. Garner had a huge shout for lbw against Gooch turned down, then he yorked him with a no-ball and finally whipped in a yorker again which Gooch managed to dig out. Gooch is a stroke-player and a very enterprising one at that, not an easy man to tie down; yet in two hours to tea he scored 17 runs. A gruesome sort of statistic which reflected pressure on one hand and real determination on the other.

Garner bowled unchanged from lunch to tea; 14 overs, one for 26, which needs no sort of comment. We made 52 runs off 28 overs – a sweating, unnerving snail's pace with both batsmen fighting hard and finding virtually nothing to hit. Gower kept the score moving with judicious ones and twos, but there was little of the flashing blade; he was the picture of responsibility.

Three hours of tremendous defiance by Gooch ended in a shower of bails five overs after tea. He was probably feeling the pressure of not scoring, the tension of wondering where the next single was coming from: in any event he pushed further forward than he would normally, was beaten when a delivery from Roberts came back, and lost his middle and off stumps. England 110 for three, and about to lose two more quick wickets.

Croft had only two men not in catching positions against Miller and gave him a terrible time, beating him outside the off stump and turning him round when he tried to play on the leg side. It looked like a matter of time and Miller was caught behind playing defensively.

Botham faced only two balls before Croft bowled him a yorker which clipped his left pad and cannoned on to his right. Botham shaped his stroke as though he was confident the ball was going down the leg side and it certainly looked that way to me, but umpire Cumberbatch gave him lbw. Suddenly we were 127 for five.

Croft, playing in his twenty-first Test match, is about to pass his hundred Test wickets and he really is an extraordinary customer to handle. In twenty years I have never faced a bowler who bowls from so wide of the crease. To get in line, you would have to take guard on off stump and still move over – but that would leave your leg stump exposed and there are few greater crimes for a Test batsman. I take middle to him and move back and across as he bowls so that I'm well over, but it's still very difficult to defend your off stump without reaching and stretching with your arms away from your body.

You want to get forward and across to him, but Croft is nobody's fool. Every so often he lets you have one in the ribs to keep you back and at 6 ft 4 ins he is not the slowest bowler in Test cricket. I suppose it would be possible to get forward to every delivery – and play him with your helmet. . . .

Croft gives the lie to so many of the accepted rules for successful fast bowling. 'Deliver the ball from close to the stumps with a side-on action,' they say. Well, Croft's feet are all over the place, his left foot is outside the return crease, his arms wave like windmills and his chest is square as he lets the ball go. A hundred Test wickets with that action? Try explaining that to some youngster in the nets.

Gower battled on despite losing another partner in Willey, caught off a thick edge at third slip, and was still there at the close with 47 precious runs. But all genuine hope of avoiding the follow-on seemed to have disappeared long ago; I didn't think we would do it as soon as Botham was out.

Gower had his moments, not least when Croft beat him with a full-length delivery which held up and simply couldn't believe that his lbw appeal was turned down. Garner was sure he had trapped him lbw when he padded up to one which came back at him but it was 'No' again. I must say they both looked out to me.

When they stopped for drinks Bairstow asked Gower how he was getting on. 'I'm all right; I think the umpires must be on my side,' Gower winked. You need all the friends you can get these days.

We lost another wicket before the close: that of Downton, who will remember his Test debut if only because of the way he got out. He played forward studiously and defensively and was bowled, not by any of the world's fastest bowlers, but by Larry Gomes of all people! Downton was mortified; an hour later he still could not figure out just what went wrong.

Fourth Day
The mist which rolled over the ridge-back hills, filling the valley and circling the ground, looked quite promising for a side still needing 68 to avoid the follow-on and with only three wickets in hand. The groundstaff, who can spot rain here ten minutes before it arrives, were already manning the covers when Gower and Emburey walked out. For heaven's sake hang around, was the message – if we don't avoid the follow-on we must at least leave West Indies as little time as possible to bowl us out again. As a brief it was straightforward enough, but much easier said than done.

Gower obviously represented our best chance, and he had already borne his responsibilities bravely. But after ten minutes he shaped to play a full-toss from Croft through mid-wicket, missed and was given out lbw. Once again Croft's angle of delivery was responsible, though Gower as a left-hander was entitled to think his leg was outside the line of the leg stump when the ball hit. As Gower walked disconsolately off, the first spots of rain arrived and the players were following him by the time he reached the pavilion; if the rain had come a minute earlier he would have been reprieved.

We gained twenty-five minutes and then lost Dilley. He plays inside to out, and all the West Indies bowlers reckon he is vulnerable to the yorker; Croft's yorker hit middle stump and we were 167 for nine. No chance of avoiding the follow-on now, even with Emburey battling splendidly.

It was a fine, gutsy performance from him, even if he suffered the indignity of being dumped on his backside by a bouncer from Roberts with the new ball. He shaped to hook, changed his mind and had no alternative but to sink (gracefully) on to the seat of his pants. We remembered what Sir Len Hutton said when asked if he hooked Lindwall and Miller: 'I once got to the halfway stage, but out of the corner of my eye I could see the local hospital. So I cut it out....' Not every day do you see Emburey following in Hutton's footsteps!

Old against the new ball was something of a catchweight contest and it wasn't too long before Roberts knocked back his off stump. He might have been out before that when he slashed Croft, and Garner at gulley leaped with both hands above his head – which must have put him about twelve feet above the ground – and couldn't hold the catch. 'If you'd only grow a bit you'd have caught that,' admonished Old....

We followed on 248 behind, but not before the weather tried to help us out again. There was a heavy shower and an inspection showed a wet patch on the pitch around a fullish length on the left-hander's off stump. The surrounds were also wet, perhaps because water spilled off the covers as they were removed; in any event the restart was delayed until 2.30 p.m.

West Indies obviously had their tails up and Holding really hurtled in – fast enough on a slow pitch to make us wonder just how pacey he will be in Barbados on a quick one. Roberts dug in a few bouncers at me, and one short delivery kept so low I almost ducked into it. Another bouncer from Roberts took the edge, dropped just short of Richards at third slip and went off his arm for four runs. It was tight, tense stuff.

Their pace was problem enough, but what made it even more difficult was an uneven bounce. Roberts dug another one in, I ducked and the ball rose only high enough to smack me in the back and ricochet away for a single. The doubt was more painful than the pain.

After we had seen off the first thirty-five minutes, Holding's pace and a delivery angled into him beat Gooch, who was lbw on the back foot. And poor Rose again looked nervous and struggling, squirting one on the ground through slips for four very early in his innings. I felt very sorry for him; he needs a confidence boost and the middle in a Test match is not likely to be the place for that. Not against West Indies.

Botham had said before we went out that we hadn't done ourselves justice and that we could save it if we fought and batted really well. 'Same batting order, better batting,' announced Gooch in his gruff imitation of Essex's Tonker Taylor. At tea

Botham asked me to keep talking to Rose, helping him through, and Kenny Barrington put in his own request. 'Do a good job for yourself, do a good job for the team, talk to Rosie and don't get out,' he said. Oh, is that all. . . .

Holding was tearing in again after tea and soon accounted for Rose, who pushed firmly at a delivery of fullish length and got a faint edge to the wicket-keeper. At 25 for two, we needed all Gower's new-found application and self control.

He batted well and rarely looked in real trouble except when Holding went round the wicket and banged the ball in hard. Gower was surprised by the pace and the awkward angle of the delivery as it chased him, and almost fell on his stumps. He tottered, stumbled, threw a leg over the stumps and fell out of harm's way; good job he's light on his feet. Rodney Hogg bowled round the wicket against Gower in Australia and gave him a lot of trouble; I've always felt that that line of attack disturbs him because it gives him less room to hit his shots on the off side.

I had an escape when I had made 15. Holding fired one in just short of a length outside the off stump, worth a hit except that it kept low and I should have let it go. But at that pace I was committed and I followed it down, edging a chance low to Mattis's left at second slip; he got both hands to it and put it down. Phew!

We simply had to see it through to the end, and I scarcely played a shot in anger when Garner bowled after tea. I took middle-stump guard, played back and across and lined him up well. I suspect Garner gets frustrated when that happens to him – he likes batsmen to give him a chance by playing shots. He dug in a couple short of a length, which is unusual for him, and fired in a few yorkers which I managed to keep out.

Mike Gatting suggested at tea that I took an off-stump guard to Croft, who still bedevils us with his wide angle of delivery. It was an intelligent thought and worth the risk, and I reckoned it worked, because I lined him up well and missed only one delivery which was a big leg-cutter. I wasn't looking to play shots, just to consume time and let the ball come to me, playing it closer to my body. (Because of Croft's angle of delivery, you tend to reach for the ball with your arms away from your body.) I felt more comfortable against him after that, and an off-stump guard is certainly worth thinking about, especially in a defensive situation.

Self-discipline was vitally important in the circumstances, and I was impressed with Gower. He obviously likes to get at the bowlers but he was very restrained and sensible, as he had to be in our position. When Richards bowled his off-spin I sensed that Gower was aching to have a go, and sure enough he tried to cut a wide, low delivery and was dropped by Murray. 'Don't do anything silly; they've put Richards on to try and tempt us,' I reminded him. He acknowledged his mistake and battled on splendidly.

We reached 65 for two at the close, still needing 183 to avoid defeat by an innings. It was a fearfully tall order, but at least we were still fighting. The heat certainly doesn't help; I was wet through by the end of the day, and as I stood in the crease sweat dripped from beneath my helmet and made a little pool at my feet. I lost count of how many times I changed batting gloves because they were saturated. Stevenson brought me a towel; I wished it had been an ice pack....

Fifth Day

How do you resist the world's fastest bowling attack for six hours on an awkward batting pitch when they are thirsting for the kill? There is always a difficult equation between time and runs, but I had not the slightest doubt that against this attack our priority was to play for time. We have never scored a lot of runs against them; there was no reason to suppose we could start now.

That being the case, I put any consideration of how I might score runs totally out of my mind. The vital thing is to occupy the crease, to defend your stumps and play only straightforward shots which involve only a minimum of risk. They must prise you out, and you must never – never – contribute in any way to your own dismissal.

Those who suggest that is 'my kind of game' underestimate the tension and the pressures involved in playing it. Like any batsman, I would rather play shots and see runs going on the board, not least because we are all judged to a great extent on averages as much as performance. Just wait until the end of the tour. But I set out to sacrifice everything to the job of consuming time – and that takes more concentration than usual. Steeling yourself not to make a mistake for hour after hour is a wearying, strenuous task, but it had to be done.

I have been puzzled by the way Roberts sometimes gets extraordinary bounce, even on slow surfaces, and I think I have worked it out. He sometimes holds the ball *across* the seam rather than along it, and if it pitches on the seam it climbs alarmingly; one delivery scuttled off the shoulder of my bat and bounced through the slips for four – and that was with a ball forty overs old!

I was a little surprised that West Indies opened with Garner rather than Holding, but it was soon clear that he was in a very aggressive mood, rolling his fingers over to cut the ball and hurling down bouncers – which is not his usual style – when he saw me trying to step forward. His prodigious height means he can bounce the ball awkwardly from just short of a length and he was obviously determined to make a quick breakthrough; thank goodness for chest-pads!

Gower had batted for two and a quarter hours and we had got through the first half-hour of the day when he was out a little unluckily. He aimed to glance Roberts down the leg side and the ball brushed his thigh-pad just hard enough to take the pace off it and allow Murray to get across and take a catch down the leg side. It was a cruel way to go after so much real hard work – and an increasingly perilous situation for us on 86 for three.

Surprising as it may sound, Miller had never faced Garner before! He asked me what guard to take and I told him just to concentrate on blocking up, take no risks and give himself time to settle in. Goodness knows, we had too much of that. Miller scores many of his runs by working the ball through mid-wicket and hooking, and I told him to forget that completely; if Garner turned him round he would be in fearful trouble.

72

In safe keeping. Paul Downton returned from the tour as England's first-choice wicket-keeper.

The heat is on in Trinidad. A pause to mop away some of the perspiration as England battle to save the Test.

He stuck at it for over half an hour, then Croft struck again. I had told Miller about my experiment with an off-stump guard to combat Croft's extraordinary angle of delivery, but sure enough, Miller stretched away from his body trying to cover the line and was caught easily at third slip.

It looked like an awful shot and, OK, it wasn't very distinguished. But it was typical of the way Croft bowls and the way batsmen had been forced to try to play him; Miller was simply a classic victim, Croft's hundredth in twenty-one Test matches.

Botham had a wind-up at Garner off the back foot and I had to remind him that we were supposed to be saving the match. 'Sorry, lack of concentration, keep talking to me,' he said. And he played very responsibly through to lunch, chipping the odd run here and there but not taking any risks.

There was a promise of rain, but I didn't think it would ever be heavy or prolonged enough to do us much good. If we were to save the match it would have to be through our own efforts, and the crunch period was approaching fast; at lunch there were only eleven overs to go before the new ball was due....

We had to accept the possibility of losing a wicket to the new ball against their attack. But it was imperative that we lost only one at most; that would leave Willey with Botham or myself to prevent West Indies getting through to the tail too soon. If we could see off the new ball we had a chance, at least a chance.

A shower of rain cost West Indies fifteen minutes and they brought on Richards and Gomes, whistling through their overs as fast as we could get down to face them, obviously intent on reaching the new ball as quickly as possible. There is a tendency for batsmen to attack the slow bowlers, especially when the new ball is only a few overs away, but this was not the day for it; Botham cut Richards for two and I reminded him it was a risky shot on a pitch where the odd delivery might keep low.

Then it happened. Botham inexplicably tried to hit Richards over mid-off and lofted the ball to Holding, who has a safe pair of hands and made the catch look easy. I could not believe it and neither could Richards; he almost went berserk with delight. Botham had played the wrong shot in our situation and the wrong shot on that pitch, where the uneven bounce made it difficult to time a forcing stroke in the air. It would have been a risky shot if we had been trying to win the match, for heaven's sake ... in our situation it was totally foolhardy. It's only fair to say that Botham was as upset as anyone, although he did say on television afterwards that it was just the way he played.

We should have been making them prise us, drag us out, and here they had picked up a wicket without a reason in the world why they should do so. No wonder the West Indians were cavorting about, hugging and congratulating each other; no wonder the crowd was stomping and cheering. It was unforgivable, and the new ball was only four overs away.

A combination of Holding, the new ball and the pitch got me out. The ninth delivery with the new ball suddenly steeplejacked, hit me on the left glove in front

74

of my throat and sped in an arc to third slip, where Haynes fell forward and took the catch. I'm not sure what I could have done about it, even after five and a quarter hours at the crease.

As I passed Willey he said, 'There was nothing you could do about that one,' and I paused and looked at the pitch. It looked as though the ball had hit one of the patches which had been re-earthed at the start of the match; it had taken a pounding and, not being compacted like the rest of the pitch, the top had crumbled. Holding had hit it with the new ball; I consider I was unlucky.

One flash of the irresponsible and another of the unexpected had thrown the match into West Indies' lap. I felt very dejected, not just at my own failure, though that was galling enough, but because there was very little chance that we would save it now. We were 140 for six with some three hours still to go, and there was no way the tail could play that well. If I had got past the new ball we might have braved it through, or at least there was a possibility. But not now, not even with dark rain-clouds approaching from the hills.

As it turned out, the umpires were very reluctant to go off and Willey and Downton had to bat through some heavy showers until they were finally chased off five minutes before tea. They defied the new ball bravely but time was against them, especially since the sky brightened and the weather showed no sign of settling in. We knew we needed them to stay together for at least thirty or forty minutes of the last session and Downton lasted fifteen minutes before he was beaten outside the off stump and Lloyd grabbed a low catch at first slip.

Emburey is a capable batsman who can battle it out, but he followed ten minutes later, pushing too far forward at a delivery from Roberts which took the inside edge and plucked out his middle stump. Then Willey was caught at first slip by a juggling Lloyd, and Old pushed his first delivery, a lifter from Garner, straight into the hands of short-leg. It was all over.

Willey's innings made me wonder why he is not played further up the order. He is a brave, durable player, but batting at seven usually gives him little chance to develop an innings because the tail is struggling at the other end. He has scored centuries and Miller has not, so there must be a case for batting Willey at five. It might be that his technique would not be up to it, but until he is given the chance we will never know, and I reckon he has played well enough in a limited role to be given the opportunity to prove himself.

Botham had to put a brave face on it. 'Never mind, lads, there are still four Tests to go, we can still pull it back if we keep our heads up.' Always assuming, of course, that we have any heads to keep. . . .

In terms of the pitches we face, Port-of-Spain should represent our best chance of winning a Test match. The slowness of its pitch deprives their quick bowlers of some pace advantage and also gives our spinners their best chance of bowling West Indies out. Yet in three and three-quarter playing days we had lost by an innings and 79 runs. How did we feel? The figures tell it all.

10

Written Off

It was unpleasant and very thought-provoking to stand at the presentation ceremony listening to the abuse of the Trinidad crowd. Unpleasant, because nobody likes to be the object of obscene chants about the ability of the team; thought-provoking, because it was so unusual.

In 1974 we lost the first Test in Port-of-Spain by an innings after losing the last Test in England the previous summer by an innings, so they obviously had reason to consider theirs the better side. But they did not abuse us then; they did not write us off as scathingly as they were doing now. The actual terms of the abuse did not concern me over-much; what worried me as a professional was that they should be so dismissive, so scornful of our ability – and so soon.

West Indians may have a very different approach to cricket than we have – hardly stiff upper lips or tea and cakes on the lawn – but their crowds appreciate the game, they have a great feeling for it and they respect performance; they are not the worst judges in the world. I wondered how far their scorn was aimed at the public pronouncements we have made since we arrived and even before that. 'The West Indian players will be tired ... England have not lost a series in the Caribbean since 1948 ... heads will roll' and so on. It is hard to claim they were realistic comments, in view of recent events, and I suspect the crowd in Port-of-Spain were reminding us of the fact. Ironically, they might have been more pro-English than most, since many were clearly angered by the omission of Deryck Murray.

Botham braved it out, as you would expect, explaining his shot with: 'That's the way I play,' and claiming he had been quoted out of context over the rolling heads business. I reckon he would have done himself more good to admit his mistakes as mistakes; nobody would have pilloried him for that.

We learned soon afterwards that Bob Willis had lost his battle against a knee injury and had to return home. It is a dreadful thing to happen to anyone on tour – and Willis had everyone's sympathy – but it seemed to make a mockery of pre-tour fitness tests and the suggestion that others might have been left behind because they were not totally fit. Willis had bowled seven overs before succumbing to an injury to a knee which had a history of problems. . . . If it was a gamble it misfired badly, and sadly for him.

Mike Hendrick and Geoff Miller were sent home from previous tours once there was an obvious doubt about their ability to continue as players; the manager suggested Willis might be kept on because he had a good influence on the rest of the team and especially, one suspects, on Botham. That would have been an unusually privileged position, even for a vice-captain.

Surrey's Robin Jackman was flown in as a replacement for Willis, and I'm bound to say that I had some doubts about this decision. Not that I underestimate Jackman's ability in any way – he has been a competitive, professional performer in county cricket for years, and has a fine record to prove it. But I do not think he will add what we need to the make-up of the party – in West Indian conditions – which is not already provided by Old or Stevenson.

The selectors presumably thought the same way, or they would have brought him out in the first place. If the pitches are receptive, any one of those three could do a good job for us; otherwise I cannot see Jackman adding significantly to the bowling strength we have.

In the circumstances I would have sent for the left-arm spin of Edmonds, simply because I feel our spin department could be improved by variety. Without being asked, some West Indian players said the same thing – which cannot be entirely beside the point. I would not have expected him to bowl West Indies out in Test matches, but I do feel he could have made a significant improvement considering the situation which now faces us. The fact is that we do not look like bowling West Indies out in any case – so it is imperative that we control them in the field, make runs harder for them to come by. We need to make them take at least three hours more to score the same number of runs, if only because that makes our first job of saving Tests that little bit easier. Then we must stand a better chance of grabbing a victory.

Our philosophy now – and it is one shared by several members of the party besides me – should be to assure ourselves of a draw and hope to spring a win from a position of safety. Plan for the worst and hope for the best, if you like. That is a realistic viewpoint, if not a very romantic one, and Edmonds could have helped by giving us more variety in spin. Every little helps when you are fighting against the odds.

The vice-captaincy fell vacant with Willis's departure, and when Miller was eventually appointed I felt I had been snubbed again by the Establishment. I do not use the word lightly or for effect.

When a man has played in ninety-five Test matches and is alone, at least among Englishmen, in making his third Test tour to West Indies it must be in the best interests of English cricket to make full use of his experience and knowledge. Especially when there are only two players in the team – Chris Old was the other – who have played a Test series in the Caribbean. If use is not made of that experience, the team has been done a disservice.

I have been accused of not helping out in the past. I have been left out of any sort of policy-making group on tours under Mike Brearley since I lost the vice-

77

captaincy. I have rarely been asked for my advice, though the impression often given to the public is that I will not co-operate – which is absolute nonsense. Individual players seek me out for advice, and I give it, but officially I am left out in the cold.

When the vice-captaincy fell vacant, a Sunday newspaper immediately ran a story claiming that I was ruled out of consideration because my fellow-players did not want me. The suggestion was quickly discounted by Alan Smith and the captain, but the mud thrown at me sticks just as hard. That article was unsigned: I wonder who was afraid to put his name to it?

Professionalism is what matters on tour. It matters for everybody, because we are all likely to be judged on our performances as individuals and as a team. I have never set out my stall to be Mr Popular, and it is inevitable that some people will like me more than others; some will tolerate me; some will dislike me. That's life!

But professional judgements should not be based on prejudice. The Establishment seem to want my *ability* but not *me*, and I find that depressing and dispiriting.

II

Gloom in Guyana

'Don't venture far from the hotel, and even then go in a group. Don't go out alone and never go out at night. . . .' That was the official warning which welcomed us to Guyana, and when we arrived it was sodden and overcast. 'Welcome to Manchester,' said Clive Lloyd.

We had all heard lurid tales of muggings and robberies in Guyana and they were reinforced by English officials on the spot and by the briefings which our tour management had received before leaving the UK. 'When you are out walking you are a target.' We were advised not to carry money in open shirt pockets, nor to wear watches and jewellery.

I'm bound to say I never felt threatened personally, but there was a sinister sense of isolation which was not helped by the grey, overcast skies and the bad weather which – inevitably, it now seemed – dogged our progress to the South American mainland.

It had rained pretty solidly for the best part of two weeks before we arrived, and there was already a real doubt as to whether we would be able to play the scheduled four-day match against Guyana. The Bourda ground was waterlogged, with standing pools of water on the outfield and soft, slimy mud on the surrounds; since the country is below sea level and protected from the Atlantic by a long, formidable sea wall, there was very little chance of any water draining away unless the weather improved dramatically.

Before the cricket ground could dry, water had to drain into a gutter beyond the boundary, then into a moat outside the stadium, and then into the main drainage channel which ran like a brown river through the middle of the town. There was at least three feet of water in the main channel, constantly topped up by torrential showers, and it didn't look as though it was going anywhere fast. Depression in the depression. . . .

Proper net practice was impossible, and after a hopeful game of tennis on the first day, I developed a sore throat and temperature from a virus infection, which confined me to bed for forty-eight hours. I lay and watched it rain – and the rest of the lads were not all that active either.

They found an indoor gymnasium where they could do loosening-up exercises and play five-a-side football – I believe Real Madrid beat Brentford in the final – but even that was short-lived. On the second day everybody was attacked by fifty-seven varieties of mosquito; arms and legs were covered in great bumps and blotches, and it was impossible to continue.

Until the weather relented there was nothing to do but read, wander round the hotel, play cards for stakes which would have challenged a Mississippi river boat gambler, and grab what sunshine there was at the hotel pool. Several of the boys were growing beards, and that threatened to be their most arduous form of exercise!

We discovered a flat, tarmac area at a local school which looked promising until it was discovered that the ball bounced only two-thirds of stump height, and the abrasive surface ruined our practice balls at a fearsome rate. Kenny Barrington looked after our practice balls as though they were gold nuggets, so there was no way we could keep up that particular form of net for long.

In the end we did get in some cricket of a sort, because it was discovered that the local police ground was above sea level and had drained surprisingly well. We were able to net and then have a practice match in the middle, and I don't suppose many England practices have ever been watched by more spectators. They turned up in their hundreds.

I felt it was important we practised under match conditions because that gives the bowlers a chance to bowl off their full run and, just as important, to judge whether they were bowling well. Constant practice in the nets is unsatisfactory for bowlers, because unless they actually knock the stumps down they never take a wicket; they need to know whether they are forcing batsmen to play to fielders, just as they would in a match.

It was agreed to play the match seriously, and that any batsman who did not make runs could stay behind and have extra practice in the middle. I had a couple of overs before Stevenson gloved me with one which whistled past my nose and Bairstow took the catch behind; you can imagine how much glee went into that decision, especially since I had already caught Bairstow, hooking, on the boundary! Butcher and I stayed behind for practice, although we were not the only ones to fail to score many runs.

The staff and management at the Pegasus did everything they could for us, and the manager provided his own video equipment so we could take in a film – *Papillon* (which seemed rather too appropriate) and *The Eiger Sanction*. But the evenings were long, especially since we knew we did not have the option of leaving the hotel; it was a confined and frustrating sort of existence and no sort of preparation for a one-day international against West Indies.

Albion, in up-country Berbice, is about seventy miles from Georgetown by road – a long, tedious trip which involves a long wait for the ferry across the wide, muddy Berbice river. The Press got up at 5.00 a.m. and set off in a clanking bus; we had a bit of a lie-in and went by air. From a small airfield at Georgetown we flew in a twenty-seater aircraft to an equally small airstrip in Berbice and made the last leg to the ground by helicopter. West Indies made the whole trip by helicopter and we

Looks like a winner ... time out for a game of tennis during our ill-starred stay in Guyana.

switched with them for the return. Everyone was looking forward to the novelty of flying by helicopter, but it was a mixed blessing, if only because the noise was absolutely deafening – no wonder helicopter pilots wear earphones even when there is no radio traffic! We landed on the ground in a great swirl of dust and grass cuttings, most of which seemed to hurricane into the Press box, where reporters already shouting themselves hoarse to make contact with England were covered in debris. 'I AM speaking up; they've just flown the ruddy team helicopter through the box....'

From the air the countryside was a patchwork of irrigation ditches serving the sugar-cane fields, mile after mile of dark green rectangles bordered by strips of brown. The locals go crocodile hunting at night, shining the headlights of their cars into the water until a curious croc comes to investigate and then aiming between the eyes. Chris Old joined them on his last trip into Berbice, but I don't recall him catching anything....

The ground itself was a revelation; modern and well kept, with good facilities and a very friendly, helpful staff. They had obviously put in a lot of work for the occasion, and it struck us that we would have been better off out in Albion for a few days than moping in Georgetown. The pitch was flat and dry, without too much bounce, and the outfield was in splendid condition. It was the sort of pitch we would have liked for a Test match – had we been in some sort of form.

But we weren't. We were desperately short of match practice, and it showed. West Indies beat us by six wickets after we left them to score only 138 to win; we should have made more runs, but nobody seemed to be able to put his game together – which was not altogether surprising. Had we won the toss we would have put them in and tried to frustrate them; in the event they put us in and did just that to us.

Willey and Botham played very well but I was most impressed by Gatting, who played a fine innings considering he has had only one long innings on the tour and virtually no opportunity for meaningful practice outside that. In all the circumstances his innings of 29 was a very valiant effort. After what he told me in Trinidad it was interesting to see that he took an off-stump guard to Croft and played him very confidently.

We discussed Croft again at our team meeting, and Butcher made the very valid point that although we had to watch out chiefly for his angle of delivery, we should not forget that Croft is a genuinely fast bowler who would let us have a few fireworks sooner or later. In front of his own crowd, Croft did send down quite a few bouncers, and it struck me – in a manner of speaking – that he may have been riled by a newspaper article which asked him to reply to my suggestion that bouncers might be over-used on the tour.

The off-spinners Richards and Gomes picked up four wickets between them, which meant that Gooch came in for some good-natured ribbing in the dressing-room. At the pre-match meeting he kept stressing that we must cash in when the slower bowlers were on, because we obviously would not score freely off the fast men. Fair enough, but Gooch insisted on calling them Mickey Mouse bowlers; if he used the phrase once he must have used it a dozen times. At the end of the game he was suitably chastened: 'Mickey Mouse and Pluto, four wickets between them. Damn good job Donald Duck wasn't playing,' he conceded in that typically drole, mournful voice.

Our spinners bowled well on a slow, lowish pitch, but West Indies never had to hurry and won comfortably enough. Richards was out by hooking, surprisingly for him since he is widely regarded and not least in West Indies – as the best player of the hook-shot in the world. But Botham did his homework well and had two men in the arc round long-leg; Stevenson took a well-judged high catch.

Greenidge was superbly run out by a piece of quicksilver fielding from Butcher and some quick thinking by Bairstow, who threw down the stumps even though he was off balance and going the wrong way. Apart from that, it was interesting to see Haynes confirm the belief that he has a lot to learn against spin-bowling. He played the seamers effortlessly, but against spin he seemed to have to whack or block; he has not yet learned how to knock them off for singles and is obviously uncomfortable when they are on.

Poor Brian Rose had already set off back to England. He developed a defect in his right eye, first suspected by Bernard Thomas who noticed he did not seem to pick up the flight of a possible catch in Trinidad. Rose is a fine squash player and yet when the opportunity arose he had seemed reluctant to play, which was not like him at all. Thomas and Rose discussed the matter, and Rose was naturally reluctant to blame his lack of runs on anything but himself. But it was felt that expert opinion should be sought, and Rose was advised by a specialist in Georgetown that remedial treatment might be necessary.

Rose would have preferred to seek a further opinion when we reached Barbados, but in view of the political climate developing hour by hour it was considered wiser to accept the Guyanese specialist's point of view. As for the political climate, we were beginning to wonder if the one-day match at Albion might be the last one between West Indies and ourselves in the Caribbean for some years to come.

Croft on bouncers:
Colin Croft was asked in a newspaper article in Guyana what he thought of my suggestion before the tour began that umpires would have to be strict in interpreting the laws of the game to prevent too many bouncers being bowled.

'Basically I think the fast bowler has got to use the bouncer. I think that if you look back to 1980 in England when we were there, not one of the umpires had anything to say about anybody bowling too many short balls – and we were in England playing against England. If they didn't take time off to tell us about it then, I don't see why this issue should be raised now.

'There are not too many people in this world who prefer facing short-pitched bowling; again there are not too many opening batsmen who could bat like Geoff Boycott. I respect him as one of the better batsmen I have ever played against, but

I think he is being carried away a bit. I don't think there is going to be a bouncer war, all I feel is that everybody will try their utmost to get the opposition out as fairly as they can. Nobody is going to "assassinate" anybody as such, it will boil down to the point of playing cricket.

'It's not the situation of our fast bowlers winning the series because as far as I am concerned there is no other choice. We have spinners like Derek Parry and Ranji Nanan making bids for Test places, but it doesn't seem likely at all that the West Indies will go into any of the Test matches with two spinners.

'The West Indies pace attack has proven that it is capable of bowling out any side on any surface. Whether the wickets are lively enough or not, I think the West Indies fast bowling attack is capable of giving any batting side the time of their lives.'

12

The Jackman Affair

The telephone rang in room 507 of the Holiday Inn in Barbados and Kenny Barrington said cheerfully: 'I suppose you've heard the news – the tour's on....' I said I'd just woken up and hadn't heard a thing. 'Oh ... oh well, laundry in fifteen minutes.' Not the most dramatic end, perhaps, to a controversy which threatened the Caribbean tour and could still have worldwide significance for cricket.

Robin Jackman, the man whose South African connections sparked off ten days of controversy, speculation and uncertainty, was receiving a phone call at about the same time. It was from his wife Yvonne in England, the first news he had that the tour was to continue. Two minutes later Alan Smith rang him to confirm it, and eight o'clock on a sunny Barbados morning had suddenly become part of cricket history. It had been a long, long ten days.

What seemed like an age before, Alan Smith had stretched himself in the team room in Georgetown, Guyana and announced to the Press: 'Robin Jackman is expected to arrive at 0:100 tomorrow.' He can hardly have suspected at the time that nine words could carry so much significance.

A day later Smith made a Press statement which was far more ominous, the first real indication that politics was about to intrude into the tour. 'I have been asked some questions relating to visits to South Africa by Robin Jackman,' said Smith. 'The questions have come from government authorities here in Guyana. I have contacted the High Commission here and explained the questions put to me and also advised Donald Carr. The High Commissioner and I have answered the questions, and there the matter rests at the moment.

'We have made no statements on the subject; the Guyana government has made no statements on the subject. I am not going to speculate; I am in touch with the High Commissioner and do not want to say any more.'

It was typical of Smith's carefully modulated language, straight out of the school of diplomacy, but the Press were under no illusions as to what it might mean. Within hours they were filing stories that the tour was in doubt; apartheid had struck again.

We were not really involved at that point. Our preoccupation as players was with the one-day international in Berbice, and it was not until we arrived in the hotel lobby on the morning of the match that we realized it was in danger. Would there be an official statement from the Guyana government? Would the match be played? Should we set off for Albion and risk some sort of explosion during the day? Local radio had already carried a report saying that Jackman was unacceptable to the Guyana government and would be asked to leave the country, but no official word had been received. They were right as it turned out, but there was the possibility that they had jumped the gun; Smith was convinced that if we went to Albion we should play, otherwise we might find ourselves isolated up country in the middle of a political row.

The West Indies players at the hotel had no more idea than we had what was going on. We sat and looked at each other while rumours flew backwards and forwards and the Press made endless telephone calls. Then the captain led the way and we were off; there was no talk of politics on the journey, or in the dressing-room when we arrived; we just got on with the match.

While we were playing cricket the politicians were playing politics. We did not know it at the time, of course, but Thursday 26 February was a day of feverish activity in Georgetown, with statement and counter-statement, high-level meetings, and poor Alan Smith fastened to the end of a telephone line with England. The High Commissioner, Mr Philip Mallet, made a statement to the Press in the morning; the Guyana government released news that it intended to deport Jackman in the afternoon; and the Cricket Council in London replied in the evening.

Statement by the British High Commissioner at a Press conference:
'The whole thing is idiotic. The fact that Robin Jackman is here as a member of a multi-racial England team to play in multi-racial Guyana against a multi-racial West Indies team is hardly a demonstration of apartheid....'

Statement from the government of Guyana:
'Following an investigation the Guyana Government is satisfied that Robin Jackman the English cricketer now in Guyana has played in South Africa recently and subsequent to the adoption of the Gleneagles Accord. The Gleneagles Accord was reached in Scotland in 1977 during a break in the Commonwealth Heads of Government Conference in London. In effect that Accord denounces apartheid in sports and frowns on sporting contacts with South Africa by Commonwealth countries.' [The full text of the Accord is printed on page 223.]

'In the Accord the member countries of the Commonwealth acknowledge that the full realization of their objectives involved the understanding, separate and active participation of the nationals of their country and of their national sports organizations and authorities.

'The Heads of Government at that time also specifically welcomed the belief expressed at their meeting that in the light of their consultation and accord there were unlikely to be future sporting contacts of any significance between Commonwealth countries or their nationals and South Africa while that country continues to pursue their detestable policy of apartheid.

'The Guyana Government has strong and well publicized views against apartheid in sports and has in the past taken appropriate action against persons who come or wish to come to Guyana hoping to participate in sports after doing so in South Africa.

'Following the confirmation that Jackman has recently played cricket in South Africa, the Minister of Foreign Affairs, Cde R. E. Jackson, received and discussed the matter with the British High Commissioner to Guyana Mr Philip Mallet on Wednesday 25 February at 16.15 hours.

'The Guyana Government knows that although attention has been drawn to the fact that the cricketer's action is not in accordance with the spirit and the letter of the Gleneagles Accord, he has neither withdrawn from the team nor has he left Guyana.

'In the light of the above circumstances the Guyana Government has been constrained to issue today an order revoking the two weeks visitor's permit which was given to Robin Jackman on arrival....'

Statement by the English Cricket Council at 6.25 p.m. Guyana time:

'The Guyanese Minister of Foreign Affairs has informed the British High Commissioner that Mr Jackman's permission to stay in Guyana is being revoked.

'The Cricket Council has informed the Manager of the England Touring Team that as Robin Jackman has been asked to leave Guyana it is no longer possible for the Test team to be chosen without restrictions being imposed. It is therefore with deep regret that England cannot take part in the Second Test due to start on Saturday.

'The Cricket Council do not consider that the inclusion of Robin Jackman in the England touring team in any way infringes the spirit or the letter of the Gleneagles Agreement.

'The Council will be seeking immediate assurances from the West Indies Cricket Board that there will be absolutely no attempt by any government to interfere with the selection of the England team or to impose any restrictions on their entry to any country included on the itinerary for the remainder of the tour....'

As soon as we arrived back from Berbice, about an hour after the end of the match and with most of us still in our whites, the captain called us into his room, told us that Jackman had been asked to leave Guyana and that the Test match was off. I suppose some of us had half expected it, but the news still came as a shock. We were asked to stay put until the manager could come and fill us in with the details; he was waylaid by the Press, the High Commissioner and those interminable phone calls for almost two hours.

Ironically, Jackman had suddenly found himself with a real chance of playing in the Guyana Test. He didn't expect it when he arrived, but Dilley injured a toe in the match at Berbice and with Old already suffering from a pinched nerve in his shoulder, there was obviously a chance Jackman would have got his first Test cap had the match been played. All things considered, it was not surprising that he was a deflated, crestfallen figure ... the entire England team suddenly broke into 'For he's a jolly good fellow', which put the fear of God into Barrington, because he was afraid the Press would hear and use it in their reports!

The noise from room 606 certainly might have given a passer-by something to think about. We laughed too loud and talked too loud, trying to hide our embarrassment, the wine went round and at one stage for some reason Ian Botham was sitting on my chest. The talk was lively and somewhat scurrilous, but understandable in the circumstances. Replacement for Rosie? Send for Alan Lamb! No, he's not available until 1982. OK, send for Mike Procter! What about Paul Parker, he's playing well for Natal at the moment.... It was affected but defiant, for we were cooped up together and trying hard to keep our spirits up.

Then the phone rang, Barrington answered it, and Jackman was summoned downstairs to receive his official notice to quit the country. The conversation palled after that, especially when Barrington went to see what was happening and returned to say that Jackman was in tears. Somebody from the team should have been with him then. We felt badly, and the music on the radio was turned off; somehow a bit of quiet seemed more appropriate.

I do not think it really occurred to any of us at that point that the tour itself might be in danger. We hadn't had time to think that far ahead or that clearly. Barrington was worried about local reaction and how difficult it would be for us to get out of the country, but I did not expect any problems. 'The people here aren't daft; they know this is about politics, not about cricketers,' I said, and the lads were inclined to agree.

Alan Smith finally arrived and gave us details of the relevant statements, though he was constantly interrupted by calls from London, and we moved to the team room downstairs for the full story. He told us we would leave as soon as possible, by charter aircraft if necessary, and we should be ready in the morning to move out at an hour's notice. We were instructed not to leave the hotel under any circumstances, not to make statements to the media and on no account to make any unguarded, critical comments about the situation in Guyana. 'Don't do anything silly and there will be no problems,' he said, and as it turned out he was right.

I was impressed with his handling of the whole affair. He did wring every bit of drama out of the situation, but he was efficient and decisive under what must have been considerable pressure for any tour manager. I think the High Commission people helped him a lot and their presence was very reassuring; they could hardly have done more than they did for us.

Only after the full statements were read to us did we begin to realize that the tour itself might be in jeopardy. We hated the thought of not playing cricket, but some of the lads said defiantly that we ought to go home right away if politicians were going to call the tune. One player, approaching his first England tour late in

Strain on the face of a man under fire. Robin Jackman returns from the one-day international at Berbice to the news that he is to be asked to leave the country.

Notice to quit. Jackman receives the document revoking his visa from a Guyana customs official.

his career, was adamant that the tour should go on if at all possible – Robin Jackman himself. He was itching to play.

We were packed and ready early next morning without knowing how long we might have to hang about, but the manager had managed to persuade the airline to put on a bigger aircraft capable of taking us all out with our baggage. It was not due out until 2.45 p.m., but we reached the airport early because we suspected there might be delays processing us through. On top of everything which had gone before, it was a hell of a day.

We lounged about for the best part of four hours and then discovered that although the plane was due it had not yet left Trinidad. Having surrendered all our local currency under Guyana regulations we had no money to buy food or a drink; in the end somebody pulled a few strings and we received a drink and a hamburger each, courtesy of the High Commission. The plane arrived late and was delayed on the tarmac; we were already tired and irritable enough, and the fact that the air conditioning in the cabin did not work was no help at all. Neither did the realization that the plane was full of passengers heading off for Carnival in Port-of-Spain.

By the time we changed flights in Trinidad, reached Barbados and got through the usual welcome of TV cameras and limitless rum punches, we seemed to have been travelling for a fortnight. Seymour Nurse drove me from the airport to the hotel, and by the time I arrived we were ten and a half hours out of Guyana, which is virtually just over the horizon. No wonder we were given the next day off.

It was inevitably difficult, in the circumstances, to escape a sense of unreality when we did get down to practice. We knew we had to carry on as though the future of the tour was assured, and heaven knows, we needed all the meaningful practice we could get. But it was not easy to sharpen our enthusiasm, knowing that at any moment we might receive word that the tour was off. We wanted to use our time profitably, but we could not be sure that we were not just wasting it.

On Tuesday, when a decision might have come through at any time, we played a practice match among ourselves, with local bowlers drafted in as reinforcements. Botham's XI and Miller's XI both wanted to bat first, because they knew that an official announcement might save them the chore of having to field!

I was batting with Gooch when we noticed Miller signalling from the boundary that he wanted to come on. Botham was already running in to bowl when Gooch stopped him and waved Miller on – this might be the news we were waiting for – but as it turned out Miller just wanted to bring out a sleeve bandage for Botham who had a bruised finger. One moment of wry anti-climax among many; perhaps the news would be communicated by a few puffs of smoke from a local factory chimney. . . .

While we were doing our best to cope with an unreal situation, the politicians were playing shots all over the place. A meeting of representatives of the Barbados, Montserrat, Antigua and Jamaica governments was arranged to take place in Barbados three days after we arrived. So three more days of rumour and speculation followed, while the Press tried to judge the mood of the governments involved, the telephone lines hummed and the world waited.

It was impossible to walk through the hotel lobby without bumping into knots of journalists. Had they heard anything definite? No. Had we been told anything? No. But the consensus of opinion seemed to be that Barbados, Montserrat and Antigua were in favour of the tour continuing without any strings attached; Jamaica, however, might not be as favourable. And since the Cricket Council had insisted that every government must accept the constitution of the tour party without conditions, Jamaica's position could be the key.

The meeting of ministers was delayed for a day because Antigua's representative, their Foreign Minister Lester Bird, could not make the original date, and because Jamaica were involved in local government elections. The local paper in Barbados announced confidently that the tour would go on because Barbados, Montserrat and Antigua were in favour, but there was no word on the potentially thorny attitude of Jamaica. The waiting game went on.

Meanwhile, one of our players slipped away for a homecoming which was doubly significant in view of the racist controversy buzzing around our heads. England's Roland Butcher went back to his home in East Point, St Philip, for a typical Bajan Sunday lunch, back to a welcome from his old mates and the grandmother who brought him up. Butcher obviously had special reasons for wanting this leg of the tour to continue; he had lots of friends and relatives on the island, cousins of his were flying in from Canada for the cricket, and his wife was among those expected in a few days' time.

Asked how it felt to be a black West Indian in an England team, Butcher said it didn't feel any different than if he were playing for Barbados. If he were playing for Japan it would make no difference. He was a professional cricketer and his job was to play cricket and cricket alone. . . . I hope the politicians took note.

Around the time the ministers' meeting was due to convene, a powerful trade union in Barbados came out against the continuation of the tour. The Barbados Workers' Union, who had strongly attacked Gary Sobers for playing in Rhodesia in the early seventies, called for the tour to be cancelled:

'The presence of individuals in the English cricket team who have been playing cricket in South Africa whether as individuals or members of a team is good enough reason to cancel the tour. Apartheid is too cruel and wicked a system for Caribbean people not to object in a most strenuous manner against cricketers who find it convenient to play and coach in South Africa.

'The detestable policy of apartheid as practised in South Africa is a cancer which continues to affect that society and which has its effects throughout the world.

'By their actions (in playing in South Africa) they have demonstrated three things: firstly, a blatant disregard for international feelings against apartheid; secondly, the plight of black people in South Africa; and thirdly, the Gleneagles Accord which was signed by the Commonwealth Prime Ministers in 1977.

'The Union feels that discontinuation of the tour is the only course open to the authorities.'

It was impossible for us to judge how far the Union's statement would influence the governments, especially since they were supposed to be upset by Guyana's unilateral action in expelling Jackman. And at the same time a former deputy Prime Minister of Barbados, Mr Cameron Tudor, came out just as strongly in favour of the tour going ahead.

'We are all opposed to the South African regime, but some of us cannot easily perceive the distinction between the death of Steve Biko in police custody and the death of Walter Rodney under police surveillance in Guyana,' said Mr Tudor.

He reaffirmed the policy of his Democratic Labour Party that while it would discourage Barbadian nationals from sporting contacts with South Africa, it would not ban individuals or teams who had played there.

'That remains our position, which was unequivocal and which safeguarded the right of the Barbadian people to decide for themselves whether they wished to entertain a visiting team or not,' he said.

There were many such statements, often representing conflicting views, in the local Press, but when they interviewed the man in the street it seemed clear that the big majority wanted the tour to go on. We could only wait for some official word and the meeting of ministers broke up in the early hours of Tuesday 3 March.

A statement was expected by the hour but each hour ticked away without any news. The Press were promised a statement at 2.00 p.m. and then at 5.00 p.m.; they gathered round the extension telephone in the hotel lobby and jumped like scalded cats every time it rang.... Their offices in England, four hours ahead and fighting edition times, were desperate for the latest whiff of news but there was none they could give. They looked tired and fed up – have you ever sat hour after hour waiting for a telephone to ring? – and I was impressed by the way they stuck to their post.

The Cricket Council meeting at Lord's had given it up as a bad job and gone home; the Barbados Foreign Minister Mr Henry Forde, who was due to make the official announcement, had gone home for dinner. There was no guarantee that any statement would be made before the next day, but the Press kept ringing and insisting gently that they must know what had been decided. They were told each time that the ministers were anxious to get the wording of their statement exactly right, and that although a decision had been made it was not quite available. Not quite ... the vigil went on hour after hour, and long after all the players had gone to bed.

Just before midnight local time the Press discovered that something might be available at the Rockley Resort hotel, where the ministers had met many hours earlier. They tore off in taxis and hire cars and about 1.00 a.m., almost twenty-four hours after the meeting of ministers had broken up, the official announcement was made. Ironically, after all the hard work they had put in, it was too late to catch the newspapers in England. And just as ironically, the principal character in the controversy was tucked up in bed, waiting for a phone call from his wife at 8.00 a.m.....

Part of a twelve-hour vigil: journalists await a decision on the future of the tour in the foyer of the Holiday Inn in Barbados. *Left to right:* Derek Hodgson (*Star*) in the foreground, Alan Lee (freelance), Pat Gibson (*Daily Express*), Peter Smith (*Daily Mail*), Paul Fitzpatrick (*Guardian*) and Ray Dye (*Press Association*). And people say reporting cricket is a bobby's job....

Questions, questions. Robin Jackman interviewed by ITN's Tony Francis on the beach front in Barbados.

Statement issued by Mr Henry Forde, Attorney General and Foreign Minister of Barbados, at 0104 (0504 BST) on Wednesday 4 March:

'The governments of Antigua, Barbados, Jamaica and Montserrat have consulted about the current tour of the West Indies by the England cricket team which includes players who have played cricket in South Africa since the Gleneagles agreement of June 1977.

'In considering the matter, representatives of the government concerned have been guided not only by that agreement which was drawn up by Commonwealth Heads of Governmment but also by the United Nations declaration against Apartheid in sports adopted in December 1977.

'Both of these agreements seek to isolate South Africa from international sporting activities.

'The agreements start from the premise that apartheid is an abhorrent practice and that there should be full support for the international campaign to eradicate it in all its forms, including its application in the field of sport.

'In pursuance of this the parties of these accords agree that there will be no official sponsorship, support or encouragement of sporting contacts with South Africa.

'The governments committed themselves to everything practicable to discourage their nationals from contact or competition with sporting organizations, teams or sportsmen from South Africa. It hardly needs relating that the governments of Antigua, Barbados, Jamaica and Montserrat fully support the principles and objectives set out above.

'The point of contention in the case of the tour of the England cricket team is whether sanctions should be invoked against those members of the team who played cricket in South Africa after the Gleneagles agreement.

'The Gleneagles agreement, however, does not deal with the question of sanctions against the nationals of other countries who engage on an individual basis in sporting activities in South Africa.

'This particular aspect of the matter referred to as the "third party principle" has been found to be one of great complexity. In fact a working committee of the United Nations has been debating this matter for over two years without resolution so far.

'The present case, raising as it does the "third party principle", must therefore be treated on its own merits.

'In view of this and after the most careful and searching consideration and having regard to all the circumstances involved, the governments of Antigua, Barbados, Jamaica and Montserrat have jointly concluded that the remainder of the cricket tour should be permitted to continue as scheduled.

'The continuation of the tour must not be interpreted to mean that the Gleneagles agreement leaves it entirely open to national sporting authorities or individual sportsmen to engage in sporting contacts with South Africa.

'We wish to emphasize that it is the obligation of the governments under the agreement to discourage such contacts by their nationals, and we expect national sporting authorities and individual sportsmen to lend their support.

'The governments also firmly believe that there is a clear need for the forthcoming Commonwealth Heads of Government meeting to reaffirm adherence to the principles of the Gleneagles agreement and to examine the manner of its implementation up to the present.

'To this end, the governments will consult as early as possible with their colleagues in the Caribbean community and the wider Commonwealth to ensure that effective co-ordination will take place with a view to strengthening the international campaign against apartheid.

'The four governments reiterate their determination to pursue the common objectives of isolating the racist regime in South Africa and destroying the inhuman practice of apartheid.

'They therefore attach the utmost importance to this examination for it is only through faithful implementation of the principles of such agreements by all parties that these objectives will be achieved.'

Robin Jackman's response to the news was dignified and considerably briefer. In an official statement to the Press, Jackman said: 'Naturally I am relieved and delighted at the news that the tour will continue, not only for myself but for the rest of the tour party who incidentally, have been marvellous in the past week. My special thanks to the manager Alan Smith, whose help over the past week I certainly could not have done without.

'I am also very pleased for my family, who had to put up with quite a lot at home. I now look forward to getting down to the job of work I came out here to do – to play cricket. . . .'

13

Taking Stock

Business as usual at last – and Ian Botham's first reaction was to take the unusual step of throwing open our team meeting for general discussion on the tour so far, the grouses and grumbles as well as the good points. 'We have to start thinking exclusively about cricket again; there are three Tests still to come, so let's get down to it,' said Botham. There was an awkward silence – in situations like that there often is, even though players will spend hours discussing the tour among themselves. So I set the ball rolling by reiterating my views about our practice facilities so far, and especially the nets.

Kenny Barrington had done a fine job at net practices, nobody could doubt that. His enthusiasm, coaching and help for the players were beyond praise – but the fact remains that the facilities themselves weren't usually up to the standard we need. To say they were poor would be to put it very mildly. Kenny had written ahead about our net requirements before every venue and checked with officials as soon as we arrived, but all we seemed to get was promises – and more promises – which were rarely fulfilled. It was frustrating for all of us, knowing as we did that we would be judged on performance without any account being taken of our problems, and it was the basic cause of a good deal of annoyance with arrangements generally. If the cricket arrangements had been up to scratch we could have smiled through other problems – poor transport, poor service and so on – but our lack of proper preparation got through to us all.

We were desperately short of extra net bowlers at most places, which meant that our bowlers had more than their fair share to do, and many lower-order batsmen never really got the sort of practice they needed against a front-line attack. Apparently local bowlers will not turn up to help out as they used to do; times have changed, and whereas once they would have regarded bowling at the touring team as a courtesy and an honour, they now expect to be paid for their services. To that I would say OK – if they want payment they should be paid, but something positive should have been done to give us the practice we needed, and there was no excuse for pennypinching when the performance and reputation of the England team were at stake.

I also suggested that we must double-check the precise facilities available.

Somebody should go to the ground very early each day and make sure that the nets were right, impress on the groundsman just what we wanted, and insist, politely but firmly, that we got our way. If, for example, the nets were damp, we could have them rolled to speed up the drying process; if they still looked like being too damp, we could postpone practice until the afternoon. Players might prefer a net in the morning and then feel they had the rest of the day free, but so what? We were here to play cricket, not to sunbathe or socialize; first things first.

I felt very strongly that good nets were essential in sharpening confidence; we needed to feel, as professionals, that we were doing everything possible to prepare ourselves for the Test matches, which would be difficult enough in any circumstances. Without our necessarily being aware of it, that lack of professional preparation had snowballed into frustration and annoyance at so many other, less important problems. It was time we stopped accepting promises and insisted on some action.

The rest of the players seemed to agree, and there was some lively discussion, often quite heated, which showed at least that they were getting things off their chest. Gooch, I remember, wanted more organized slip-catching practice, because we hadn't done much; Jackman made a very sound point that, as a newcomer, he had noticed players hooking a great deal in the nets. Did they intend to hook the West Indian fast bowlers in the matches, or was it just self-indulgence in the relative safety of the nets? If it was, it wasn't genuine practice. Butcher reminded us that we were guests in the Caribbean and might have to put up with inconveniences without complaining – a fair point, as they all were, but the players were still adamant that we must insist on good net facilities.

There were many other points at issue, of course, and at least the discussion gave everyone a chance to thrash out complaints and put a point of view. Botham deserves credit for encouraging us to clear the air, but then, as Alan Smith rightly said, he is young and inexperienced and he needs everybody's help....

A fifty-over practice match was arranged next day against a Barbados XI, and we were delighted – or something – to find that their side included Clarke, Daniel and Garner. But we needed practice against good-class opposition and an eleven-run victory didn't do our confidence any harm, especially since Gooch, Gower and Gatting all made runs. I felt in decent form without being really as sharp as I would have liked; as I have said, it is difficult to pick up the threads when politics and the weather have combined to make us all feel a bit flat.

Yorkshire's Bill Athey is due to arrive as a replacement for Rose, and it will be good to see him again. I would have brought him out in the first place, because technically he is the best equipped young batsman in the country. Having said that, however, I'm not sure he is the best choice in our present circumstances. Gatting and Butcher were brought as first choices, and they haven't had all that much cricket so far; Athey has a right to expect some opportunity to prove himself out here and it cannot be easy to fit him in. As things have turned out, I would probably have gone for a more experienced player with a proven record – but Athey has the character to take his chance when it arises.

It is a wry thought, but as the four-day match against Barbados approaches we have played only fifteen days' cricket on a tour which has already spanned fifty days. Politics and the weather have certainly stacked the cards against us; it just goes to show how vitally important our practice and preparations for the Test matches are.

14

Back to Business

Barbados are acknowledged as the strongest team in the Caribbean, so it says a lot for the general standard of cricket out here that before last year they went five years without winning the Shell Shield. In any circumstances they are a formidable proposition – with players like Clarke, Marshall, Daniel, Haynes and Greenidge they are bound to be, and Alleyne, who would get into most Test sides, could not even command a place against us. The way we felt, a match against Barbados was like playing a Test match in preparation for a Test match.

The pitch was of particular interest to us because the signs were that Barbados pitches have changed character. The nets had grass on them, and so did the pitches on which we played our practice matches; this was most unlike Barbados, and an ominous portent for the Test. But the pitch against Barbados had been shaved of grass; they won the toss and put us in, as they usually do, to enable their quick bowlers to make use of any early moisture.

There was pace and bounce and we spent a fair amount of time ducking and weaving – this seems to be where we came in – until Gooch was gloved by a delivery in front of his face and the ball fell on to his wicket. There was no respite: Daniel bowled an excellent line and length at awkward pace; Marshall was 'slippery' as ever, skidding the ball on to the bat and moving it disconcertingly; Clarke made the ball bounce a lot and smacked me on the chest-pad to prove it. Neither Clarke nor Marshall is the biggest fast bowler in the game, in fact they are surprisingly streamlined and slender, and I have often wondered how they generate their pace. Perhaps the answer lies in their incredible looseness around the neck and shoulders; Clarke, for instance, is very wristy and open-chested, yet the odd delivery really whistles through. They say he can rub his shoulder-blades together without any difficulty, and it may be that freedom in his upper chest which makes the difference. When you consider our stereotyped image of a fast bowler – muscular and very strong in the thighs, chest and backside – Marshall and Clarke simply do not fit the picture.

Gower was out in a bizarre way, and I felt sorry for him. He drove the last ball of an over from Padmore to King at mid-off, we made no attempt to run and the umpire at my end moved tentatively off towards square-leg. Gower tapped the pitch, obviously assuming – as anyone might have done in the circumstances – that the ball was dead, but King whipped in a throw and the wicket-keeper took off the bails; Gower was run out! I went over to the umpire, now at square-leg, and asked him: 'You did call over, didn't you?' but he insisted he did not. I reckon he should have stayed put at the bowler's end until he called 'over'; by walking away he deceived Gower, and that cost him his wicket.

Butcher was under a special sort of pressure – and it showed. It was obvious from the moment he arrived in Barbados that he would be the centre of a great deal of publicity. One newspaper featured the local boy who made good in a pullout with a huge colour picture and the headline: 'Our boy – their bat'. He was on show and determined to do well – but it was hard to impress with flowing shots against this bowling attack, and he became frustrated, which added to his understandable nervousness. He got out as I did later, trying to hit Padmore over the top, and both catches gave an interesting little insight into cricket tactics in this part of the world.

We both thought our shots would clear deepish mid-off and mid-on, but as soon as we showed our intention of attacking the spinner, the fielders turned and ran back several yards – looking over their shoulders in case we hit in their direction. By the time we played our shots, the fielders were quite a bit deeper than we expected. It was unusual, and it worked – one to watch for the future.

Padmore bowled tidily and well but it was significant how little real effort he made to spin the ball. He concentrated on bowling tightly, wicket to wicket, with the ball never quite up to be attacked, and that seems to be typical of the West Indies' attitude to spin in teams dominated by fast bowlers. The spinners know they are simply 'spelling' the quicker bowlers, and they know also that batsmen will try to get after them, so they just bowl tight and invite batsmen to get themselves out. There is not a lot of flight or subtlety, rather the intention to use batsmen's frustration against themselves.

Batting against almost unrelieved pace bowling for hour after hour is a soul-destroying business. Duck one, weave the next, block one, ignore a wide one . . . and all the time the sun is beating down and the frustration mounts no matter how you discipline yourself. We cannot hope to score quickly, for the simple reason, I believe, that we are not brought up to hook and cut.

In English conditions they are danger shots, played very sparingly if at all, in deference to the kind of surfaces we play on and the type of bowling we usually face. To hook and cut well you have to do it instinctively or develop the skill through constant practice; we certainly don't play those shots instinctively, and our conditions at home are far from ideal for developing them. So we are limited in that respect.

And this becomes vitally important on West Indian surfaces where the ball bounces and hurries through. Without an instinctive readiness to hook or cut we lost at least two balls an over which we might otherwise have scored off; from the point of view of getting runs we are virtually facing four-ball overs, and that seriously slows down our scoring rate. But what can we do? If we hook and get out

A typically awkward delivery from Wayne Daniel during the match against Barbados - and he can't even get into the West Indies team.

In the firing line again, Graham Gooch gains height for a fine defensive shot against Daniel.

- always on the cards because the shot doesn't come easily – we are accused of being irresponsible. If we cut those shots out, we are accused of being boringly slow. We scored some 300 runs in eight and a half hours, and the reaction of Greenidge and Haynes when Barbados began their reply underlined a crucial difference in our make-up.

Greenidge is a magnificent cutter, and when Botham dropped the new ball a fraction short and wide he smashed it through point and gulley with tremendous power. Haynes is a brilliant hooker who attacks anything short; the bowlers had to keep it up to him, and then he drove mercilessly. It was a classic dilemma for our bowlers, based on the batsmen's ability to hook and cut; the new ball disappeared in a smoke-trail of runs.

It was a far cry from our innings. I felt I played really well – I played and missed at only one delivery, a widish one from Marshall immediately after I reached 50 – but it still took me four and a half hours to make 77. Willey played really well, too; he's a good, undemonstrative pro who shows a great deal more tenacity and application than some players higher in the order, but his 50 took him three hours. When Barbados batted it was suddenly a different game.

Stevenson, like Botham, is basically a bowler who bowls line and length and lets the ball do the work. Here he seemed to feel the need to strive for an extra yard of pace, to give us some sort of answer to their fast-bowling attack, and his accuracy suffered; then they picked him off. Even at their fastest, bursting a boiler to compensate for lack of movement off the pitch, our seamers cannot generate enough pace to make life really uncomfortable for the West Indies batsmen; the only time we looked capable of exercising control in the field against Barbados was when Emburey and Jackman bowled.

John Emburey is, in my opinion, the best off-spinner in the world. It is fascinating to watch him bowl now. He is a tall, strongly built man, yet his delivery stride is tiny, a dancer's step barely half the width of the crease. The whole of his bodyweight rests on the ball of his left foot and he is perfectly balanced and in total control at the moment of delivery, commanding the ball right up to the instant it leaves his hand so he can adjust if necessary. Perfect control, beautiful to watch.

Robin Jackman got off to a flying start on the tour – at last – partly because Haynes was going so well that he couldn't wait for the next boundary and gave away his wicket by flashing at a wide delivery. But I was very impressed by Jackman's professionalism and total commitment in the match.

Jackman made a virtue of his limitations. He obviously does not have the pace to intimidate batsmen, so he buckled down to the only job available to him – containing and frustrating batsmen into mistakes. The right line – a few inches outside the off stump – and a nagging length, never quite full enough to hit; the only time he was punished was when he strayed on to middle stump and was whipped away on the leg side. He was puffing and blowing a bit, clearly not quite match fit, but he used every ounce of his experience to tempt and draw the batsmen without losing accuracy.

Our boy, their bat. West Indian crowds warmed to Roland Butcher and wanted him to succeed – provided, of course, that England failed!

When he took a wicket he was characteristically delighted; when he thought he might have an lbw he was deafening. We were used to it, but the poor umpire nearly jumped out of his skin when Jackman first unleashed one of those foghorn appeals which last for twenty seconds. It was undiluted enthusiasm, and the locals took to him instantly; more than that, it is the sort of competitive attitude which disgruntles a batsman or perhaps annoys him into doing something rash in reply. There is method in Jackman's brashness.

He could have had five wickets in his first bowling spell on tour and deserved every one of them, but he dropped a hard chance off last man Daniel. As it was, he used his ability to the full, and no professional could help but admire that.

We had been criticized in the local Press for batting slowly, but it was noticeable that Barbados did not score their runs very much more quickly. In fact, had Gooch at slip not dropped George Reifer, a very promising twenty-year-old who makes runs consistently, they would have struggled to pass our first innings total. On top of that, Emburey had several appeals for lbw turned down when he used his 'arm' ball – good shouts against batsmen on the front foot – and we suspect West Indian umpires are reluctant to give lbw against batsmen on the front foot. OK, says Botham, as long as they are consistent and don't give us out on the front foot ... Hell, says Gooch, when do we ever get on the front foot....

The match ended in a draw, long since a foregone conclusion, but the behaviour of the pitch was interesting with the Test match only a couple of days away. As it wore, small chips broke free from the surface and the bounce was never entirely predictable. I dug one out from Clarke with the toe of my bat on the Monday night, and then faced a few low deliveries next morning, which suggested we might think in terms of getting forward a bit. Then one took off from just short of a length and gloved me to second slip. Gatting was bowled by one which scudded along the ground. In circumstances like those it is not difficult for a side to become demoralized, especially if they are short of practice, as we were, and therefore already vulnerable.

There was a postscript to our preparations in Barbados which might not be unconnected with the events at our clear-the-air team meeting. Kenny Barrington went searching for good batting nets and discovered two concrete strips, one unusable because the run-ups were hopeless and the other because it was fifteen miles away. But he persisted, and finally he came up with an artificial strip which was laid along one of the nets at the Kensington Oval. The bounce was slow but high, and we could probably have done with something a bit quicker, but at least the surface was true. It was certainly an improvement on many we had used so far. If at first you don't succeed....

On the front foot for once, if only against Albert Padmore's off-spin! I get in a drive during the Barbados match.

15

Opportunities Wasted

Kensington Oval, Bridgetown, is not the most attractive of Caribbean grounds, which often comes as a surprise to the thousands of English cricket fans who pour into Barbados for the Test match. For the third Test they were there in strength again, braving the hot sun in search of an instant tan, risking the local rum, fluttering a Union Jack from the Three Ws stand and sitting in bright pink expectancy under a motley collection of floppy headgear. They were probably well pleased with England's performance at the end of the first day, but I couldn't share their satisfaction.

Jackman forced his way into the Test side, which reflected tremendous credit on him but suggested to me that somebody had got the selection of the original tour party wrong. After all, Stevenson and Old were picked in front of him, and they were both fit and better acclimatized; if Jackman was to be preferred to them he should logically have been out here in the first place.

The pitch was as grassy as we feared, quite unlike the shaven one on which we had played the Barbados match, and I asked the groundsman why it was so different these days. He said they usually left grass on because of the fast-bowling attack in the island team, and it was even suggested that they had prepared the surface specifically because I had made inquiries and wanted the grass off. A rum sort of compliment, I suppose, but I don't believe it; I reckon the instructions about pitch preparation came from 'upstairs'. In any event we were glad to win the toss and put them in; it was the sort of surface on which our seam bowlers should be able to do some damage.

Hard and grassy – the sort of Test pitch batsmen have nightmares about. You can handle bounce from a hard surface and movement off a grassed pitch, but put both together at this level and batting is the devil's own job. The ball immediately went through at shoulder height from just short of a length, it seamed about and both openers played and missed frequently. It was the sort of surface on which Botham should be very effective, and we had cautioned him at the team meeting against trying too many bouncers; lively fast-medium with seam and swing is his game; at his pace anything short is meat and drink to players like Greenidge and Haynes.

Above: Gordon Greenidge caught by Graham Gooch at first slip ... Robin Jackman's first Test wicket, and the England fielders obviously enjoyed it as much as he did.

Not a shadow of doubt. Everton Mattis concedes the inevitable as Ian Botham asks 'politely' for lbw in the Barbados Test.

Greenidge hooked Botham for six but didn't hang around long. Knowing that the ball was likely to bounce, he did not get right into line but left himself a little room; he was hanging back and not far enough across when Jackman's fifth delivery took the edge of his bat and skidded to Gooch at first slip.

Richards came in to the sort of ovation which signifies something between idolatry and hysteria. The word had got round that he rarely makes runs in Barbados, though Richards himself points to centuries there both against Pakistan and in island cricket and shrugs off his recent failures. Still, it may be that the slight to his reputation had got through to him – especially when, at a function earlier, the Governor-General diplomatically told him that George Headley would be remembered as the best batsman West Indies ever had, and that I would be remembered as the greatest stonewaller of all time! Whatever the cause, it was a strange sort of shot that cost him his wicket.

We deliberately posted a fine-leg and a man behind square for the hook. When Dilley bowled his first ball widish and just short of a length, Richards seemed to have committed himself forward and could not resist flashing at it; Botham took the catch well, shoulder high at second slip.

West Indies 25 for two and Richards gone for a duck! No wonder the locals looked a bit mortified and the Three Ws stand was full of pink glee. We could hardly have made a better start, and the way Mattis was shaping, I didn't expect him to last long. Jackman bounced him and hit him on the head – goodness knows why he doesn't wear a helmet, because I don't think he has the class on this sort of surface to do without one; perhaps it's a macho thing. But he straight drove Jackman for four and I went over to have a word.

I don't know what interpretation was put on it by anybody else, but the conversation went something like this: 'We're a couple of old pros, Jackers, let's have a chat and they're bound to think we are cooking something clever up. Let's just slow it down a bit, make 'em wait for a while. Probably think we're talking tactics. I only want to know where you spent your honeymoon. . . .' Jackman grinned and ran in to bowl; I never had chance to speak to him again, because Botham moved me from mid-off to long-leg.

Haynes worried me. He looked in fine form, even by the time he had 20 on the board, hooking Botham and driving Jackman for boundaries. I mentioned to him during a drinks break that I thought the pitch had too much grass on it. 'No way, man,' he said, 'it will settle down' – so I bet him twenty dollars I was right. He conceded the point later, but I don't recall getting my money. . . .

Haynes is always saying to me that he will teach me to play the ball forcefully off my hip if I will teach him how to concentrate. He knows he still has to sort himself out in that respect – heaven help somebody when he does – and I reckon it was his impetuousness that got him out. The better he plays, the faster he seems to want to score, and when he had made 25 classy runs he drove extravagantly outside the off stump and was caught behind. 'Beat the ball, man; beat the ball' is a favourite Carribean expression, and Haynes epitomized the philosophy when he got himself out.

Mattis, never comfortable, had got a thick edge for four and slogged another straight boundary off Jackman. But he got too far over towards off stump trying to counteract Botham's swing and was trapped lbw, though his reaction suggested he thought he had got a nick. With West Indies tottering on 47 for three Lloyd promoted himself in the order, which was the right decision since he is obviously a much better player than Gomes, who followed him when Mattis was out.

West Indies were in trouble on 65 for four at lunch, and it was clear that we needed just one more wicket to open an end. On that pitch, and with all their real batsmen gone, we would have been in a pretty commanding position. But it didn't work out that way.

Lloyd attacked. Jackman tried to york him and Lloyd clattered the full-toss for four; he drove a half-volley for four and then got a thick edge for two – in no time at all he had doubled his score and gained the momentum which every batsman needs. It struck me that our thinking was going astray.

Lloyd is a big man who sees a diminutive figure like Jackman as a challenge: he wants to get after him. On this occasion he was clearly looking to get on the front foot and clatter anything pitched up to him. The only way Jackman might get him out was to frustrate him, to tie him down by bowling a nagging line and length and force him to make the mistakes. Time wasn't important, we had barely started a five-day Test, yet Jackman was trying hard to bowl Lloyd out when he should have been trying to fret him out. Jackman did not bowl badly, but I felt sure the tactics were wrong; there are more ways of skinning a cat, even a Big Cat, than knocking his stumps over. Lloyd's confidence and momentum grew, he felt established enough to attack Dilley from the other end with square cuts and in no time he was in the thirties.

We desperately needed a wicket now, and Gomes should have gone when he had made 14. Botham, bowling over the wicket, drew Gomes wide playing defensively and Bairstow got both gloves to a straightforward catch a little in front of first slip. But as his momentum carried him on, Bairstow's knee jarred against his gloves and the ball squirted out. He claimed a catch on the grounds that the ball had settled in his gloves, but the umpire would have none of it and Gomes escaped. A costly miss for us, especially since Gomes had already been fortunate to escape when a shooter from Dilley bowled him – he could never have kept it out – and the umpire signalled a no-ball.

Gomes is a limited player with few shots apart from the drive to mid-on or mid-off and the ability to work the ball off his legs; the sort of player you can keep quiet but who is not easy to get out once he sets himself to play a solid supporting role. And with Lloyd going well he did just that, content to hang about and do a steady job well while Lloyd took the game away from us – fast.

Gooch was tried for a couple of overs and Lloyd punished him. The idea of a bowling variation was sound enough but Gooch was, in my opinion, not the man for the moment – not at his pace and with Lloyd flexing his muscles. In any case, if Gooch was going to contain, he should have bowled round the wicket to Lloyd;

Clive Lloyd with a raking back-foot drive against John Emburey, as David Bairstow positions himself, just in case.

we should have been making them graft for every run on that pitch; instead Lloyd was banging four after four while we insisted on trying to bowl him out, and the advantage we had at 65 for four slipped into history. You can take wickets from a defensive posture – the right kind of defence, after all, can be a positive tactic – but that did not seem to occur to anyone.

Even Emburey could not put the brake on. I was fielding with Gatting for the cut on the off side, and we were amazed at how much work we had to do. Emburey was bowling off stump or just outside, and Lloyd was able to stay on the back foot and cut him with ease; I could not understand why Emburey bowled that line, and I asked him what on earth was going on.

He said that after our experience in Trinidad, where Lloyd struggled against that sort of attack, Botham had instructed him to bowl the same line. It was an extraordinary instruction, considering the quite different nature of the surface; it would have made far more sense for Emburey to bowl wicket to wicket, and he would have preferred to bowl that way. Instead, a very fine off-spinner was being played with something approaching contempt. There is nothing wrong with Jackman or Emburey as bowlers, but the way they were used appeared to be simple rule of thumb. I thought Botham's lack of experience and lack of fine tuning in Test-match situations showed through. And I say that as a fact demonstrated by events, not as an easy accusation. We were tactically naïve.

We conceded 101 runs in the afternoon session and completely lost our grip on the match, not through lack of endeavour but through tactical shortcomings. Bairstow's missed catch did not help, of course – and he was to miss stumping Gomes later – but that happens and always will; nobody will be more critical of Bairstow than he is himself. But we tried too hard to outgun West Indies when we should have been trying to outfox them ... Jackman, Gooch, Emburey – all very capable bowlers but not well used. Emburey could have been given a spell at the other end, where the breeze would have helped him to drift the ball out and spin it back, although in fairness that was the end the quicker bowlers needed because they were expected to take wickets. West Indies were 166 for four at tea, with Lloyd 78 and Gomes 24.

Gomes escaped again when he had made 38. He attempted to go down the pitch to Emburey, who saw his intention and bowled a quicker yorker outside the off stump. Gomes, momentarily stranded, tried to jab down on the ball but it hit the bowlers' footmarks on the batting crease and, fortunately for him, leaped and hit Bairstow on the shoulder.

Dilley had bowled well after tea, going round the wicket to the left-handers, which was a sensible way of keeping them quiet. Then Jackman bowled the kind of spell he should have been encouraged to bowl all day. He had one slip, four men in a ring in the covers, mid-off ten yards deeper than normal and Butcher at extra cover also a few yards deeper than usual; and he bowled at off stump, just short of a length. Nothing pitched up, nothing to hit.

Lloyd tried to get forward to drive on the up, but had to check his shot; when he did get the drive in, it was cut off easily because the fielders were those few yards deeper; the only runs he got were off a fine edge to third-man. Jackman should have bowled that way in the afternoon; there cannot be any disgrace in accepting one's limitations and making experience count. He was obviously tired, and Chris Old had to empty a flask of cold water over him during drinks to help keep him going, but he battled on without any complaint.

Four hours after walking into a near-crisis situation, Lloyd reached the century he deserved – and it was remarkable but not insignificant that 68 of them came in boundaries. It was a very fine innings in any circumstances, especially valuable on that pitch and in view of the situation when he went in. A few minutes later he was gone – and very annoyed with himself.

Lloyd tried to slog Jackman over mid-wicket and was caught by Gooch just in front of square-leg – not a very distinguished shot, and one which will have angered him for more reasons than one. He had allowed Jackman to frustrate him out; he had fallen when West Indies had us by the throat; and he had exposed his tail-enders to the new ball, which meant the possibility of a quick end to the innings.

Gomes fell to the old ball after batting almost as long as Lloyd. His was a very different innings, but a professionally admirable one, worth its weight in gold as far as West Indies were concerned. Eventually he pushed forward tiredly and was caught at second slip, a bonus for us at that stage since the new ball was due.

It bounced and swung again, and I could not understand why Murray did not wear a helmet. Against the new ball on a pitch like this, he is really not a good enough player to do without. Dilley beat him with one which bounced and hurried through, and Bairstow took a straightforward catch, but we did not make particularly good use of the new ball up to the close. Roberts and Garner were able to ignore several deliveries when they should have been forced to play at every one.

We tend to use our bowlers in blocks of an hour or so, and I would like to see us chop and change a bit more, especially when we are not getting wickets. It is another way of putting pressure on batsmen – notice how often a bowler who looks innocuous at one end suddenly takes a wicket when he is switched to the other. The breeze, the background, the angle of delivery; any one of them can upset a batsman just enough to induce a vital mistake. I have never underestimated the importance of *making* something happen in a Test match, and shrewd bowling changes are one way of doing it.

West Indies 238 for seven might sound in most contexts like a good day for England, but all things are relative and I believe they have a winning score. We have said before that to beat West Indies, we have to perform to the very best of our ability and they have to fall thirty per cent short of theirs. I reckon they were around seventy per cent today, but we were not at our best – and now the opportunity has gone.

The pitch will be cut tomorrow morning, rolled before the start and again before we bat. But I cannot see it changing its spots too much, and that looks like a dreadfully difficult prospect for us. On that pitch we should have been looking to dismiss West Indies for 160, or 180 at the most. That's how difficult batting is going to be.

Second Day
For the first time in my life, I can look at a scoreboard with a duck against my name and not feel a profound sense of failure. For the first time I remember, I can write off an innings, whatever the history books and Test records may say, as being as near to irrelevant as any Test innings will ever be. Because a Kensington Oval pitch prepared to favour the fastest bowling attack in the world turned Saturday 14 March into a lottery and a farce.

I also feel angry, angry for the thousands of English supporters who ploughed a lot of money, perhaps even their life savings, into the holiday of a lifetime in order to watch Test cricket. Real Test cricket, that is, with shades and meaning, skill and counter-skill. They already had to put up with enough: there were unfortunate stories about reserved seats being occupied when they arrived, of locals forcing their way in without paying, and tickets being sold twice over. And then they were presented with a spectacle which might have sent the West Indians wild with delight but which had damn all to do with Test cricket as I understand it.

England were bowled out for 122, their lowest score in a Barbados Test and a record which will probably stand only until they produce another Test pitch like this one. The bowlers' figures will stand for ever – Roberts two for 29, Holding three for 16, Croft four for 39, Garner one for 30 – but, magnificent performers though they are, those analyses were given rather than earned. In retrospect they will probably admit it themselves.

West Indies added 27 runs for their last three wickets in the morning, amid much playing and missing, wafting and edging. Roberts wafted at a wide one and was caught behind; Holding tried to turn Botham off his legs two balls later but was beaten as it seamed, and Gatting took a head-high catch back-pedalling behind square; Croft blocked studiously, while Garner worked a few off his legs, but Botham finally changed ends and had Garner caught behind playing forward. Botham's spell was three for 10 in 25 balls, and West Indies finished on 265. It was just a prelude.

I knew the pitch would be a killer, and Roberts, bowling downwind, soon gave a taste of things to come. Gooch got a four and two off thick edges, played and missed and was turned round completely by one delivery which just missed off stump. Holding's first over to me is already a part of Test history.

The first delivery was short of a length and gloved me, bouncing well in front of the slips; the second was short and I played and missed as it bounced; the third nipped back and hit me on the inside of the left thigh; the fourth bounced and I played it down in front of gulley; the fifth was an action replay of the fourth; the sixth plucked my off stump crazily out of the ground. It was a bit rapid, to say the least, in fact it went like a rifle bullet and I may just have played a fraction inside it, expecting him to pitch it up.

Graham Dilley celebrates an overdue success against Larry Gomes in the Barbados Test. Gomes made full use of a couple of escapes to play a long, valuable innings until Dilley had him caught at second slip.

Six good reasons why I would never advise anyone to become a Test opening batsman! There are many easier ways, even in cricket, of earning a living....

Facing quick bowlers on a pitch with pace and bounce it is almost inevitable that one opening batsman will fall to the new ball, so you have only a fifty-fifty chance of survival at best. Not the best of odds; better to be a mid-order batsman and come in when the ball is old and there is a chance the spinners will be on. You think about things like that on days like this.

Not that there was any respite in this innings. No batsman could ever consider he was in; everyone played and missed, tried to summon all his skills simply to survive, and pinched a run or two where he could in the unhappy knowledge that every delivery might be his last. The innings became a catalogue of wickets and near misses, of guts and sweat, with precious little evidence of the subtlety which normally makes Test cricket the highest form of the game. We expect that against the West Indies attack, but on this surface the odds were stacked hopelessly in their favour.

The local fans were dancing on the rooftops, spilling on to the field hugging and kissing each other at my dismissal – and the pandemonium had scarcely died down before Gatting was out. It was a fearful test for him, going in at number three in the third over, and he barely lasted five minutes before he pushed forward at Roberts and Greenidge claimed a catch ankle high at third slip. Gatting hesitated, unsure that it had carried, but the square-leg umpire confirmed the worst and we were 11 for two.

Gooch obviously decided to get on with it when he could. With so many men in catching positions, the leg-side field was invitingly unpopulated, and Gooch flipped Holding off his legs for four, then hooked Roberts for four and hooked him again off the splice for a couple. We were beginning to think that perhaps the ball wasn't bouncing quite as extravagantly any longer when Gower got one which sped off the splice over the slips for three and Gooch had to fend another off his chest. It was hard work, relieved only when Gower unleashed a glorious off-drive for four which left even Holding applauding.

Even the ruddy weather seemed to be against us! A sky which had been blue and clear suddenly became overcast, which did not help our cause at all – and Gooch was out five minutes before lunch. He had left a delivery from Garner which nipped back and almost took his off bail, and the next delivery was a repeat which bounced as Gooch tried to steer it down to gulley. It took an under-side edge on to his stumps and we were 40 for three.

Butcher received a warm ovation and a warm welcome in front of his 'home' crowd. Mattis dived to his left and got a hand to one shot which slipped through him at fourth slip for four, and Butcher played at and missed a full-toss and another delivery wide of the off stump. Play a couple, miss a couple – there was absolutely no certainty, and Gower was experiencing the same sort of difficulty, until he was out in the same bizarre circumstances as in Trinidad.

A thin shower of rain swept the ground and the umpires might have come off at any time. Before they did, poor Gower pushed forward at a delivery from Croft, who was bowling a fairly full length from over the wicket, and Mattis grabbed the catch as it bounced through his hands into his chest at fourth slip. The West Indies followed Gower off the field while the groundstaff raced to put the covers in position.

We lost about twenty-five minutes to the rain, but it was only a stay of execution, hard as Butcher and Botham tried to give the innings a bit of stability. Botham had an escape when he edged Croft chest high between second and third slip; Richards half went for it and Haynes made a valiant effort, but they were too far apart, and I noticed they closed the gap after that chance had bolted. Butcher sensibly resisted the temptation to pull or hook short stuff, except when he tried to pull Garner and got a single off the splice. Mostly he was content to block and hang on until he drove at Croft and Richards took the catch low at second slip.

With half the side gone for 72 we desperately needed a respite, but there was precious little sign of that. Botham, looking to get on the front foot, was startled by a bouncer from Garner and lost his helmet as he ducked hastily out of the way; it almost rolled on to his wicket, but Botham pounced and flicked it away with his hand. Then Willey shaped to duck Garner, changed his mind and was hit as he turned away. The crowd hooted with glee and Willey flung up a V-sign, which at least suggested he was in a typically defiant mood. Garner really ran in at Willey after that, trying short deliveries, a bouncer and a yorker – which surprised nobody.

Botham soldiered on, hooking Croft for four, cover-driving him for another and top-edging him for runs when every one was precious. He rode his luck, too, almost edging a delivery from Croft on to his stumps and then escaping when a delivery from Holding flew off the edge high to Murray behind the stumps. Murray flung up a glove and parried it, but was hopelessly off balance and could not grab the ball as it fell behind him.

The next delivery was a bouncer, Botham swayed out of harm's way and threw his bat away in disgust, planting his hands on his hips and glaring down the pitch. Two balls later Botham was gloved by a delivery which bounced again; Murray knocked it up and caught it turning round and England were 94 for six.

But not for long. Bairstow was hit on the pad and there was a big shout for lbw; he drove hard at the next ball from Holding and it flew low to Mattis at fourth slip. Not a very distinguished shot, perhaps, but an understandable one in a situation where batsmen know they must grab every opportunity to score a run. Had Bairstow been in for five overs he would probably have played that same shot off the meat of the bat for four, but it is hard to be patient when the ball is bouncing and moving about and five overs is as many as you can realistically hope to survive.

The light faded again, Holding sat Emburey on his backside with a bouncer, then Roberts returned for Croft and Emburey gave a straightforward catch to Lloyd at first slip. It began to rain at tea; from our position on 99 for eight we would have been happy for it to rain for three days, but this is Barbados, not Blackpool in the holiday season. . . .

Willey had already batted an hour for five runs and it seemed like an eternity, not least to him. He had ducked and weaved, braving the onslaught with characteristic courage and determination, a far better player in my opinion than many give him credit for. 'There must be easier ways of earning a living,' he said. Now where have I heard that before?

The last session was interrupted by smoke blowing across the ground from a department-store blaze in the centre of town. Willey made a fine show of being unable to see the pavilion from the middle, and later absorbed a bit of time by insisting a row of shutters which form part of the pavilion sight screen should be closed. But there was too much time and not enough wickets, even though Jackman stuck around manfully and Willey picked up useful runs with fours through cover off Holding and through mid-wicket off Garner and Croft.

Jackman turned a chance into a four when Richards let a nick off Roberts scuttle past his left hand at second slip; he battled well until Richards had a word with Croft who bowled a wide half-volley which Jackman sliced to gulley. Dilley, trying to work Croft off his hip, got round too far too quickly and lobbed the ball off the back of his bat to short leg. England were all out for 122.

West Indies faced about ten minutes' batting to the close and lost Greenidge – who can bat a bit – when he played back to Dilley and was lbw. Just another addition to some pretty damning statistics which said it all about this so-called Test pitch.

In all, fourteen wickets had fallen during the day for 155 runs. West Indies are a formidable batting side, no doubt about that, and even they had lost eleven wickets for 271 runs so far in the match. Only Clive Lloyd had made an appreciable number of runs and he faced only one quick bowler and did not have to battle through the new ball.

I cannot believe that this sort of surface does an ounce of good for Test cricket, least of all in the West Indies, where they are desperately short of money and must want matches to be entertainingly fought over the best part of five days. Or do they prefer to win at any cost? This pitch said so.

Clyde Walcott and I had a chat at the end of the day, and I told him I thought there was too much grass on the pitch. He disagreed, insisting that they were looking for pace and bounce to entertain people and ensure a Test-match result. 'But West Indies have an attack capable of bowling out any side in the world, even on good pitches. They have proved it time and time again, even at Trinidad where the pitch was much slower.' He still refused to agree. 'You wouldn't have scored many runs on that pitch yourself,' I said, and he did not answer.

We could have made some firm representation about the state of the pitch before the Test started, as soon as it became clear that they were preparing a strip, quite foreign to Barbados, with an unusual amount of grass. Of course we could not tell them how to prepare a pitch – that is entirely up to them – but we could at least have made our misgivings known, politely but firmly, and informed them that we would take the same view in our official tour report.

Robin Jackman, battling on without complaint as usual, produced a real old pro's spell of bowling to frustrate Clive Lloyd out in the Barbados Test.

The worst day of the tour. England stand in silent tribute to Kenny Barrington, whose death hit everybody tragically hard. MCC coach Don Wilson is on the right.

We did nothing, and I maintain the Test match has already suffered as a spectacle and a genuine contest of cricket skills. I do not even think the West Indian batsmen have enjoyed it – Richards, Greenidge, Haynes and Mattis can't be exactly over-joyed. How much pleasure can anyone take when the dice are so heavily loaded?

I told the groundsman on the first morning that I reckoned the match would be over inside four days. When a cheerful, smiling Desmond Haynes said what a beautiful over Holding had bowled to me he also added, 'But what would a young batsman playing in his first Test match have made of it? He would have wondered what sort of a game this was.'

I repeated my conviction that the pitch had too much grass on it, and Haynes winked. 'You could be right,' he said, 'but I'm going to get some runs tomorrow because you only have one fast bowler. . . .' That just about says it all.

Third Day

England and cricket everywhere suffered a terrible loss with the news of Kenny Barrington's death a little before midnight on Saturday 14 March. Most of us did not know about it at the time because we were already in bed, but Alan Smith called around at 7.30 the next morning to break the bad news. It was a tremendous shock, as you may imagine: the sort of situation in which it is easy to pour out words and very difficult to find the right ones.

We were stunned, not simply because of a man's death but because Kenny was very much an integral part of the team. His main job, which was organizing the nets and practices, meant we saw a lot more of him than we did of anyone else on the tour management; he was one of the boys, always ready to bowl in the nets – and woe betide anyone who actually got out to his leg-spinners! Kenny and I did not always see eye to eye, and I do not think he would expect me to say we did, but I had the greatest respect for him as a player; he was a very fine cricketer and a totally dedicated professional.

There was a minute's silence before the match started, and several of the players were in tears. Kenny's death cast a pall over the match which hung heavily all day. It was a dreadful situation, but we still had a job to do.

Croft the nightwatchman made it fearfully hard for us. He was content at first just to defend his wicket, to ignore any delivery he did not actually have to play, but his confidence grew until he was able to outscore Haynes. Botham and Dilley strained hard to get him out and bowled him a fair amount of short stuff; Dilley even went round the wicket and hit him on the arm, but Croft showed a tremendous amount of courage and did really well. He played and missed, of course, but any tail-ender was entitled to do that on a pitch where so many better batsmen had done the same.

Wearing out our best bowlers, helping to take the shine off the new ball, was exactly what West Indies wanted from him, and I would have been inclined to set a defensive field earlier and attempt to prise him out with Emburey or Jackman. In the event he made 33, his best Test score, before he tried to hit Jackman back over his head and lobbed a catch which I took, taking a couple of paces forward and stooping low, at mid-off. It was, fittingly, Croft's birthday. . . .

Haynes again looked formidably solid, and I wonder just when Botham will stop trying to bounce him out. The hook is one of Haynes's best shots, and he never looks like being bounced out by bowlers of our pace; he hooked a short one from Botham for four, hooked a bouncer for four and when Botham positioned two men for that shot he simply hooked him effortlessly down for singles. Haynes also likes to work anything just short of a length off his hip, and that was his undoing when he went on to the back foot to work a straight delivery from Botham and was lbw for 25. He is worth a lot more runs than that, and I suspect that once again it was his concentration that let him down.

Mattis survived a big appeal for lbw before he had scored and I'm still not sure how. We reckoned it would have missed off, missed leg – and hit middle. Bairstow sank to his knees and Botham sat on his haunches, unable to believe his bad luck, but Mattis had got his foot fractionally forward and that might just have made the difference. There was no other explanation.

West Indies were 71 for three at lunch, and Botham bowled at Richards immediately afterwards – a good move as far as we are concerned because there is a lot of rivalry between the Somerset team-mates. Botham likes to get Richards out, while Richards might just help him by accepting the challenge and doing something rash. At least, that's the theory. Botham bowled very sensibly, a good line and length, but Richards was able to gain his momentum at the other end.

Dilley had switched to the pavilion end, at his own suggestion I believe, because it was felt the wind might help his in-swinger. Fair enough, but it meant that he could not afford to drift towards middle or leg stumps, or he would be in real trouble. Croft had already taken quite a few runs off him on the leg side, and there is no way you can give Richards anything to hit in that area. I feared the worst.

Perhaps Dilley was badly affected by Barrington's death. He was very fond of the Colonel, and it may have hit him especially hard – I don't know, but the fact is that he never approached anything like his real pace; there was none of the fire and brimstone of the previous evening. He drifted down and Gower had to make a superb stop at mid-wicket; the next delivery was short and not very quick, and Richards was on to it like a flash with a magnificent pull which sailed out of the ground for six. Richards examined his bat like a gunfighter inspecting his six-shooter . . . 'Good bat, this,' he muttered.

With our bowling resources, I could not see how we would get him out unless he played a rank bad shot, especially if he got off to a good start. Then the adrenalin flows and his macho takes over until it is impossible to see him failing to score a century. We had to pressure him at both ends, and although Botham did a good job, Dilley's tendency to drift down the leg side – on to Richards's strength – made real containment impossible. In the circumstances, Jackman or Emburey would probably have done a better job.

Botham's only really bad delivery to Richards came after he injured his hand attempting to stop a fierce drive from Mattis. He could have gone off straight away, but he completed the over off a short run and Richards pulled a short delivery fiercely for four, which was unfortunate for Botham after he had bowled so well. Botham came over to me before he went off. Perhaps he was going to ask me to bowl...?

No, I was to be captain in his absence – which at least helped to answer some speculation. Ever since Miller was not selected for the Test, the Press had wondered who would take over if Botham had to go off. Alan Smith told them it had been decided, but refused to name the emergency captain, and as far as I know there was no official announcement to the team. Puzzle, puzzle, and I was conscious of a buzz round the ground when Botham approached me. The fact that Gooch was already absent with a bruised finger might not have been entirely insignificant....

Like any decent captain, I took my responsibilities seriously. I marked out my run carefully, loosened both shoulders – because you never know when you might need to bowl left and right arm in an over – turned my cap peak to the rear for an uncluttered view of the unfortunate batsman – and then lobbed the ball to Jackman so we could get on with the game. The crowd seemed to like it, and I don't think it did any harm. Botham made a speedy recovery.

Having seen Mattis a few times now, we know he likes to get outside the line of the ball and hit it very straight on the on side. So Emburey intelligently gave him problems by bowling round the wicket to him, with Butcher a bit deeper and wider than usual at mid-on and a deep mid-wicket. It worked in so far as Mattis could not score any boundaries in that area – but Richards was a rather different problem!

Jackman bowled pretty tightly at him, but it needed only a slight error in line or length for Richards to explode one of those fearsome shots. Slightly down the leg side – and we are talking about a matter of inches, not a foot – and Richards belted him through the on side; slightly wide, and Richards went on to the back foot to whack him on the off side. Fractions are vitally important when Richards is in this form and mood.

We brought Butcher in a yard or two and Richards suddenly lifted Emburey for a huge six to long-on. From where I was standing it didn't even look like a fierce hit, just a firm one! I asked Botham if Emburey had lobbed it up a bit and he said, 'Don't think so. I reckon Viv's insulted because we have a man deeper for Mattis than for him.' For heaven's sake, don't insult him again! Richards already had his sights set on a century; he played carefully and sensibly and executed his more aggressive strokes quite beautifully. A master at work.

Mattis obviously does not have his power or range of strokes, and was frustrated by some good bowling to defensive fields. When he had made 24 in ninety-five minutes, Jackman suddenly bowled him an off-spinner, well pitched up, and Mattis was half-way through a drive before he spotted it. He tried to stop his shot, slipped a little in the crease and spooned a catch to Butcher at cover, obviously angry with himself for not spotting the delivery sooner. West Indies 130 for four.

I thought Jackman bowled particularly well. He has bowled abroad a lot and

A magnificently violent shot from Viv Richards on his way to an overpowering 182 not out. Perhaps it serves us right for getting him out for a duck in the first innings. . . .

Far left: David Bairstow at his best. Gomes still had quite a way to go when Bairstow gathered a quick throw from Roland Butcher, dived and threw down the stumps from mid-air. A spectacular and brilliant run out.

Left: Some of the thousands sardined into Kensington Oval with the inevitable transistor radios.

Bottom: Former West Indian and England Test players at the Barbados Test match.

Below: Private box ... An unobstructed view from the roof of the stand and protection from the sun for one inventive customer in Barbados.

knows all about line and length on overseas pitches, and more than that, he is a tremendous competitor who refuses to acknowledge defeat even when he is near exhaustion. He bowled a long spell before tea and fifty minutes afterwards, and by then his little legs were like lead, his pace very strictly medium. Bowlers like him are the workhorses of the game and expect a lot of donkey-work, but I would have bowled even him in rather shorter spells, especially with the new ball in prospect. I still believe in the virtue of variety, especially when you are not taking wickets, and especially when a man like Jackman has crowded a lot of bowling into a relatively short time on tour. In this heat, and particularly when bowlers are not having much success, variety is a must.

Emburey had an off day and was annoyed with himself afterwards. He bowled a little too short, allowing both batsmen to get on the back foot, and for a straight-forward, orthodox batsman Gomes scored off him far too quickly. He hit him off the back foot square and through the covers for boundaries, and I reckon we could usefully have swapped bowlers, changed ends or done something to enable a man like Emburey to catch his breath and think his bowling over for a while. There is a lot of merit in that when things aren't going quite right, even for the best of bowlers.

Richards oiled along, sweeping Embury for a couple of fours and driving him off the back foot, through the covers. We never really looked like getting him out, in fact the only false strokes I can remember were when he tried to hit Jackman off the back foot and missed, when he whipped a full-length ball from Jackman through mid-wicket just wide of Gower about three feet from the ground, and when he tried to force on the leg side again and got an inside edge for two. Not much to feed our optimism there, though we felt he might be a little vulnerable to Emburey's arm ball since he likes to work the off-spinner right round to leg and sometimes gets a leading edge. A couple did pop a bit, but not enough to matter.

Gomes should have been run out when he had pieced 31 together. He drove at Emburey who deflected the ball into Dilley's patch at straight mid-wicket, set off and was sent back by Richards. A good throw would have left him high and dry, but Dilley tried to return it off-balance when he might have steadied himself, and the ball arrived miles above Bairstow's head in a slow lob. Simple and safe would have been better than clever and quick.

As it turned out, Gomes was run out quite spectacularly when he had made another three runs and Richards acknowledged he was the man at fault. Richards played the ball behind square, saw that Dilley was the man deep for the sweep and called for two. He turned and ran a few paces before he realized that Butcher had hared after the ball from just behind square, and was about to pick it up – so he sent Gomes back. Butcher made a quick return as he pivoted and Bairstow finished the job splendidly by gathering, diving for the wicket and throwing the stumps down from mid-air!

Lloyd came in with West Indies 212 for five and the new ball available in one over. Botham asked me if I thought we should take it immediately in the hope of grabbing a couple of wickets, but I said not – Jackman was spent, Botham himself had done a fair bit of bowling and Dilley was nowhere near his normal pace. Unless we bowled well through the last forty minutes with the new ball, Richards was quite capable of smashing the shine off it – especially since he has a habit of thumping it against the concrete on the boundary. After a bit of that treatment, any ball looks as though it has been through a potato-peeler. I suggested we keep it tight for a while longer and perhaps give ourselves four overs with the new ball at the end.

When the new ball was taken, Dilley bowled to only one slip which hardly said a lot for confidence in his ability to knock a couple of wickets over. Had I anticipated that I would have advised against taking the new ball at all, or for more than one or two overs at the most.

Our habit of using bowlers in long spells probably stems from county cricket, where you know you are only going to field for around six hours at the most. It is very different in a Test match, and I believe in taking a man off before he's spent, especially when you have only four main bowlers to play with. That way each one has a little bit in reserve – it might just be the ability to come on and bowl three or four significant overs which means that the captain has that much more manoeuvrability when it matters.

West Indies finished the day on 245 for five, with a lead of 388, already a hell of a mountain for us to climb. Viv Richards crashed Dilley through mid-wicket for his century off the fourth ball of the last over of the day. He left it late but there was never much doubt that he would make it.

Fourth Day

Clive Lloyd said before the start that he was aiming for a lead of 500 before considering a declaration. It seemed like over-kill in our situation and in view of our batting record against them, but that is Lloyd's way with this side. He grinds the opposition down and further down, perfectly confident that he has the bowlers to dismiss any side – and especially with a day and a half at their disposal. Sad to say, we did not make it any harder for them.

West Indies made 134 off twenty-seven overs before Lloyd's declaration at lunch, and that was every bit as humbling as it sounds. We would have done better than that, even against Lloyd and Richards, on a Sunday afternoon in England but there was a dispiriting air of resignation about our bowling and fielding. It was as though we were going through the motions, just waiting for them to declare.

That is not to say our bowlers did not try. Botham strove hard for control and line, while Dilley looked no more than lively fast medium, and Jackman was clattered around fearfully; there was no edge to our bowling, no sign of the 110 per cent competitiveness we needed. And there was precious little sign of any real plan.

Dilley was a good example. He can be really quick on his day, but he is still young and very inexperienced and lacks the maturity or the stamina to sustain his best for long periods. Suddenly he looked very much like a boy.

Botham set him a predominantly off-side field and asked him to bowl outside the off stump, to Richards's weaker side. But Dilley drifted, was hit through the leg side, tended to over-compensate and was hit on the off side off the back foot. Botham took out the only slip and put him on the off-side boundary, and then Dilley really did not know where to bowl. His inevitable lack of experience showed through and I felt Botham could have helped him by being more decisive.

It was a situation which cried out for consultation between a bowler and his captain; I saw it develop and was aching to talk to him, but that's not easy from the depths of third-man. 'Look, Graham, I want you to bowl wide of the off stump and I will give you extra protection on that side. Do you feel you can do it, because only you can know for sure? If you can't, then bowl fairly straight and we will pack the leg-side field. Let Richards hit you there for singles and bowl at the other man. . . .' It is a tactic we often use against Richards in one-day cricket at home, and it would have made sense to employ it here. As it was, Dilley drifted and West Indies galloped away towards their declaration.

It looked at first as though Richards had set his sights on a double century and nothing was going to stop him. He took ones, twos and threes at will and occasionally unleashed one of those smouldering boundaries, but as lunch approached he had already made his highest Test score in the West Indies and perhaps he was happy to make do with that; 182 not out wasn't all that bad. . . .

West Indies made their runs at five an over and with ridiculous ease, except when Lloyd was almost run out. He blocked Botham and answered Richards's call for a quick single, since our fielders were well spread out, but Bairstow ran to square-leg and shied at the bowler's stumps. He missed by a fraction, with Lloyd still straining to get in. Richards gave a technical chance of a return catch to Botham – a hint of a chance, no more – and Jackman made painful contact with a drive from Richards which ricocheted off his shin for four! Apart from that we simply waited on events, and it was a really lacklustre morning for us when we looked dispirited and ragged in the field and bowled without any real fire.

Lloyd eventually tried to lift Botham over mid-wicket and was lbw on the back leg; Roberts fell second ball to a fine diving catch by Bairstow off one of the few deliveries which pitched and bounced. West Indies were 379 for seven at lunch, with a lead of 522, when their manager Steve Camacho came into our dressing-room to announce they had declared.

Psychologically, our poor performance in the morning was very damaging to our now slim chances of saving the match. The onus had been put on our batsmen, as though nobody else was capable of affecting the course of the match, and it is terribly difficult for batsmen suddenly to shrug off an established sense of depression and bat as though their lives depended on it. You simply cannot suspend your competitiveness for a couple of hours and then expect it to flood back when you strap a pair of pads on; a gloomy mood gets through to everybody.

West Indies had been allowed to play through the morning session as though it were a benefit match; now we had to bat for more than a day and a half to save the match, and nobody was going to do us any favours. We had no illusions about the size of the problem – and especially not after a couple of overs.

Gooch negotiated a maiden from Roberts; I played a couple of balls off Holding and got a run off the third; we ran a leg-bye from the fourth. Then the fifth delivery reared from just short of a length, hit me on the left glove in front of my throat and lobbed gently towards the waiting slip cordon. It was Trinidad all over again – I have two bruises on exactly the same spot to prove it – except that this time the ball sailed to Garner at gulley.

Poor Gatting didn't have much chance with his first ball. He pushed half forward to a delivery of fullish length and the ball simply squatted and hurried through. It scraped the bottom of his bat before hitting the leg stump – what a way to go! – and we were 2 for two. Gooch and Gower had a hell of a lot of damage to repair.

Could they see it through? It was almost two and a half hours before the next wicket fell, after a partnership full of guts and determination, laced with some streaky shots, quite a bit of the luck they clearly needed and several strokes of real quality. The minutes seemed as though they would never tick away; every delivery might have been the one to break the stand, and with it England's back; the bowlers turned and wheeled in with wearying repetitiveness while we watched grim-faced and hoped they would cling on.

Every heart in our dressing-room missed a beat when Gower had reached 17. Croft went over the wicket and bowled him a wide, full-length delivery which Gower shaped to push into the covers, but the angle of delivery – with Croft so wide of the crease – deceived him and he nicked it. Richards at second slip barely moved, neither did Greenidge at third, and the ball sped waist high between them for four. Far too close for comfort, that!

Croft bowls a wide full-toss and Gooch slices it through gulley for four; Gower glides Croft off the back foot through backward point for four; a huge lbw shout against Gower when one keeps low, and Croft pummels the air in annoyance when it's turned down; Gooch, always looking to get on the front foot to Garner, runs him past gulley for four; Richards comes on and Gower drives him uppishly through cover for another boundary . . . and at tea they are still together, absorbing valuable time with England 94 for two. Suddenly you realize how hot it is.

Gooch reached his 50 in the first over after tea after batting for 123 minutes, the century partnership came up at the same time, and soon afterwards Gower reached his 50 after 130 minutes at the crease. Keep going, lads, there's a full day tomorrow . . . but Gooch can't resist lifting Richards over unpopulated long-on for four. Looked good, but what if he had mis-hit it? Steady, steady.

The pitch was much easier now – the fact that West Indies bowled Richards in preference to the quicks showed that – but there was still absolutely no room for error, not in our situation. Roberts pitched one short and wide of the off stump and Gooch attempted to hook, which was ominous. He played and missed at another wide delivery, which was another danger signal as far as I was concerned: Gooch was trying to get after the bowling, when his job was to stay, and stay – and stay.

Gower was going for his shots, too, and I feared they were being lulled into a false sense of security. Against such an attacking field, with nobody at mid-on or mid-off and with no third-man, it was not difficult to play a firm shot for runs, in fact the scoreboard was ticking over pretty quickly. Both batsmen were in danger of forgetting their priority, which was to bat all day – for 30 if necessary. So long as they were playing shots, there was a chance that they would make a mistake – just one – and get out. That was exactly what Clive Lloyd wanted.

In a saving situation you have to make the bowlers work, not play shots which might be appropriate in other circumstances but which invite errors; you have to remind yourself again and again that the job is to stay there and never mind the scoreboard. Play shots by all means, but only safety shots – and the hook and the hit over the top certainly do not come into that category. I felt the batsmen were playing too freely for our good.

Gower fell to a stroke which would have been dreadful in any circumstances, and he acknowledged as much afterwards. He tried to run an innocuous-looking slower ball from Richards with a horizontal bat and without any attempt to use his feet, and chopped it half-way up his off stump. It was a horribly tame way to get out after nearly two and a half hours' work, and Gower asked me afterwards where I thought he had gone wrong. 'You were starting to feel good because the runs were coming; you were looking to score rather than remembering the priority was to stay there; they tempted you to play shots and you started to fall for it. . . .' It's a hard lesson.

Butcher never looked settled, playing and missing twice in his first three deliveries off Richards, and there was little permanence about him until he played back to Richards and was lbw for two. Suddenly we were 139 for four, with Botham gritting his teeth to resist the temptation as Richards tantalized him with some invitingly flighted deliveries. He kept himself in check well, but Roberts beat him with a delivery which bounced a bit and slithered off the face of the bat to Lloyd at first slip. A good delivery, especially to a new batsman who is wary of committing himself forward, the sort of line and length which caught Botham in two minds.

Willey is a fighter, never one to give his wicket away, and while Gooch continued playing his shots, he concentrated on staying there to the close. There were plenty of hairy moments, and it was obvious he was having some difficulty picking up Croft, especially as the shadows lengthened, but he battled through with typical tenacity. At the close we were 166 for five and a long, long way from salvation.

In situations like this, England obviously miss an experienced player in mid-order to give the talented but inexperienced batsmen a helping hand. I was lucky when I started to have players like Barrington, Cowdrey, Graveney and Dexter around, so that there was always somebody with a fund of knowledge and technical skill at the other end. England have only one really experienced batsman at the moment, and it has been made abundantly clear that 'officially' he is not required to offer the benefit of his experience. Certainly I give it readily whenever it is sought – that has always been my practice.

Colin Croft bowling quick and wide of the crease again during a destructive spell in the second innings. Umpire Douglas Sang Hue is as inscrutable as ever.

The cry is always for youth, but there are so many Test situations where experience is of crucial importance. Lloyd is an experienced Test campaigner and he outsmarted Gower in the end, making it seem easy for him until he allowed himself to forget the realities of the situation. It took him a while, but Lloyd won through in the end.

Gooch might have gone the same way. He played a lot of shots when he should have been thinking in terms of playing for his stumps and cutting out every possible risk – and I say that in full recognition of the quality of his unbeaten 88 at the end of the day. It is impossible to cram real experience into relatively few Test matches, it has to be passed down in the way that it was passed on to me, by listening to older and wiser players and sifting their experience, learning from their mistakes as much as their successes. Then you learn not only how to play but also how to think your way through Test match situations, how to apply your mind to the next problem and the one after.

Pure ability is not enough at Test match level. A player has to learn – and the faster the better – how to think round problems and get out of tight situations. He will do that better if he can listen to and play with more experienced players who are encouraged to give their views – I know because it is the way I learned. But I am not encouraged to pass my experience on. And the more I mull it over, the more I wonder how that can be in the best interests of English cricket at a time when we have many talented players with little deep experience of the Test-match scene.

Fifth Day

At 12.59 p.m. John Emburey attempted to hit Garner over mid-wicket with a tail-ender's shovel-shot, missed and saw the ball deflect off his pads on to his stumps. England had lost the third Test match by 298 runs.

Our last five batsmen held off the inevitable bravely enough, but there was never a realistic hope that we could bat all day to save it; even on a now-good batting surface where Emburey was prepared to accept odds that he would stay to tea, our last flurry of resistance was a forlorn hope. The match was lost and won long before the last wicket fell.

Gooch and Willey took over where they had left off the previous evening in their contrasting styles: Gooch looking for runs and playing and missing with blithe frequency; Willey quiet and undemonstrative, defending well. Gooch was determined to keep his score moving along, perhaps aware that the second new ball was only a handful of overs away, and played and missed at Holding with unnerving regularity – twice in successive balls, three times in one over, four times in another. Willey had gritted through ninety-five minutes when he was out, unluckily considering the shape of the match so far.

Nobody had been given out on the front foot, yet when Willey played forward to work Croft on the leg side, the umpire considered an lbw shout for some time and then gave him out; from where we were sitting it looked a very rough decision.

Bairstow, on a pair, worked his first delivery off his legs for two but fell to the second. The ball from Croft was well pitched up, he drove at it and was given out caught behind very low by Murray to a decidedly muted appeal. Bairstow said he thumped the ground and did not hit the ball but we were 198 for seven and there was no arguing with that.

Then Gooch fell, after batting for just over five hours and hitting thirteen fours. He square-drove hard at a wide half-volley from Croft, and Garner at gulley made a potentially difficult catch look easy. No sooner had Gooch completed his stroke than Garner was throwing the ball up from his bootcaps and England were 201 for eight. Just a matter of time now. . . .

West Indies had bowled Richards to hurry them towards the new ball and they took it soon after Gooch was out, which meant poor Emburey and Jackman faced a doubly difficult and uncomfortable passage. Croft had Jackman in several sorts of trouble, but Jackman stuck at it with typical pugnacity which probably provoked Croft even more. He dug out a couple which kept low, ducked to avoid a bouncer which didn't bounce and got two runs off his rear, stood up to bouncers as Croft went over and round the wicket. Emburey fought it out, too, having taken forty minutes to get off the mark. He sent for a new pair of batting gloves after only three or four overs because those he had on were already wet with sweat; the sort of situation in which every minute seems like an hour and there are far too many hours in the day.

They braved it through to lunch, which was a good deal longer than many people might have expected, but Jackman was out soon afterwards. He went on the back foot and jabbed down hastily at a delivery from Garner which didn't bounce, but the ball squirmed from beneath his bat and on to the stumps; the end of a characteristically optimistic and defiant innings.

Dilley wasn't too surprised when Garner and Holding ambled across, taking a particular interest in his feet. It is not that they are frustrated chiropodists, just that Dilley knows he is vulnerable to the fast yorker and has a habit of stopping the ball with his big toe. West Indies know it, too: Garner's first two deliveries were yorkers but Dilley kept them out. He profited from his weakness in a way, because Garner over-reached himself attempting to fire in his yorker, and both Dilley and Emburey were able to despatch full-tosses for runs. But they could not expect miracles and neither could we; Emburey stuck it out for seventy-five minutes before the end came.

It strikes me that the biggest single difficulty England teams have at the moment is suiting their batting to the needs of a particular match, especially in a situation which calls for defensive awareness. They simply seem to go out and bat for runs – no bad philosophy, perhaps, but one which cannot hope to cover every contingency we are likely to meet in a Test match. Graham Gooch's innings was a good example of the trend; his runs were precious, and the time he spent at the crease even more so, but he did not set himself to stay for as long as it took to finish the job; he just played for runs and accepted his good luck as part of the game. I would not criticize

Gooch's innings except to say that he could have been out many, many times playing shots which, in the circumstances were heavy with risk.

But Gooch is a product of a system of cricket which seems perversely intent on not producing Test-match players. In the name of so-called entertainment, we are set on producing batsmen who are encouraged to hit everything in sight; they build reputations on a Sunday afternoon when bowlers are restricted to laughable run-ups and there are no slips or gulleys, then they are pitched into Test cricket and expect to do the same against Test-class opposition. Don't blame the players; blame the system that breeds them. If ever a competition was invented specifically to stunt the growth of the real cricketer it was the John Player League, which has absolutely nothing to offer a batsman or a bowler in terms of genuine technical experience or improvement. Those who want to redeem it say it has improved running between the wickets and fielding, and I agree – but at what a price. And it is just one, albeit the worst, of several limited-overs competitions we have to play, and the county championship has restrictions which make it less and less likely to produce Test-match attitudes. I know this is no new thought, but it is on days when you have just lost a Test by 298 runs and people are writing you off as second class that you pause to consider the real reasons, the fundamental causes of defeat.

Even county-championship cricket doesn't help as much as it used to, partly because of a fixation with phoney restrictions and bonus points and partly because the surfaces on which we play are usually quite different from Test-match pitches. That is not true in Australia or West Indies, where Sheffield and Shell Shield matches are played on hard, true surfaces which encourage players to develop exactly the sort of technique they will need in Test matches at home. When they play in England we produce good Test pitches which help them; and when we don't – as at Headingley a few years ago for instance – there is hell to pay. So West Indies or Australia can play their normal sort of game in Test matches, while we, even in England, have to adjust.

And not just in regard to the pitches we play on. County-championship regulations have militated against Test-type players for some years; I remember that Graham Dilley spent a full day in the field for the first time in his cricket career after he had made the Test side, which is funny if you don't mind laughing at England's flair for self-destruction. In Australian-grade cricket it is common for players to field for five and a half hours, and it is common for bowlers to bowl for ages on very good surfaces. They learn how to bowl sides out or how to contain them; they learn how to spread themselves over a long day in the field, just as batsmen learn how to contend with the problems of a long innings. In England we bowl a hundred overs and troop off; perfect grounding for a five-day Test. . . .

There were loads of former Test players in Barbados, many of them ready to hand out a lecture on how they would have played the West Indies fast bowling, usually how they would have taken the attack to them and scored runs, etc, etc. That is nonsense; I really do not believe that the old timers would have clouted this attack around – but they would have made it more difficult for them, and that

Robin Jackman's tenacity in Barbados riled even Joel Garner, and the result was predictable another bouncer and Jackman takes hurried evasive action.

supports my argument about the type of cricket we play now and the type of cricketer it produces.

I have never been one to harken back to the 'good old days' and to suggest, as some do, that players of twenty years ago were so much more talented than the modern ones, partly because I just don't believe it. But they were undoubtedly better players defensively, and in a situation like ours in the third Test they would have made it harder for West Indies than we did.

Test batsmen of the early sixties were built around a solid defence. They learned their trade without the benefit of limited-overs competitions where a defensive stroke is looked upon as the next thing to a failure; they did not have to fret about bonus points or hundred-over limitations. Bowlers were encouraged to learn how to bowl people out; batsmen were expected to bat for big hundreds, basing their innings on a solid defence and playing their shots from a well-established base. Defensively they were undoubtedly better players, with a better attitude to working for long periods – either as batsmen or bowlers – because the cricket they played encouraged them to be. Contrast that with the apprenticeship that a young player gets with counties nowadays – all flash and ferment, anything to bring in the cash – and you can see that the system is to blame, not the player.

Good players will always come through in any era but I have maintained for a long time that our domestic system does not get the best out of players, certainly not in the sense of equipping them to play in Test matches. Graham Stevenson is a product of his time – a strike bowler with Yorkshire on seaming pitches, a very aggressive batsman in limited-overs competitions, yet he finds it terribly difficult to step up to the high level where surfaces, attitudes and requirements are so different. Is that Stevenson's fault?

Clive Lloyd won the Man of the Match award and I would not quarrel with that, but I suppose the match will be remembered by some people for two or three amazing overs from Michael Holding. His first over in the first innings, and then the one in which he dismissed Botham and Bairstow; his first over in the second innings when I was caught and Gatting was out first ball. They may not have actually won the Test match themselves, but they were huge psychological blows in West Indies' favour.

I have looked back over my dismissals, of course, watched them on local TV a few times, dropped into a room in the Holiday Inn one night where the BBC team ran through their film of my dismissal in the first innings. In a professional sense, the first-innings dismissal concerns me more, because I was bowled, and that is not how I get out very often. I watched replays of the second-innings dismissal, caught at gulley off a lifter, and I really don't know what I could have done, how I could have played that particular delivery with safety, no matter how long I had been in. It was a delivery which I reckon would have got most batsmen out, unless by good luck the ball were to drop wide of a fielder.

When I am bowled I always want to know why, and Holding's over in the first innings was very interesting. It goes without saying that the pitch had a great deal

West Indies' Rolls Royce Michael Holding reckons Jeff Thomson just shades him as the fastest bowler in the world. Not sure that I entirely agree....

The end of the best over I have ever faced! Bowled by Holding in the Barbados Test – and where has the off stump gone?

to do with it; hard and pacey and grassy – far too grassy to be considered a good Test surface. But looking back, the extraordinary thing is how Holding produced a first over which was so fast and so accurate in terms of line and length. Now that is most unusual. Most fast bowlers find it difficult enough to combine pace, line and length perfectly at any time; to dovetail all three as he did – in his first over – was an incredible achievement.

No doubt many people who saw the over and the delivery which got me out will talk in terms of pace and pace alone. If they do, they will sell Holding short. There was a good deal more to it than that – in fact there usually is. It often annoys or amuses me how people talk about a batsman 'beaten for pace'; apart from tail-enders, they rarely are beaten for pace alone. It is like watching a spinner take a wicket and saying the batsman was beaten for lack of pace; there are always subtleties involved.

So why was my off stump knocked out of the ground? Basically, because I played fractionally inside the line of the ball. And there was a reason for that which goes a long way beyond a simple sort of misjudgement.

My natural inclination is to get in line as far as possible. But having played two deliveries which bounced somewhere round throat height I tried to get a little more on the leg side, a little out of line because it is impossible to avoid the bouncing delivery if you stay in line, and you cannot hope to play it down or wide of the catching cordon for ever. That is not timidity, it is a style which many batsmen accustomed to facing fast bowling on bouncy pitches adopt as a matter of course.

I remember some years ago when England played in Perth, where the pitch was hard, bouncy and true. England came up against this chap called Bobby Simpson, who stayed leg-side when the ball bounced and got across very quickly to anything pitched up on or outside off stump. A certain bowler of ours called Fred thought Simpson was chicken because he did not get in line, and really fancied firing him out. I can't remember offhand how many runs Simpson scored, but I know who won the contest – and it wasn't Fred!

When Holding bowled me, I expected a delivery well pitched up after so many short ones. I got back and across my usual amount but since I was already favouring the leg side, that was not quite enough. So I played a fraction inside the line . . . and goodbye off stump. An error of judgement? Up to a point, yes, but at least I had tried to think it through, and to suggest that I was just beaten for pace is to underestimate the subtleties of the situation. Whichever way you look at it, however, it was a very fine over – the best I have ever faced.

Most of the spectators on the last, mournful day were English visitors who had already paid for their seats; there were very few locals there, even though the price of admission had been cut by half, and I feel that is significant. I still feel sorry for those people who travelled so far; the match could have been over inside four days had Lloyd not batted on in search of a lead of 500, and they were entitled to better than that.

West Indies have the best side in the world at present, there is no argument about that. But if they seek to rub it in or perhaps prove it to themselves by producing unbalanced pitches, they will simply do themselves a disservice in the end. West Indian crowds love to see their heroes win, but they also like to watch a cricket contest; if they just wanted to watch an easy victory, where were they on the last day?

Of the two Tests we had played, one was arranged in virtual competition to Carnival in Trinidad, which was nonsense, and the other was played on a pitch which favoured the West Indies fast bowlers, who needed no help at all. Whatever the merits and demerits in a purely cricket sense, the logic of that from a financial point of view totally escapes me when West Indies are so short of money and need every penny they can get. They reckon they have already lost a million dollars, taking the unplayed second Test into account. Next they will be asking England for some relief from the financial guarantees made before the tour started, but I for one can't find much sympathy for them.

Michael Anthony Holding is too slender and slim-shouldered to be a fast bowler – until he lets go of the ball! His T-shirt, announcing that he was a member of Joel Garner's fan club, hung loosely round his ribs, he smiled a lot and spoke in a gentle Paul Robeson tone. Not exactly the popular image of a man generally accepted as the world's fastest bowler....

'The fastest? Well, I'm aware they say that, but I'm not so sure myself, not with Thomson around. When he gets everything together I reckon he's probably the fastest, but I suppose I'm the fastest playing Test cricket. I try to bowl within myself, keep a bit in reserve, because I know I'm going to have to bowl seven or eight overs at a stretch. If Clive Lloyd said he only wanted three it might be different – I could really let it go then but if I bowl really quick I tend to lose my line. I'm not all that accurate, so I keep a bit back.

'Nobody really took me in hand and told me what to do when I was a kid. I just played local matches, that sort of thing. I have always been pretty loose and I don't seem to stiffen up after a spell, which is fine. The long run developed in England in 1976; I don't know why really, I just kept on walking further back. But it definitely helps because I can build up momentum without using body strength; if I bowl off my short run I have to use body strength, and I don't really have much of that.

'I think the first time I bowled really quick was in Australia in 1975, especially against New South Wales in Sydney. The wicket was very grassy and I really ran in; I took six wickets and they said I bowled quicker than Andy that day. That's when I saw myself as a quick bowler; up to then I'd bowled a bit of out-swing, the odd one coming back, not much real pace.

'Since then I reckon my best bowling was at the Oval in 1976, in the second Test in Melbourne in 1979, and in Barbados – especially that first over! Yes, I rate that with the best, and I'm still not sure just what happened.

'The previous match in Trinidad I couldn't get my run-up at all, and once I start having problems like that it's impossible for me to bowl well. I just put them all over the place. In Trinidad I even used Andy's footmarks because I couldn't get it right, and I was thinking of asking him to run up in Barbados but there wasn't time or something. So I was very tentative, but it worked out OK ... I know by the time I get half-way through my run-up if it's right, and suddenly it felt good – you probably remember it. ...

'We enjoy winning, we've been successful with four fast bowlers, and there's no reason to change. And we're all aware that we have the fastest; if anybody's going to do any terrorizing, it's going to be us. In 1975–6 in Australia all we got was bouncers – Lillee, Thomson, even Gilmour bounced us all the time. In 1979 we got everything in our half – a welcome change. When we go in to bat it's reassuring to know that not many fast bowlers will bounce us because we have the fire-power. We get a couple but not many. And we relish it while we can.

'I can see us going on together for another four or five years. After that it may change, but I know several young fast bowlers who are coming through, so perhaps they will just take over. We have one in Jamaica now, a lad called Mark Walsh, who's taking eight or nine wickets an innings! There are two or three I know of in Antigua, too, so we'll have a few fast bowlers around for some years – and don't forget Andy is the oldest of the present bowlers and he's only thirty.

'Standards of batting seem to have dropped; most young players these days don't get behind the line of the ball at all. If I bowl a delivery outside off stump they miss it completely, which may be a good thing as far as they are concerned! It's not just England players, it seems to be the same everywhere, perhaps because there's so much emphasis on fast bowling. When you bowled at Cowdrey all you could see was a bit of the off stump; when you bowl at young players these days you can see all three. I like that. I remember Derek Randall always went the other way – all you could see when you bowled at him was his feet; I didn't like that very much.

'You can always sense when a batsman doesn't like what you're doing. Some stand very still, some back away, but you can always tell. Once England had players like Cowdrey, Graveney, Barrington and May – I never saw much of them but from what they tell me they were really good players, world-class players. Of the present England side there are only four that I consider to be good batsmen: You, Gooch, Gower and Willey.

'I wouldn't say Willey had a good technique, but he's a very difficult player to dislodge and he doesn't seem afraid. He's always getting across. I have been hearing a lot about Athey since 1976; he has a good reputation so I suppose he must be a good player, though I've never seen him make runs. But there aren't very many around. I don't know how long I'll be around; four years seems a long time when you've a long way to walk and a long way to run. I know there's a story that I could have represented Jamaica in the Olympics, but that's just one of those stories ... my partner in junior cricket was a feller called Seymour Newman who ran in the 800 metres in the Olympics, but there was never any chance of me doing that. I wasn't very good – as an athlete I was just mediocre.'

16

Extinct Volcanoes

Montserrat is a perfect spot for those with nothing to do and half a lifetime to do it in. A green, hilly island with three volcanoes – two thankfully extinct – explored by hairpin roads and ringed by beaches of black volcanic sand. The kind of place where nobody travels far or very fast, where there are few hotels and where the relatively few visitors relax round the pool at their holiday villa or play the charming eleven-hole golf course.

Several of the players were soon out on the course, and a big challenge match was arranged for the morning of our departure – Bairstow and Stevenson versus Gooch and Gatting. A bit of a contrast in styles, I expect; Bairstow and Stevenson were winning handsomely until their game fell apart – noisily – and the others came from behind. The lizards and land crabs which scurried through the undergrowth and popped out of their burrows for a look are probably still talking about it. . . .

Boredom is always a potential problem, ridiculous as that may sound to anyone braving an English winter, and it becomes particularly acute when the weather closes in. The black clouds gathered on top of the hills and a mist crept slowly down into the valleys, bringing torrential rain; then relaxation is enforced and becomes tedium. Montserrat is not exactly a jumping place and is proud of the fact; we read, sunbathed when we could, and I played a couple of games of tennis at a neighbouring hotel.

Our own hotel was pleasant enough, and the staff really tried hard to make us feel at home; the food was simple but superbly prepared so we had no complaints on that score. None of the rooms had air conditioning, which opened the door, so to speak, for those particularly voracious mosquitoes which seem to have followed us round the Caribbean. We were bitten – and then bitten on top of bites – until we started to make use of those coils of scented material which burn slowly and give off a smoke to keep the bugs at bay. They work, too, even if the room smells a bit like an opium den.

Botham left with his family after a couple of days because he had been invited to Antigua's wedding of the year, or perhaps of the century, when Viv Richards got married. Meanwhile Miller the crossword enthusiast was always looking for clues;

he made a point of asking my opinion about plans and tactics, and I felt involved – I appreciated that.

The match against Leeward Islands lost a lot of its public appeal when Richards and Roberts did not play, but a public holiday was declared, all the shops closed and there was a fairly good attendance on a couple of days considering the size of the island. The ground was unpretentious, nicely situated on the edge of the sea about two miles from the capital, Plymouth; the pitch was grassy and very firm, and after winning the toss we put Leewards in.

Rain delayed the start until 2.00 p.m. Then we bowled badly, owing in part at least to a chronic lack of match practice. Old had not played since the Test match in Trinidad; Stevenson was little better off with roughly one week's work out of the last five; Dilley went for 27 off his first three overs, including 16 runs off the second, and we should have concentrated on bottling them up, but the bowlers were pitching much too short and the ball sat up invitingly to be hooked, pulled, cut or hit through the covers off the back foot. When the bowlers tried to correct themselves they overpitched and were driven again – a familiar enough formula, especially for men not in the best of practice.

Nobody took advantage of it better than Luther Kelly, a policeman from St Kitts, who went galloping off like a member of the flying squad. It was only after he was out – we had a word at tea and Stevenson went round the wicket to have him caught at slip soon afterwards – that we gained any real measure of control. Leewards included a local man, one Everton Ryan, who looked suspiciously as though he had made the side chiefly because he had only to walk up the road from Plymouth ... suffice to say that he did not look the thirteenth best player in the Leeward Islands and in fact had the greatest difficulty guiding the bat on to the ball late in the day in murky light. After he had played and missed for the umpteenth time one of the umpires inquired solicitously what he thought of the light. 'It's not the light, man, it's my eyes,' he said mournfully. It was one of the less sensational facts of the match that he got a pair – but then he did run me out, so I reckon his trip was not altogether wasted.

The groundstaff showed no inclination to cut the pitch at the start of the second day, so I asked the manager to remind them. They eventually brushed the grass proud of the surface and a chap went over it swinging a machete! Amazing how much grass they got off before his arm got tired.

The tail collapsed quickly to Dilley and Stevenson, who bowled a good line and length and skidded the ball off green patches, and Leewards finished their first innings on 161. Before we could start our innings there was a heavy shower of rain, squalling across the ground from the tips of the volcanoes, and when the sun came out soon afterwards the new ball bounced appreciably. We hopped about a bit; I was hit on the gloves a couple of times and fended one away from my throat; Downton was caught behind off one that bounced.

Athey looked determined to attack, a bit desperately so, hooking as soon as he came in and getting a few bruises on his arms for his trouble. But he made the shot

A square cut with a difference - the groundsman in Montserrat used a machete to cut the pitch before the start of play.

Viv Richards, bowled over at last, watches pensively while his bride signs the register after their wedding in Antigua.

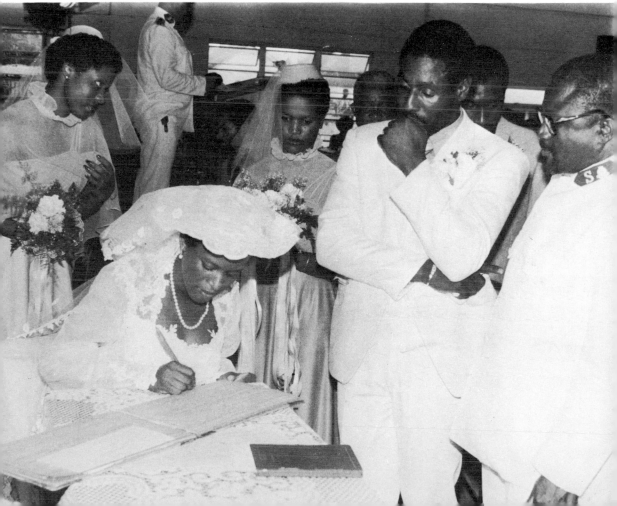

pay off later, and although he never looked comfortable against the spinners – Parry had him dropped by mid-on running backwards – he made 41 before playing loosely at one of the quicker bowlers and giving a catch to gulley.

I felt in good form: playing compactly, scoring off the quicker bowlers and keeping on top of the spinners. In fact I didn't see myself getting out until Miller called me for two and I was run out by an accurate throw from the laughing policeman at wide mid-on. Centuries do me good in terms of positiveness and self-confidence, and I was more annoyed at missing the 23 than I was pleased at scoring 77.

We stumbled a bit towards the close, the off-spinner Noel Guishard picking up three quick wickets. Gatting pushed too firmly and was caught off bat and pad; Butcher played for the spin and was bowled by a straight one; Stevenson launched himself into a slog with his head thrown back. Bairstow had already pulled the opening bowler White straight into mid-wicket's hands, so it was left to Miller and Jackman to steady us to 211 for seven.

Miller battled hard for his first first-class century next morning, but Jackman, Old and Dilley got out, leaving him high and dry with an unbeaten 92. Our lead of 90 was very valuable now that the pitch had settled down under two days' hot sun. The grass had become straw-coloured, and the bounce was much more manageable; there were plenty of good shots to be played.

However, it turned out to be a frustrating and fractious sort of a day. When we had four wickets down for 123 we thought we might finish it very quickly, but then Shirlon Williams went to hit Miller over the top and Downton missed a stumping – which proves at least that it doesn't only happen to Bairstow. Williams was nine then and went on to make 62, helped, we were convinced, by some bizarre umpiring decisions. We were sure Bairstow caught him off his gloves at short-leg, sure also that Jackman had him caught behind. Amoury likewise made 56 after we felt sure Old had him caught behind early in his innings . . . several players began to get annoyed on occasions – typified by sarcastic comment and clapping when Williams played one in the middle of the bat.

Williams resented that. He hit out angrily, and it came off – Miller went for four and six, and Dilley was thumped for six – at least until Dilley knocked back his off stump; then Williams turned, and as he strode off there was an exchange of words.

The mood of annoyance was taken up next day when Dilley went round the wicket to dislodge Leewards' last batsman and was no-balled twice for stepping outside the return crease. He did not like it, and asked Stevenson at mid-off to watch his feet. No umpire likes to have his judgement challenged like that, and between innings he came to the dressing-room and explained that Dilley's back foot was outside the return crease at the moment of delivery, so it had to be a no-ball. 'What about Colin Croft, he seems to get away with it?' said Stevenson. And the umpire explained patiently that Croft's back foot was OK, even if his front foot often cut or went outside the return crease. He was perfectly right, of course, but by questioning his decisions we had rubbed him up the wrong way. And at team

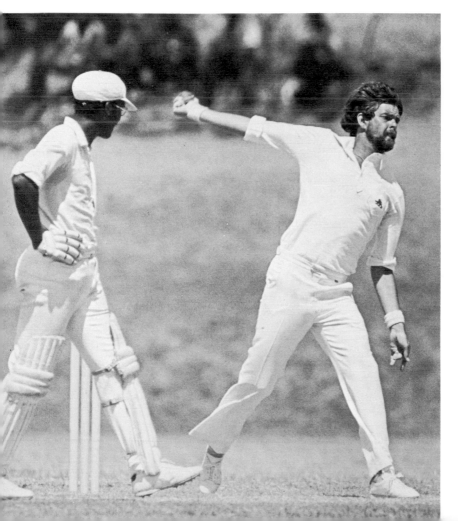

Above: Yorkshire's Bill Athey joined the tour as replacement for Brian Rose and did well in the first innings at Montserrat. Judging by the wicketkeeper's reaction, that's runs.

Geoff Miller captained the side in Montserrat, his only match after being named as vice-captain in succession to Bob Willis.

meetings we had been warned repeatedly against challenging umpires' decisions for that very reason. When we batted I tried to engage the umpire in some sort of conversation, but he was edgy and upset and muttered about the players not accepting his decisions. I felt we had stored up some trouble for ourselves, and the first delivery the off-spinner Guishard bowled to me confirmed the worst. He was bowling wide of the crease and the ball pitched well wide of the off stump, so I padded up – and even the crowd couldn't believe it when I was given lbw. Athey from the other end later confirmed that the ball wouldn't even have hit another set of stumps. It was, I am afraid, the worst decision I have ever had.

Miller was unfortunate, too, to be given out playing forward to the slow left-armer; then Butcher was caught at short-leg off the off-spinner and was given the benefit of somebody's doubt! Butcher got away with a few head-high drives over cover but otherwise hit the bad ball well; he clearly made out a good case for inclusion in the fourth Test, when it seemed that his position was under pressure from Athey. Now it looks as though Gatting is the one in danger.

We won comfortably enough by five wickets, but it was a pity that the match had to be marred in the end by some poor umpiring and by the ill-feeling which affected the umpires and players on both sides.

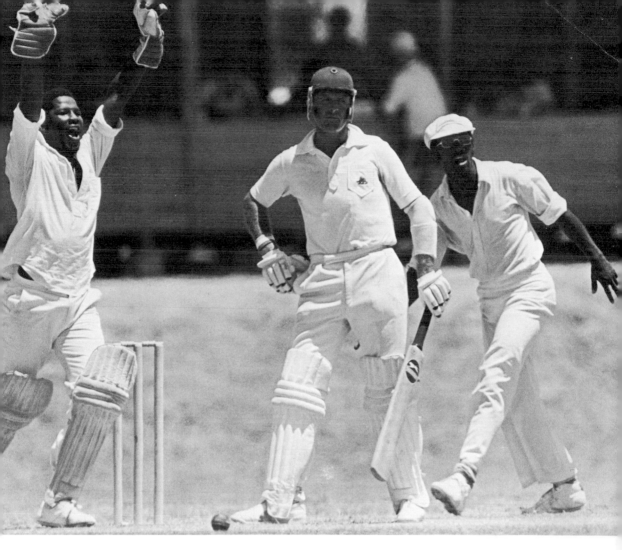

Happiness is Sherlon Williams and Vance Amory plus a successful lbw appeal. Can't say I was as impressed – it was the worst lbw decision I have ever had.

17

Memorable Hundreds

Time and a lot of really hard work have completely changed the face of the compact cricket ground at St John's, Antigua. When I first went there in 1968 there was a pavilion and no more; in the absence of stands the crowd simply spread themselves along the grass surrounds, and the most prominent building in sight was the local prison, now partly masked by a fine new public grandstand and white retaining wall. The ground has been developed to the point where it is arguably the most attractive of the Test venues in West Indies and the island was buzzing in anticipation of its first-ever Test match. By 5.00 a.m. there were 5,000 queueing outside the ground; by the time we got there it was almost full to its 15,000 capacity and we had to pick our way gingerly through the throng.

Colin Milburn was there, bluff and hearty as ever, which reminded me of the 1968 match against Leeward Islands and the umpire who made a point of seeking him out before we started. He pumped Milburn's hand, told him how much they were looking forward to watching him on the tour, how much they hoped he did well and so on. Can't be bad, thought Milburn: it never does any harm to have an umpire on your side.

I pushed a single off the first ball, the second took a thick edge on to Milburn's pad and there was his mate the umpire firing him out lbw without a second's hesitation! So much for the power and entertainment of a long innings from Milburn – and to make matters worse for him I scored a hundred, so did Barrington, and he never managed to force his way into a Test on the tour.

The prisoners from the local gaol were used as labourers on the ground in those days, and one of them was rolling the pitch when I went out for a look. 'Mr Boycott? I'm a big fan of yours, man. I roll you a good, good pitch. You come back here in six years' time and I'll roll you a good pitch then, too – I'm in for life . . .' At least it gave him something to look forward to!

Bill Athey won his place in the side for the fourth Test, which was not entirely surprising since he had made runs in Montserrat and Gatting was low on scores and confidence himself. Butcher was chosen to bat at five, though I would have given that spot to Willey, who has looked too good so far to be relegated to seven in the order. Willey is solid and combative, he stands upright against the short stuff, plays straight and with no flowery shots. Even the West Indies team cannot understand why he has been used so low down the order. With Willey at five and Botham at six, the choice of seventh batsman would fall between Butcher and Miller, and I don't think there's a great deal to choose between them. But in view of Miller's 92 not out in Montserrat I would have given him preference; he must be pretty confident, and apart from his batting, I feel we will need an extra spinner in the Test match. Once the new ball is out of the way Botham and Stevenson do not have anything like the pace of the West Indies attack, and I fear they could be pretty easy meat on a good batting pitch; we need two spinners up our sleeve, all the more so this time since workhorse Jackman had a slight leg strain and was ruled out.

I understand that the choice of wicket-keeper led to a long discussion in the selection meeting and that Botham's preference for Downton was the clinching factor. Bairstow was very unlucky in my book; he has done well for England in his relatively limited appearances and he has the ability to lift others but first he needs to be lifted himself – and his belief that Botham does not regard him as first choice can only damage his confidence and his performances. Given support and encouragement, Bairstow has it in him to work little miracles for a side, but he does need his own confidence boosting from time to time – and there is nothing wrong with that. Perhaps that is because he worked so hard to make the England team in the first place, and I cannot help thinking that Downton is having it a bit easy by comparison; things which come hard are usually better appreciated, and I feel Downton should have to force his way into the side by the sheer, unmistakable force of his performances. He is a fine prospect and he has the years on his side; time will tell.

The pitch for the Test match was grassless, rolled mud, just as I remembered in 1968 and certainly more typical of West Indian pitches than some we have encountered. Botham asked my advice on what to do if we won the toss, and I suggested we should bat.

It was bound to be difficult – against this attack it always is – but the pitch was good and we saw off their initial onslaught very well. Holding still produced some deliveries of real pace – Gooch played and missed, and I had to weave out of the way of a couple of nasty bouncers – but it was significant that after only four overs Roberts had to resort to his trick of turning the seam across to get extra bounce from the pitch. It is quite amazing how well that works, and it also means that Roberts is more likely to put the ball exactly where he wants it, unaffected by the new ball's tendency to swing off line with the seam in the conventional position. More bad news for the batsmen.

Still, we were doing pretty well: I steered and off-drove Holding for a couple of fours which prompted him to try a few deliveries round the wicket, Gooch lay back and hit Garner splendidly over the slips when he attempted to dig one in. There was even a suggestion of over-confidence when Gooch tried to hammer Croft through the covers and missed; I told him to cool it, because we were doing well, and he acknowledged the caution.

It is important for batsmen to talk to each other – even criticize each other – in situations like that, and we do it without anyone taking offence. Gooch told me I was playing a bit wide to Croft; I felt it was necessary because Croft's angle is so awkward and there is always the danger of lbw padding up, but the point was well taken. After my gentle admonishment about playing too freely at Croft, Gooch studiously ignored a couple of tempting deliveries and then eased a controlled shot through the covers for four: a very fine stroke played with just the attitude we needed.

Holding passed me at the end of an over with a big smile and 'Nice pitch, Geoff.' He knew they were in for a struggle if we established ourselves firmly, and we looked like doing it – until Gooch was run out unnecessarily.

He had made 33 when he drove Croft towards the empty long-on position and set off with three on his mind. Holding gave chase from mid-wicket and by the time I completed the second I could see Gooch might struggle to make it, running to the danger end. I shouted 'No' at least three times, but I could see Gooch was determined to make the third so I set off . . . and before I got to the other end I heard the roar which signalled Holding's throw and Gooch's dismissal.

Gooch said afterwards that he heard my call but felt confident he could make it. But he is not the fastest thing on two legs and Holding probably is – certainly, I have never seen a bowler, and a fast bowler at that, who covers the ground so swiftly and with so little apparent effort. He just glides along, and his stride eats up the yards with amazing speed; add to that a beautifully accurate throw on the turn and Gooch really didn't have a chance.

The sort of self-inflicted blow we could well have done without, especially when we had already done so much of the hard work. Athey strode in and I had a quick word: had he faced Croft before? He said he had. 'Watch his angle; I usually try to cover my off stump a bit more than usual. . . .' Athey negotiated a yorker from Garner and a bouncer from Roberts, Croft switched ends and struck again, just as we feared. It was an unremarkable delivery in itself, except for that extraordinary angle which confounds batsmen time and time again. Athey pushed forward defensively, the angle pulled him a bit further and a bit wider, and the ball flicked off the edge low down to Lloyd at first slip. 60 for no wicket had become 70 for two.

Gower's second ball from Croft bounced, but not enough; Gower ducked, but not enough, and the ball smacked his helmet before flying away for four leg-byes. Who says batsmen do not need helmets? Only those who have never faced this sort of situation – this sort of fast bowling delivery after delivery, match after match.

I felt good. I felt I had played all the bowlers pretty solidly and without any real alarms, I had driven Holding and Roberts for four, worked Croft for four off my hip, and never missed a delivery from any of them. I was just beginning to feel they would not get me out when Lloyd and Croft had a word just before lunch and Haynes was brought from mid-on to a position just in front of short square-leg. Predictably, the next delivery was dug in really short, and I played it down. Another

Left: Aggressive as ever – Graham Gooch in Antigua. Sadly, he discovered that three into two simply will not go. . . .

Not much evidence of 'limited ability' there! Peter Willey crashed Croft over gulley for six during his magnificent century. Perhaps he will now get the recognition he deserves.

very short one and I shaped to play it the same way, but it got bigger than the last, clipped my thumb and slowed just enough to give Murray an easy catch on his knees. The assurance of our early play and the solid base of 60 for the first wicket had evaporated to 95 for three and we were in trouble again. Backs to the wall, up against it – this is where we came in. . . .

Butcher does not inspire me with much confidence in situations like this. He lacks an air of permanence, tending to play and miss rather too much. He is what I call a static player, who is not tight enough when he's defending or playing his shots. Against bowlers of this calibre batsmen have to move their feet quickly and decisively into position and Butcher doesn't do it; I may be wrong in my reading of his game, but that's how it looks to me and I have told him so.

He was dropped early in his innings, a thick edge off Roberts which flew very quickly to Richard's left at second slip. Richards dived and got a hand to it, while Lloyd at first slip never moved. It would have been a great catch if it had stuck. And when he had made 17 Butcher was dropped again, this time by Mattis off Croft at fourth slip. Butcher drove at a wide one and the ball sped slightly to Mattis's left, certainly not a difficult catch and he was fortunate to escape. His most memorable shots, perhaps not surprisingly, were a couple of hooks for four off Croft – one played firmly and downwards and the other over the head of Holding stationed half-way to the boundary. After batting for forty-three minutes Butcher played back defensively to one which got big on him and looped a catch to Greenidge diving forward at third slip. 'I just couldn't make any more height,' Butcher explained; it was clearly coincidence that he was using one of my bats!

We needed a strong, steadying innings from Botham, especially since Gower was going nicely and had reached 31 when Butcher was out, but alas he faced only five deliveries before Croft deceived him with the angle of delivery – again – and Lloyd took a superb catch, juggling and then diving at first slip.

'Dammit,' said Botham when he got back to the pavilion. 'In future I'm going to whack the damned thing. If it's pitched up it goes, and if it's short I'm hooking and never mind the man back. That's how I've got my runs in the past and I'm not going to play his angle any more. . . .' Every man to his own . . . Botham may have a point.

Gower had batted for seventy-five valuable minutes when he pushed forward at a delivery from Holding, perhaps a fraction wide, and slid a catch low to Mattis at fourth slip. England 138 for six. Gower is still something of an enigma as a batsman; he plays so effortlessly and so beautifully that at times it's a pleasure to watch him – and yet I cannot sit through one of his innings without fearing for his safety. There is an indefinable element of self-destructiveness in him, moments when he seems to lose himself and play almost as though he is watching somebody else.

I notice that, especially early in his innings, he gets a fair proportion of his runs along the ground behind the bat; he got fours off Croft and Roberts between fourth slip and gulley, then between third and fourth slip in this innings. Perhaps that suggests the ball runs off the face of the bat more than it should and could account for the way he got out. It's a puzzle and I don't claim to have worked it – or him – out.

Willey set about establishing himself with typical pugnacity. His attitude was clear when Holding brought Haynes in to silly-mid-off, a strange sort of position and one which Willey wasn't going to tolerate for any longer than he had to. Willey whistled a beautiful cover-drive just past Haynes, who must have felt the draught of the shot; then he cracked the next delivery head-high over cover for another four and again Haynes must have felt he was standing at the wrong end of a coconut shy. Haynes made a diplomatic withdrawal; Willey had made his point and left no one in doubt about his attitude.

I worked with Downton for twenty minutes in the nets on the day before the match, advising him basically to play straight: block straight and hit straight and don't look to work the bowlers around. Downton said he got most of his runs last season by 'looking to stay in', and I reckoned that was just how he ought to approach his batting in the Test, especially since he had played relatively little cricket.

He stuck to it manfully and played a couple of nice firm pushes for four until he looked to give himself room to hit his favourite shot square and nicked a delivery from Garner towards first slip. Murray dived across, thrust out his right glove and held on. England were 176 for seven, but Willey was already fighting magnificently and Embury is level-headed and brave enough to stick it out when the situation demands.

Garner attempted to york Willey and was cover-driven for two fours in succession; he spread his field, bowled the next three deliveries short in annoyance at himself for giving him two half-volleys, and then pitched the last ball up – and Willey promptly drove it straight for another boundary. Three fours off the Big Bird in one over.... I was seventy-five yards away in the pavilion and I enjoyed that!

Croft and Willey were having something of a battle, perhaps because they are both hard, unrelenting characters who don't like to see the other man on top. Willey shaped to block and got a thick edge down to third-man for four, while Croft fumed; a vicious-looking bouncer followed, then Willey knocked a short one down to third-man for a single while Croft waved his arms, convinced that it was a false stroke. Willey ambled past waving a hand at Croft as if to say 'Aw, shuddup; I played it there.' A tough nut, this Willey. Richards replaced Roberts and Willey lay back and hit him square for four to reach his 50; a short pause for applause and the next delivery was driven through Roberts at mid-off for another four – Willey really was playing supremely well.

So was Emburey, in a very different sort of way. His job was clearly to hang on in support, and he gritted it out bravely while Croft put men close to the bat and tried hard to bounce him out. One painfully off his gloves; another threatening his throat – it would have been hard work for anybody, but as a tail-ender, Emburey showed tremendous guts. He slipped off during a drinks interval and put my chest-pad on, announced that one delivery which leaped into his throat hadn't hurt him a bit and remarked that he was afraid he was becoming over-confident! Frankly, Embers, you could have fooled us. . . .

One of the points from the team meeting was that if somebody got in, it was vital he was encouraged, advised and cajoled if necessary towards a century; we knew we needed somebody to play a major innings to keep us in the match. I noticed that Willey was becoming too aggressive and I sent a cautionary word out with Jackman, the twelfth man. Willey acknowledged it and swished his bat in self-annoyance when he played loosely.

Croft looked as though he was becoming increasingly rattled, both by Emburey's doggedness and by Willey's provocative habit of plonking a hand on his hip and staring back down the pitch in a show of defiance. Croft bowled shorter and shorter, he went round the wicket to bounce Emburey and gave the tail-ender a really rough time; yet there was no hint of any action by the umpires. To me it was clearly intimidation, reducing bowling to a matter of brute force without any pretence of subtlety, and I am sure an umpire like Dickie Bird would have stepped in and reminded Croft of the regulations. But Emburey was peppered by four bouncers in one over and a total of seventeen in his innings, yet still the umpires made no move. Ugly cricket, that.

Emburey braved it out for eighty valuable minutes before he was out in a very odd way. Croft, bowling wide from over the wicket, loosed a full-toss and Emburey pulled out of the way as though he had not picked up the flight of the delivery. He confirmed later that he lost the ball among the multi-coloured crowd at the edge of the sightscreen; there was a huge sightscreen at the far end of the ground, but the one at the pavilion end was much smaller, and when Croft went wide the ball came out of the relative gloom of a walkway leading into one of the stands.

Stevenson had already ducked one delivery from Croft – with the periscope up as they say – and he soon fell in a similar way to Emburey, pulling away from a yorker as though he could not see it. Croft walked back grinning hugely at his good fortune. It was an unfortunate way to get out but I have already told Stevenson that he cannot hope to score runs at this level until he gets his foot to the ball. That could be important to his future. It takes raw courage to face fast bowling of this calibre, and no batsman can hope to survive without it.

England were 235 for nine, Willey was 69, and it was obviously imperative that Dilley hung around because every run was vital and not one ounce of Willey's ability should be wasted. Dilley pushed forward to a delivery from Holding, there was a deafening appeal for a catch behind and Holding glared murderously when the umpire turned it down; Dilley looked blithely unconcerned and determined to sell himself dearly.

Willey played splendidly. It takes guts to face this sort of attack over after over, and Willey has that – in fact I think he relishes the challenge; it takes ability to survive and by the end of the day he had glared back at them for over three hours. And when they gave him the slightest opportunity, Willey smashed the ball with

Mean, moody, magnificent? Colin Croft certainly likes the image, and those eyes don't look as though they belong to Father Christmas!

the conviction of a man bred in a hard school where somebody has to be the boss and show it.

Croft dug one in short and Willey, on his toes and meeting the ball just below shoulder height, crashed it over gulley for six; Roberts was thumped through cover for four, Holding bowled short of a length and Willey gave himself room to thunder the ball square for four; another delivery from Holding was full length on the off stump and Willey threw his left leg across and clubbed it straight on the on side for another boundary.

Roberts withdrew from the firing line like an exhausted volcano. 'The fire's gone out,' remarked Downton sardonically. But Willey was still there, 91 not out at the close as England hauled themselves to 260 for nine.

Second Day

'That's my job; that's what I get paid for.' Peter Willey's view of his vitally important innings was as down to earth as the man himself – but any man in any job deserves a bonus and Willey deserved a century on the second day. Even before he set out in search of those nine tantalizing runs he had a decision to make: should he play normally and put himself in Dilley's hands, hoping that the tail-ender would survive long enough, or should he attempt to settle it himself quickly and perhaps get out playing a rash shot? Willey need not have worried; Dilley obviously felt his double responsibility heavily and played his part admirably.

Even Willey's heart must have missed a beat in the second over of the morning, when he glanced Roberts down the leg side and Murray sprawled to take the catch. The umpire's finger had already gone up when the ball dribbled out of Murray's glove – perhaps he was trying to throw it up – and a hasty cancellation of the signal meant Willey was reprieved. He needed a bit of luck like that, and he made sure it wasn't wasted.

While Dilley steeled himself to stay – skipping in the air to keep down a couple of short-pitched deliveries, letting a bouncer from Roberts whistle beneath his nose, leaving the ball outside the off stump with precise selectivity – Willey edged towards his century.

A quick single to mid-off; a fine square drive off Holding which looked like four but was stopped a foot from the boundary by Haynes; a great shot off his toes, but only a single because Greenidge made a good stop at deep square. Thirty-two long minutes had elapsed before Willey hooked Roberts to long-leg, raced for two in defiance of Croft's throw and reached the century he richly deserved. It had taken him three hours and thirty-nine minutes and included a six and fifteen fours; it was a magnificent effort and I was delighted for Willey, who is a good pro.

Dilley was caught low and one-handed behind the wicket soon afterwards, having batted for seventy-two minutes in all, but not one second of that would be under-estimated either by us or by Willey. England were all out for 271.

The spotlight switched instantly to Viv Richards, even though Greenidge and Haynes strolled out to start West Indies' innings. They were just preparing the ground, warming up the audience until the star attraction of the afternoon was ready to make an entrance: the local boy who made good enough to be accepted as the world's greatest batsman, playing in the first Test match in Antigua. A man who could conceivably have hoisted the ball into his own backyard in St Johns and who must, *must* get a century to satisfy an expectant crowd and his own sense of occasion. Haynes faced eleven deliveries before he was beaten by Botham's out-swing and Downton took a good catch low to his right; Richards ambled arrogantly into the din.

A statistical record of the fourth Test will show that West Indies made 73 runs in the hour to lunch. It will reveal that West Indies scored fifteen fours in that hour, that Greenidge and Richards hit seven fours each, that Dilley went for 30 runs off five overs. It will suggest that England were murdered and that will be close enough to the truth – but not the whole truth. Because the key to West Indies' amazing onslaught was the sheer presence of Viv Richards, the psychological battle which he created and won.

Dilley reckons he bowled well in that period and, unlikely as it may sound in terms of bleak statistics, I agree with him. Greenidge would probably agree, too, in that he stole his runs off a couple of thick edges past gulley, ducked, weaved and worried while Dilley steamed in forcefully and made him look for all the world like one of our batsmen facing the West Indian pace attack. If we had four bowlers like Dilley in this mood, it might be a very different series. . . .

But Richards was incredible. He smashed Botham for two fours on the off side and on-drove him for another; he slashed Dilley past gulley for four, then drove fiercely through mid-on for another boundary. In twenty minutes he had galloped to 29, and 28 of those were in boundaries; the fact that not all of them came off the middle of the bat did not trouble him in the slightest.

'I wanna impress them here, Boycs,' he told me during a delay while shiny advertising boards near the pavilion were covered up – and there was absolutely no mistaking his determination not only to score a century but to impose his will. Dilley went round the wicket to him and Richards was almost lbw, he had to check a couple of violently intended hooks as the ball followed him, and he was brilliantly caught down the leg side by Downton – cruelly it was off a no-ball. But that only slowed him down momentarily; he was determined not to be stopped.

Richards against the quick bowlers and the new ball is an intriguing phenomenon. He does not even play them on their apparent merits, he simply sets out to dominate – and the faster they bowl the more ferocious his reply. It is a matter of personal pride, ego and macho that he should take the initiative and be seen to do so; if anyone bowled at 200 mph, Richards would set himself to hit them for 12! It is beneath his dignity to duck or weave; fast bowling is a challenge, and he must fight fire with fire. He pulled Dilley's bouncer out of the ground for six, and then sauntered down the pitch, ostensibly to pat it down but really for the deep satisfaction of confronting the man he had just defied and defeated. His victory was obvious in Dilley's downcast face, but Richards simply had to rub it in.

Master stroke – the irrepressible Viv Richards on his way to a century in front of his home crowd in Antigua. Food for thought for Paul Downton.

It cannot be just coincidence that Richards' sporting hero is Joe Frazier, the heavyweight boxer who typifies aggression, courage and the compulsion to go forward, always forward. Frazier is proud of his conviction that he fears nobody; even when he is wounded he is not hurt. Fast bowlers have an inbuilt intent to do batsmen physical harm – there is no doubt about that – and Richards the batsman, like Frazier the boxer, regards it as a matter of pride to walk into the blows. Everything else is suspended while Richards establishes his superiority, even to the point where other batsmen can score readily and be practically overlooked.

Greenidge seemed subdued, but only by comparison, because he played strokes which were recognizable as normally aggressive cricket shots. Botham pitched wide and short and Greenidge cracked him through the covers off the back foot for four; a shortish one was worked off the hip for four, then Greenidge leg-glanced Dilley for another boundary. At lunch he was four runs ahead of Richards and had hit as many boundaries, but the talk and the memories were entirely of Richards, Richards.

I have talked to fine old players like Yorkshire's Bill Bowes, and they tell me that the abiding memory of Bradman was how quick his reactions were; he hit the ball when it was pitched up but was incredibly quick to cut or pull if it was pitched short. There must be a similarity with Richards there. He is always looking to get on the front foot and drive, and yet if anything is bowled short he has the reflexes of a snake. He is back in a flash to play those marvellously aggressive strokes; his score simply rolls along.

A century partnership was established in only 105 minutes but Stevenson replaced Dilley and bowled really well at Greenidge. I was fielding at mid-off and told Stevenson to concentrate on line and length because Greenidge was fretting; he seemed determined to show he could dominate the bowling like Richards and the medium-pacer must have looked like easy meat. Greenidge kept trying to hit Stevenson too hard, he lost his timing and played several fierce drives on to his pads or off inside edges to fine-leg.

Finally Greenidge got himself out, trying to force his shot like an indifferent golfer. The catch sailed to Athey at mid-on and West Indies were 133 for two. Greenidge had forgotten one of the golden rules of batting, which is never to try and compete with your partner; instead of complementing Richards, and even enjoying the relative lack of pressure at his end, he tried to compete with him at Stevenson's expense. That must always be a temptation, when you spend a fair bit of your life batting in Richards's shadow, but it was a mistake nevertheless.

Once he got through the new ball and proved his superiority, Richards was far more circumspect, not least because Emburey bowled superbly at him, very straight and with two men in the box as at Trinidad. Richards has too much respect for Emburey to do anything silly, especially when he was looking for an impressive century, and perhaps spin does not represent the same sort of challenge to his masculinity that fast bowling does. It's a fascinating thought.

When he had made 70, Richards attempted to pull Stevenson and got an underside edge; the ball did not bounce and I reckon if he had not laid a bit of bat on it he would have lost his off and middle stumps. That seemed to caution him for a while, to remind him that his century was only 30 runs away, and he played studiously forward in defence or on the drive. Stevenson was miffed. 'What the 'ell's going on now? Is he taking the mickey out of me?' he asked. But Richards knew that on a good batting pitch and with the new ball subdued, a century was his for the taking if he played with reasonable care.

Even so, he did not relish Embury's accuracy and the fact that his favourite areas for taking singles – square-leg and mid-wicket – were patrolled by Butcher and Gower. Richards suddenly broke free, mis-hitting Emburey in the air dangerously close to Gower, and the ball just had enough momentum to reach the boundary for four. Then a straight four, then one off the back foot through the gap, well placed rather than well timed – and after a period of relative idleness he had zoomed from 70 to 82.

Stevenson finished a tenacious spell of bowling with the figures 14-3-51-1. Good, but not good enough. With Yorkshire on county pitches he will always be an effective strike bowler, but on better Test-match surfaces he does not have sufficient pace to make that the basis of his game. He must learn – and quickly, because England will not wait over-long – how to bowl an immaculate line and length; how to vary his pace subtly; how to frustrate batsmen until they make a mistake which gives him or his fellow-bowler a wicket. His pace alone simply will not carry him through. Instead of bowling five good deliveries and one bad one, he has to learn to cut out the ragged score-ball and bowl four maidens in a row. If he concedes runs it should be down to the batsman's good luck. In simple terms he should be aiming to bowl, at the age of twenty-five, the way Robin Jackman bowls at thirty-five; I know that's a tall order, but it really is the way to an England career. Instead of conceding 51 runs off fourteen overs he should have conceded 28, even against Richards. That's the sort of ability England seek from a bowler of his type.

Willey did a fine job against Mattis after tea, in fact I can remember only three obviously bad deliveries in the spell, when first Mattis and then Richards were allowed to get on the back foot and hit him through covers. Mattis was confronted with two men positioned for the drive, one orthodox and the other so straight as to be nearly on the pitch, a square-leg, mid-wicket and mid-on.

Since he likes to score most of his runs on the leg side but does not sweep, he really did not know where the next run was coming from. His only answer was to try and hit over the top – the sort of act of frustration which Willey wanted – and he was almost caught and bowled when he had made 25. Willey, deceived because the ball came back to him slower than he expected, spilled the catch just wide of his left shoulder. Mattis almost holed out to me at short, straight mid-on soon afterwards; I tried to scoop it in but it didn't quite carry.

Richards had arrived in the nineties and the crowd was praying for him to hit a ten off every ball; he was prepared to take his time even if they weren't. On 98 he steered Willey to third-man and Stevenson challenged him to try for a second. Nothing doing. Botham ran in and then pulled away as if something in his run-up was not quite right, and the crowd groaned in frustration. Then Richards drove hard through mid-off, Stevenson misfielded in his anxiety to prevent a single and the ball sped away for four while the ground erupted.

I thought for a minute that half the Antigua police force were staging a demonstration of their own, haring on to the pitch from every quarter of the ground and heading straight for the newly-crowned hero. But no – they were just anxious to get there before the crowd enveloped him and they won by a short head. One Rasta resplendent – or something – in brown cavalry boots and a blue and red striped shirt went through a ritual on the outfield which was somewhere between a prayer meeting and a Tiller Girl rehearsal . . . while Richards was wreathed in smiles and patted half to death. For the record, his century took 237 minutes, included nineteen fours and a six and was created off 174 deliveries.

The new ball was available but our experience in Barbados warned Botham against taking it, sensibly enough. He also showed a willingness to use his bowlers in shorter spells and put me on later in the day for variation – he probably also thought that the crowd might react and disturb the batsmen's concentration. I went through the old reverse-cap routine, but they were a pretty dead-pan audience and Richards politely informed me he was prepared to block forever rather than get out to me!

I told Richards that Jack Hobbs, then England's best batsman, used to make a point of giving his wicket away to the most deserving bowler once he had reached a century, and I reckoned, of course, that I was the most deserving case! 'Can't do it,' said Richards. 'I need another 20 for 4,000 Test runs. Sorry about that. . . .'

Richards was 110, Mattis 56 and West Indies 236 for two at the close. Saturday was Richards Day in Antigua.

Third Day

'If I get a hundred I'm going to get 200 and not get out. . . .' This ominous prophesy from Richards to a mutual friend suddenly looked all too likely. I suppose everybody expected West Indies to bat all day and build a massive lead, but in the event it went horribly wrong – for them and then for us.

By lunch West Indies were 301 for seven, five more wickets having fallen for 65 runs. The English supporters in the crowd were crowing, as they were entitled to, and even the Union Jacks seemed to be fluttering with their chests out from the double-decker stand. Nobody could really have foreseen that, nor the utter frustration which was to follow. . . .

Sensationally, Richards fell to the fourth delivery of the day, the fourth with the new ball which was taken at the start of play. He cracked the first delivery for four off his hip – here we go again – but then attempted a massive, ugly pull and lofted a top edge straight to Emburey at mid-on. Richards smacked the bat angrily against his pad as he walked off – and no wonder; it was a tremendous psychological lift for us, and it showed.

Mattis amazed me. On that good pitch he should have been looking to get

Left: Local boy makes good – and a century. Viv Richards is obviously delighted with a hundred in front of his home Antigua crowd.

Below centre: Gordon Greenidge: not quite the force we might have expected in the series, but who's complaining?

Bottom: Crazy, man, crazy ... a local Rasta celebrates Richards's century in inimitable style. No doubt he'll receive an invitation to the next police ball!

through the new ball and then press on for a big score; instead he seemed determined to thump everything out of sight. Short, pitched up or good length – it made no difference to Mattis, who suddenly seemed to want to bat like Richards, without anything approaching his ability or experience; he even went to hook a delivery which was so wide of the off stump that Downton had to take it in front of first slip!

He was bound to come unstuck before long, and Dilley missed him at fine-leg when he hooked Botham firmly. It was a more difficult chance than it might have looked because the ball went hard, flat and very fast, forcing Dilley's hands apart above his head and bouncing off the retaining fence for six. But he was out soon afterwards, when Botham went round the wicket and he tried to get across to crack the ball off the back foot. It sliced away to point, where Butcher took a low catch, even if Mattis seemed unwilling to believe it had carried.

It was a strange, immature sort of performance and certainly not a good innings for his side; if Mattis imagines he can bat like Richards he has an inflated opinion of his ability – but perhaps he fell into the trap of thinking our new-ball attack was ordinary just because Richards often makes it look that way.

Gomes didn't last long. He likes to plonk a leg down the pitch and push into the area of mid-off, and Botham reckons he can draw him slightly wider and further forward, putting him in trouble by making him reach and play away from his body. He did it perfectly and Gower took the catch waist high and slightly to his left at third slip. West Indies were 268 for five, and the face of the match had changed dramatically.

Like Mattis, Murray seemed to be suffering from the copy-Richards syndrome. With only one run on the board he launched into an ambitious pull and lollipopped a catch to me at wide-ish mid-on. He really does not have the talent to play that kind of shot so soon in his innings; I don't think it is disparaging to say he is the sort of batsman who will make useful thirties and forties if he works very hard at his game, but here he was trying to come in and play like a millionaire. Botham had taken three wickets in five balls, while Clive Lloyd looked on like a man who couldn't believe his eyes.

He had a pretty rough ride himself from Dilley and I couldn't help wondering again just how their batsmen would fare against four genuinely fast bowlers, but he picked up a couple of fours just before lunch when Stevenson and Emburey were on and that helped him into his stride. Stevenson went round the wicket and Roberts, trying to whip across the line to square-ish mid-wicket, lost his off stump for his pains. West Indies were 301 for seven at lunch, and we were entitled to feel pleased with ourselves.

We had done far better than anybody expected, even if West Indies had contributed to some extent to their own downfall. That's the name of the game; they can give their wickets away any time they like, as far as we are concerned! And we could be forgiven then for thinking we would be batting around mid afternoon, perhaps chasing a West Indies lead of 50 or 60. They had to bat last . . . if we batted well we

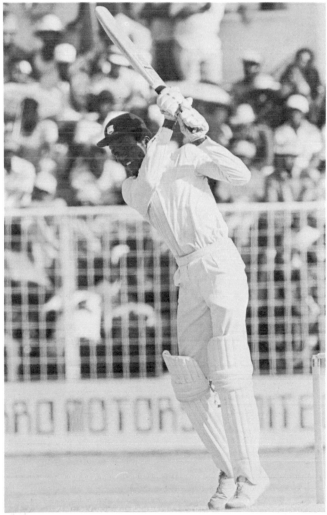

Above: Everton Mattis hits Peter Willey over the top – an effective-looking shot but it was born of frustration as Willey tied him down.

That's better, a more handsome shot – and judging by his smile, Mattis knows it.

might put them under real pressure for the first time in the series. It was an attractive thought – until everything began to go demoralizingly wrong.

Lloyd tried to play Dilley circumspectly and didn't have too much success; typically he decided to wind up and attack him, but that didn't work either. The ball sliced off inside edges and rattled his pads; he was obviously in trouble but he hung in there against Dilley and kept clattering Emburey at the other end, so much so that we had to put square-cover almost on the boundary to cut off the four.

Garner clung on like a giant limpet. We tried everything we knew against him and he certainly did not get every delivery in his own half, not by a long chalk. Yet when Dilley bounced him he just leaned his 6 ft 8 ins forward, picked up that long-handled bat and blocked! It was staggering ... and anything just short of a length was hip-high to him: he simply whipped it wristily away. Early in his innings Botham crowded him with five men when Emburey was bowling, a good tactic psychologically against tail-enders, who do not have confidence in their ability to avoid a bat-pad when they can hear fielders breathing around them. Garner panicked and tried to thump it – high and handsome towards long-off but Stevenson could not get back far or quickly enough, the wind was carrying it away from him and the chance went down. Lloyd strode down the pitch and had a word, and you did not have to be psychic to guess that he was saying: 'For heaven's sake play sensibly....' – and Garner did.

It is always aggravating when you cannot get tail-enders out, but you have to accept that in the modern game they are often fairly competent players who know how to defend. What is unacceptable is when the scoreboard begins to rattle round, when a stand extends to 30 or 40 and there is no sign of a breakthrough. Lloyd and Garner put on 30 runs in forty minutes at one stage and their partnership had reached 85 in 103 minutes – too many too fast – when Lloyd drove at a delivery from Stevenson just short of a length and was caught behind.

West Indies were 108 runs on at that point, which was bad enough. They had scored 99 between lunch and tea, an incredible striking rate in the circumstances remembering that even Richards and the recognized batsmen had not been able to push the scoring along that fast at any time in the match! Something had gone badly awry.

In a way, our success laid its own trap. Bowlers had looked as though they might get a wicket at any moment; the ball was fizzing about hitting pads and inside edges; it was the sort of situation in which you feel you must attack because you are bound to break through. And then the breakthrough doesn't quite happen, and the score goes up; the batsmen tempt you with false strokes, and the score still goes up....

We had established a good position and we should have defended it, not simply by setting defensive fields but by adopting the right attitude. Bowlers should have told themselves: 'I'm going to bowl two maidens from my end,' and worked at giving absolutely nothing away. Twenty minutes without a run is a lifetime to a tail-ender; not being able to score is an insidious form of pressure. We bowled to

A bear hug for Graham Stevenson from Ian Botham after Stevenson bowled Andy Roberts. No doubt Graham's ribs will mend in time. . . .

A demon bowler whose name escapes me . . . but not quite as fast as Michael Holding.

get Garner out when we could have put pressure on him in a different way – and the commanding situation we had developed slipped away.

When we saw the initiative was draining away fast we should have closed the match up, stopped the game for a while and made the batsmen think hard for every run; tail-enders aren't especially good at that! We had to get them out or stop them scoring, and since wickets did not fall that left only one avenue open. I do not blame Botham for the tail-enders making runs, because there will always be a day when tail-enders get runs – even when you feel the next ball will be their last. But I didn't think he seemed to be alive to the danger or to the tactical alternative open to him. The fact is that at tea West Indies were 400 for eight; it was just as though Richards had got his 200 and the tail had contributed next to nothing.

The afternoon period was chastening enough; the eighty minutes after tea were little short of demoralizing. Garner went quickly when he tried a wristy flick off the hip, got into the shot too quickly and lofted a catch off the leading edge to Butcher at mid-wicket – but Croft, and especially Holding, really made us look foolish. Holding pulled, cut, played every aggressive shot in the book and cracked three sixes and five fours out of 58; Croft blocked industriously and refused to be budged. They piled on 67 in sixty-five minutes before Lloyd declared on 468 for nine, leaving us an awkward half-hour to the close. As it turned out, the light gave out after four overs, with England 190 behind.

The hour in which Holding was going full throttle highlighted another of Botham's problems as captain. There was no question of any lack of effort from the bowlers; they all gave everything they had, and nobody put his back into it more than Botham himself. But just when he needed to be at his freshest and most alert, he was tired and sweaty after a long spell of bowling; when his mind needed to be clear he was unavoidably jaded and I thought there was a lack of attention to detail in the field placings.

Stevenson bowled round the wicket into the tail-enders' ribs without a man catching round the corner or saving the single – which made no sense; Emburey fielded too deep at square-leg, and the batsmen were able to take two to him without difficulty; short singles were taken at will. Details, perhaps, but important ones which illustrated how difficult it is for any bowler, particularly a seam bowler, to combine the job of captaincy, where theoretically at least he has to check eight fielding positions and keep his mind right on top of the job no matter how physically hard he has worked himself. That is not nit-picking, and not a jibe at Botham; it is a problem which would affect any bowler and must take some toll on him.

Antiguan rain is as spectacular and uncompromising as Antiguan sunshine. Naturally enough, the weather waited until the rest day before it turned English – endless squally showers, the occasional deafening downpour, a chill wind which whipped the sea into whitecaps and brought dark clouds hurrying over the promontory near our hotel. When the sun did break through John Emburey tried his hand at one-man sailing and very nearly did a Chichester – he was disappearing fast towards the horizon, quite powerless to bring himself back to shore, when Mike

Gatting alerted the locals and they sent a glass-bottomed boat out to retrieve him. Emburey admitted he had shouted and waved without anybody apparently noticing and was getting a bit scared by the time the rescue boat arrived; another couple of hours in that wind and he might have arrived in Jamaica three days before we did. . . .

The fourth day's play was already in danger, and it was obvious when we arrived at the ground that we could not start on time. The outfield was still very wet and water had crept under the covers, leaving a couple of dark tramlines just around the length that Croft would hit from the pavilion end. No sooner had the groundstaff got the covers off than another storm swirled in from over the hills; the covers were hastily replaced and in no time they were puddled with an inch of water as the rain beat down.

Any chance of starting at all was swamped when the covers were removed again and a couple of gallons of water spilled on to the run-ups at the pavilion end. The groundstaff spread red sawdust over an area five yards square, it rained again and in no time there was a glutinous swamp right in the middle of the bowlers' path. Even given three or four hours' hot sunshine it was doubtful if that would have dried; as it turned out there was more rain, and although the umpires hung on hopefully, by late afternoon they had to accept the inevitable abandonment for the day. I can't pretend we were exactly despondent about it.

Fifth Day

Batting a full day to save a Test match should not be beyond a Test-class side on a good batting pitch, given the right sort of approach and application. But our track record so far wasn't exactly impressive: we had lost heavily in Trinidad and Barbados, and there were only two periods in those Tests when we had looked like taking a grip on the game. We needed an honourable draw in Antigua to boost our morale. Not a feverish scratching sort of survival but a sound batting display, and although we knew it would not be easy we were pretty confident that we could see it through.

The pitch was good, too good for the liking of Roberts who dearly wanted to make a big impression in the first Antigua Test in front of his home crowd. It was interesting how much support we received from the locals; they were forever wishing us good luck, wanting to shake our hands, saying they hoped we played well and so on – even the local ground administrator admitted he came under criticism from the locals when England struggled! Like them, he wanted the first Test in Antigua to be remembered as a good match, preferably with a result on the last day, so that Tests would be taken there in the future. Nobody really wanted a three-day wonder on a poor pitch.

Lloyd had got runs to challenge the suggestion that he does not make enough for West Indies at home; Richards had made a century in front of his home crowd so there was no complaint about the pitch from them. But Roberts seemed disgruntled and complained that all the grass had been taken off; the spark was missing from his bowling for most of the day, and that obviously helped our cause. I cannot say that I was disappointed with his performance, but he must have been!

Garner was really trying. I had spoken to him earlier and he was aware that he had not taken a bucketful of wickets so far on the tour; he wanted a big haul and it showed in the way he knocked the ball into the pitch, speared it at us and tried hard to extract every last ounce of life.

Croft was up to his old tricks again. He bowled two bouncers in his first over and three in his second, and when we stopped for drinks I asked the umpire just how many bouncers Croft was allowed to fire down. I don't know if he took any notice but at least it drew his attention to the way we felt, and that seems to be important. When Croft went round the wicket he ran on the pitch and yet nothing was said until we had a word with the umpire again. . . . There seems to be a tendency to let things drift and we often had to have a polite word for the sake of self-protection. It is not as though Croft's bouncer is the easiest in the world to face; he seems to get the ball up from nowhere, not really short enough to duck underneath, and I was credited with four byes off my armpit taking evasive action. We determined to see it through, conscious not only of the short stuff but of the likelihood that the odd one would keep low on a pitch now over four days old. There were no histrionics, no flashy strokes; we just played it sensibly through to 91 without loss at lunch.

I had slid one delivery from Holding between third slip and gulley for four; Gooch edged one short of Garner at gulley – minor alarms, perhaps, but little moral victories for the bowler and enough to remind us again that this West Indies attack is always capable of snatching a couple of wickets quickly and turning a match on its head. We had to keep our priorities firmly in our minds – and our job was to save the game.

So Gooch began to concern me. Not long after lunch he was trying hard to hit Roberts for four; at least four times in an over he drilled fiercely aggressive shots straight to fielders – extravagant shots in the circumstances. And when Richards came on Gooch went for him as though it was the Sunday League.

Suddenly he was playing shots all round the wicket: a four through cover, a full-toss clubbed over mid-wicket – seven runs off Richards's second over, and I had not taken strike against him yet! Richards bowled Gooch a delivery on leg and middle and he ran round it to get inside and lofted him over cover for four. Not a business shot, as they say, not off the middle of the bat and not a shot to be playing in our situation. Somebody was not thinking.

It is always tempting to attack the slower bowlers – Richards and Gomes in this attack – because you know it's a respite from the quicker stuff. You can score as many in three overs against them as you can in two hours against Holding, Croft and the rest.

But that, after all, is precisely why Richards is used, and why he often bowls so slowly and tantalizingly. His job is to tempt, to encourage batsmen to make a mistake and get themselves out – and I was not totally surprised when Gooch fell.

He went down the pitch to attack a big, looping delivery, half changed his mind and spooned a catch which just carried to Greenidge at mid-wicket. Richards was on his knees in jubilation; whatever the score, he clearly considered he had won that particular round.

It might seem churlish to criticize a man who made 83 runs and batted well, and I do not want to be accused of that. But as in Barbados, Gooch seemed momentarily to forget what his first job was; he did his own thing rather than disciplining himself to do the job his team and the situation demanded. People seem to imagine I enjoy batting defensively for hour after hour and that is simply not so, but I reckon I can get my head down and do it when I have to. That is a very important part of Test cricket, and however unglamorous and taxing, it is something which has to be learned. And it has to be learned by everybody. Gooch is a good enough player to know that, and a good enough player to take runs off bowlers like Richards without indulging in risks which threaten the best interests of the side.

Croft was due for a return and, sure enough, he was put on as soon as Athey arrived. It is clear that Athey, like most of us early in the tour, has not worked out a defence to Croft's extraordinary angle of delivery; he played and missed three times in an over and I was already anxious for him. In fact he pushed so wide at one delivery that the bat slipped out of his right hand. Predictably, Athey pushed again outside the off stump, the angle beat him and Richards took a low catch at second slip.

It was 2.00 p.m., West Indies still had a lead of 51 and we had suddenly lost two wickets in a matter of minutes: a testing period. Richards wheeled and tantalized, Croft galloped in; there was a tangible heightening of tension and I felt it very strongly. I knew that if I got out then we might struggle with two new batsmen at the crease and Holding fresh to return ... hang on or we could be under pressure again.

The match became static, with Gower trying to play himself in very sensibly, leaving anything he did not have to play, and with me concentrating on staying there while he did it. Richards fancies he can tempt Gower out – a slow one outside the off stump, then a quicker one which almost invariably hit Gower's pad. But Gower played very responsibly; I passed 50 and just kept ticking over; we were there at tea with England 181 for two.

Roberts had his best spell of the day now. He began to wobble the old ball in the air, drew me wide and made me play and miss as I drove – it was the only delivery I missed all day. Gower played and missed at a couple and padded off to one very close to the off stump; he almost edged a delivery from Croft into his stumps and had to knock it away pretty sharply but he kept his head and maintained his concentration marvellously well.

The trouble was, he overdid it a bit! That may sound an extraordinary thing to say, and I admired the way he disciplined and checked himself – it was a first-class example of a man playing for the team. But he had gone from one extreme to the other, playing in a very static way to the point where he stopped looking for a single for himself and did not call me from the other end. Now that is a dangerous mood, because it leads to boredom; it makes both batsmen go flat, and nothing is more likely to produce a mistake and a wicket.

It is vital to play carefully when the situation demands and this one clearly did, but it is also important to stay alive to opportunities to score with safety, otherwise you vegetate. Even as the calling non-striker you can keep involved in the game and in fact it is important to stay on your toes, to be constantly aware, to keep your mind alert even if every shot being played is a safety shot. I cautioned him against becoming too defensive-minded – imagine me having to say that to David Gower! – and I reckon that was a compliment to the way he was trying to do the job.

By the time he was out the match was saved, and I felt sorry for him. He tried to leg-glance Croft, hit it too fine and was well caught by Murray diving to his right – a cruel way to go after he had batted so responsibly and so selflessly. People keep looking for a new, responsible Gower and I think they often see that quality when it doesn't really exist, but there was absolutely no doubting the character of his innings today. He obviously found it hard to strike a balance between defence and picking up the runs which keep your concentration going – it's not as easy as people seem to think – but I was very impressed with his attitude in this innings.

Getting out the ways he did might tempt him to wonder, 'What the hell, what's the point of trying to play like that?' but the way he disciplined himself was absolutely right; he deserved to be not out at the end.

With half an hour left to the scheduled 4.30 close the match was safe. By no stretch of the imagination could West Indies take eight wickets and then knock off the runs for victory in an hour, even if we went on until 5.00 p.m. Half an hour meant something like seven overs and I was 82 not out; should I set out to make a century and risk getting out in the process?

Statistically, it might not sound too difficult, but I didn't fancy my chances all that highly. For a start, Richards coolly informed me – as acting captain, because Lloyd was off the field – that he had no intention of letting me get a hundred. And more than that, it is always difficult suddenly to adopt an aggressive attitude when for so long you have been concentrating on saving a match. Croft would bowl at least half the overs left, and he wasn't exactly cannon-fodder; if I was going to strike quickly it would have to be against Gomes.

Jackman came out with the drinks trolley, and I mentioned to him that I was wondering whether to see it out or make a determined effort for a century. I don't suppose I could have asked a better man at a better time.

'Look mate, when you've been retired five years and you look back on this game, I reckon you'll want to look back on a hundred,' said Jackman. 'What's another ninety to you? The sort of player you are, you can get it without slogging; go for the hundred, mate. I know what I'd do....'

The match was saved, I'd done the job I was supposed to do and nobody gets centuries against this attack every day. Jackman gave me the fillip I needed, and soon afterwards Marshall helped with a raking throw at the stumps which scuttled

Above: The satisfaction of a job well done – on my way to a century in Antigua.

A feeling in a hundred!

through Garner and went for five overthrows to take me to 94. I lifted Gomes over mid-wicket for four, took a single to mid-off and then slid a single round the corner to reach my century at 4.25 p.m. after five and three-quarter hours.

We had saved the Test, which was very satisfying in itself, I had done a job and made a century, which had to be a bit special against an attack like this one. I don't think I have to say that I was very pleased.

Isaac Vivian Alexander Richards suddenly looked very much like his hero Smokin' Joe Frazier, dressed in a casual shirt and a pair of multi-coloured knee-length shorts. He looked fit and fierce enough to come out of his corner and go fifteen rounds with anybody. But Richards was in a reflective mood, draped across a sofa in the deserted England dressing-room after his historic century in the fourth Test. Here was the local boy who returned as a legend and gave his native Antigua a day it would never forget....

'Sure I wanted a century here, I wanted it very badly. I've never done particularly well in Antigua, do you know that? Got a few runs here and there, nothing much – so I really wanted to score a century in the first Test match in front of my own people. They put pressure on me, you know; they stop me in the streets and want to talk about cricket all the time. It doesn't bother me, I'm used to it, but it's pressure just the same.

'Most of them probably hadn't seen me play much. They'd heard cricket on the radio or maybe seen me on television, so it would be a real letdown for·them if I failed and I was aware of that. I slept well enough, but I was more nervous in the middle here than I have been anywhere else in the world. I could hear the crowd and sense the atmosphere. I decided to do my own thing out there – I've tried playing myself in carefully, taking my time, and it hasn't worked too well for me. So I decided that if it was there to hit I was going to hit it. Once I reached 50 I knew this was it; I had to go on for that century.

'The most difficult spells were against Emburey. It was a good wicket and you tend to take things for granted a bit, you want to hit through the ball all the time, but he was bowling with the breeze and getting it to straighten up and it was never easy against him. Stevenson bowled well, too – steady and straight; he didn't give me room to hit, like some of the others did. Man, I enjoyed that hundred, I enjoyed it ...

'When I was a kid I used to practise a lot, you know? I never went anywhere without a bat and a ball. I never wanted to bowl, only to bat, and they said I was bat-minded because I never wanted to get out and give somebody else a chance.

'I went to Alf Gover's school in London in 1973, and he wanted to change my stance – with my elbow down the wicket, I was pretty open in those days. He wanted to change my grip, too, but I didn't feel comfortable, I was restricted to playing a few shots. Alf helped me to tighten my defence but he never managed to change my style....

'Sometimes I'd get Andy Roberts to bowl bouncers at me: not every ball, just mixing them up so I never knew when the bouncer was coming. I never used to hook; if it came on to my body I just used to push it away but I got out quite a lot doing that. I first began to hook when I reached Shell Shield cricket in 1972 – not very well at first, but I worked hard at it and Andy helped. I suppose it was still not a genuine hook, more of a quick positional thing to pull.

'Australia in 1975–6 was when I really learned to hook, against Lillee and Thomson. Sometimes I'd block, but most of the time I'd hook. You have to be careful out there, especially on the big grounds like Perth; if you don't get it right you can be caught in the deep whereas on most grounds it would be four or six.

'I know I can hook and break people's hearts. I can see it in some bowlers' faces; they wonder what's going on and they have to pitch it up ... yes, you can break some bowlers' hearts. Like Len Pascoe. I used to hit him through there regularly and he didn't know what to do. Then he was bowling wide half-volleys, the lot – real rubbish, man.

'Dilley got me out hooking in the one-dayer at Berbice and I promised myself, "I'm going to hit you out of the ground next time. ..." So I did. It gets me out sometimes but it gets me a lot of runs too.

'I never used to play on the off side at all. I'd try to cut and I kept getting out, so I stopped the shot altogether. But my old man knew what was going on, and he told me how to put it right. When I got into Shell Shield cricket I found it was coming OK.

'Something went wrong with my game in the second year with Packer. I'd had a magnificent time in the first year, but the second was all wrong. The heart was willing but I just couldn't concentrate. I don't like to make excuses but I had a couple of bats that felt bottom-heavy; mentally I didn't feel right, I couldn't get into my stride. They were beautiful pitches but I just played bad shots; they didn't really bowl me out – I got myself out.

'You have to go out there every day and tune yourself in; you're expected to get runs and it's hard, hard. Nowadays I try to pick the matches where I want to do really well; I try in them all but I put a bit extra into some innings. Touring is hard, really hard.

'I'm fit, you're fit, I feel really good, but sometimes it's wrong in the mind. No matter how good you feel the mind seems to work on its own and there's nothing you can do about it. When it comes right it's a great feeling ... you can break a bowler's heart, man. ...'

18

Billy the Kid

From the air Jamaica is a striking contrast of rugged, green mountains and sparkling white beaches washed by an ultramarine sea. The approach is pretty spectacular in itself, because Norman Manley international airport sits on a long finger of land opposite Kingston harbour; our aircraft overflew the coast, turned sharply and drifted in to land with panoramic views of the capital on one side and the Caribbean, dotted with islands, on the other.

The idyll was spoiled, sadly, by our reception committee. Not by the local cricket officials who were welcoming and helpful but the sight of armed guards loitering – with intent – round the corridors of the airport and ready to escort us to our hotel. It does not take long to realize that Jamaica has a recent history as a violent island; the newspapers invariably carried daily reports of shootings on the streets, and even our hotel corridor was patrolled by armed guards.

When we went to the ground we were escorted by a jeep full of armed police – armed in a distinctly business sense, that is, with rifles and submachine-guns as well as regulation pistols. The locals accept it as a matter of course, but it was a distinctly ominous sight to our unaccustomed eyes; one of our bodyguards had discarded his regulation holster as too functional and wore a custom-made one slung low on his thigh, weighted for quick use with a thong round his leg. He was left-handed, too, so naturally we quickly christened him Billy the Kid. Glad he was on our side. . . .

Sabina Park will undoubtedly be the most impressive ground in the West Indies when it is finished. We arrived slap in the middle of a huge rebuilding programme aimed at increasing the size of the playing area and providing lavish facilities; skeletal girders sticking up everywhere, concrete stands in the process of completion, cranes on the outfield and the dusty smell of drying cement. It seemed impossible that a Test match could be housed among the piles of rubble and brickwork in a little over a week, but as we have seen before a bit of ingenuity and a lot of hard work can produce miracles out here.

The sightscreens from which Wes Hall used to launch himself into his run have disappeared, to be replaced by two huge walls painted a functional shade of duck-egg blue. The dressing-rooms, still unfinished, were bare and inhospitable concrete

Very West Indian . . . Lawrence Rowe hooks Ian Botham during the Jamaica match.

Very Middlesex . . . Roland Butcher unleashes a muscular hook against Jamaica.

boxes, and since the only means of locking the door was a bent six-inch nail, we were instructed to take all our gear with us every day. Work had not progressed as far as the completion of a scoreboard, but when our match against Jamaica started they were working on it. . . .

Six years ago the pitch was rolled, dry mud with a polished sheen – quick, but with a true bounce. Since then it has been dug up and relaid, and the pitch we played on against Jamaica was bare at the ends (spinners' length) and grassy in the middle (quick bowlers' length). It was not quick, but the new ball bounced like a tennis ball and the spinners got a lot of turn, especially the left-armer Donovan Malcolm, who made the ball leap about disconcertingly – a decidedly awkward customer.

I made 98 in the first innings and four not out, batting at number ten, in the second – not a case of instant relegation but the result of a throat infection which kept me out of the match for two days. Gatting, needing a good score and very tense early on, was dropped by Rowe at first slip when he attempted to cut the off-spinner Tucker, but he went on to make 93 and looked increasingly impressive on the way. Butcher scored 44 but got out needlessly again. Even so, both of them increased the pressure on Athey for a Test place.

The match meandered to a draw, but not before Gooch made a century in the second innings – coolly, sensibly and valuably, with the Test to come – and not before Rowe made one of those classical hundreds which remind you what a fine player he is. He made 28 not out overnight, really attacking the ball with his long-handled bat and the local Press went into raptures about the possibility of a century from him. He played far more steadily next day with that obviously in his sights and finished with 116. He keeps very still until the bowler bowls and then moves into position with lightning speed, back at first but always ready to come forward. His favourite back-cut really is a beautifully executed stroke and brought many of the runs in his innings, as it usually does. Rowe is more English than most West Indian players, except when he shows his origins with a characteristic and practised hook shot; unfortunately for him, he has suffered from too many injury problems abroad and seems to have been written off as far as Tests are concerned. He is still only thirty-two, and his total of seven Test centuries is not a lot for a man with his ability.

Talking of ability, I had a chat with Emburey before the match and tried to remind him just how much talent he has. For me, he's the world's best off-spinner, but I think he is sometimes a little bit lazy and doesn't quite do himself justice. I told him he should demand a world-class performance from himself every time he bowls, that he should never be satisfied with competence but aim always for excellence, because that is his standard. He has the ability, since he's no mug with the bat either, to be remembered among the very best of his type in the world. It was meant as encouragement, and Emburey bowled superbly for his six for 92 and made 34 with the bat: just what we want from him.

Jamaica's left-arm spinner Malcolm is a player well worth watching for the future. He jumps into a high action, spins the ball a lot and in this match bounced it much

Left: Lawrence Rowe again, and this time it's Mike Gatting on the receiving end.

Centre: Donovan Malcolm bowls – and look at the bounce from a left-arm spinner!

Bottom: This time it's four runs – on my way to 98 against Jamaica.

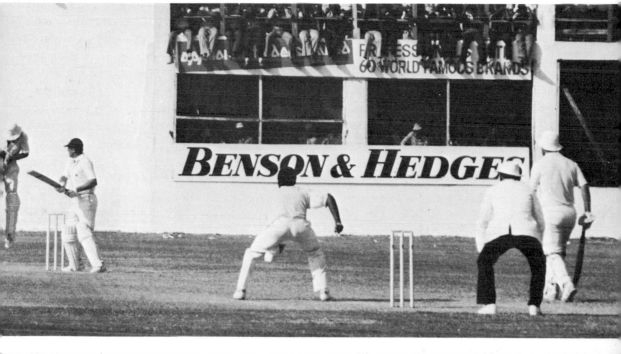

more threateningly than any other bowler on either side. I was beaten several times by deliveries which leaped – sometimes shoulder height – and yet when I looked at the pitch there were no tell-tale marks to be seen, which was amazing. Malcolm already has a lot going for him; if he continues to improve I am sure we will hear a lot more of him.

I found it odd when I was batting that the ball seemed to get harder to hit the older it became! The bounce became more pronounced, and it was difficult to force away on the ground because the grass was long and the ball just seemed to die. I got bogged down in the afternoon and made the mistake of trying to hit the ball harder and harder when I should have been knocking it off for ones and twos. Finally I was caught in the gulley by Mattis.

Unsure whether the ball had carried, I waited until the umpires had consulted before setting off. By the time I reached the pavilion there were quite a lot of boos, and it reminded me just how volatile the Jamaican crowd can be. I remembered the 1968 occasion when Basil Butcher was caught down the leg side by Alan Knott and hung around until the catch was confirmed. Perhaps the crowd interpreted that as a suggestion he thought he had been cheated, I don't know, but in no time at all there were bottles on the pitch. A small incident, misinterpreted, can set them off.

There was a fair amount of coming and going as far as the England team was concerned. Miller, who was due to play, went down with a heavy chill and upset stomach, so Emburey had to be drafted in; Downton caught a chill very early in the game and Bairstow fielded substitute wicket-keeper; Old tore a muscle in his thigh; and when Emburey had to go off for a couple of overs we had pressed all our reserves into action, including the manager Alan Smith! Goodness knows what would have happened if somebody had chosen that moment to tread on a nail; perhaps we could have sent for Billy the Kid.

The match was heading towards an inevitable and pretty aimless draw and I advised Botham at tea on the last day to make some sort of token gesture by declaring. It would have meant nothing in terms of the result, but Jamaica had been in the field for two-thirds of the match and I reckoned we might lay ourselves open to criticism if we kept them out there to the bitter end. Emburey would probably have enjoyed another bowl on that pitch and we could have given men like Gooch and Gatting a chance to turn their arm over for four or five overs each; whatever happened, at least we would have made a gesture.

Botham said he wanted our middle-order batsmen to get more practice, which seemed sound on the face of it. But there is batting and batting, and it was obvious that Jamaica would not waste their best bowlers in the last session; unless they did, any batting practice would be of strictly limited value. Sure enough Jamaica bowled Mattis, Basil Williams and an off-spinner called Neita, and the match degenerated slowly into farce. Worse than that, we lost four wickets in the last session, so any thought of useful practice went completely by the board. Draws, even rather tedious ones, are inevitable in cricket, but I do not like to see matches reduced to nonsense and tedium if it can be avoided. That lowers the tone of the whole game.

19

Gower's Triumph

Graham Gooch almost talked himself out of a memorable century on the first day of the Jamaica Test match. He did not know it at the time, of course, but Gooch was one of those most strongly in favour of fielding if we won the toss.... There was quite a bit of discussion and when the time came for a decision Botham was ready to put West Indies in.

I was in favour of batting. Whatever we do against this class of opposition we are going to have a tough time, but on balance I reckoned we had to make them bat last if we could. The pitch would wear, it might turn, and if we batted well – and first – we had a chance of getting Emburey into the game, one of the few potential advantages we have. More than that, we had to decide whether we wanted to win the match or try and play safe, and batting first was our only hope of a victory; a slim one, perhaps, but this was the last Test match and we had nothing to lose. 'Whatever we do, let's be positive about it,' said Alan Smith.

As it turned out, our deliberations did not count because West Indies won the toss and Lloyd put us in. That didn't surprise me, because Lloyd always likes to use his fast bowlers when they are fully rested – and that means on the first day of a Test if possible. If things go according to plan, West Indies then bat for two days, the rest day intervenes and the bowlers have had three days' rest by the time they come to bowl at us again. The fact that there might be a little bit in the pitch on the first day is a bonus as far as Lloyd is concerned; he backs his side to bowl us out in most circumstances and just likes to get the sequence right!

West Indies changed their side for the first time in the series when they brought in Malcolm Marshall for Roberts, swapping one threatening fast bowler for another. It might mean that Roberts is near the end of a very fine career, or it might simply annoy him and sharpen him up for the future; either way West Indies will not lose out if Marshall bowls as well as he can. Athey had been under pressure for his place - at number three, and it was even suggested that Botham might grasp the nettle by batting there himself. But Athey kept his place; he has got out to Croft twice, and in fairness to him it does sometimes take time to work Croft out.

Some things don't seem to change at all. The pitch was quite heavily grassed and I asked the groundsman on the day before the match to shave it a bit; the nets at the ground were very poor, and we had to use a strip of concrete behind the pavilion in a nearby school play area. The attendance on the first morning was disappointing, too, in comparison with what I remembered on previous tours.

The pitch was not particularly quick, but the ball was likely to bounce a fair bit off the grassier patches, as Gooch soon discovered when Holding hit him nastily on the gloves. Holding and Marshall quickly went round the wicket to me and fired in some short stuff which I had to fend off; it was obviously a pre-arranged plan and both quick bowlers were running in as though breaking the opening partnership would be the key to the innings. When Croft bowled over and round the wicket, and inevitably short, at me I could hear Richards at slip urging him on: 'C'mon, Crofty, c'mon, Crofty....' But Crofty didn't have any more success than the rest of them.

It certainly was not for the want of trying – he bounced Gooch five times in his first two overs, and I asked umpire Douglas Sang Hue, 'How many of them is he allowed?' Sang Hue just smiled – inscrutably, as they say.... Gooch ducked, weaved, swayed out of the way; he left one in-cutter which didn't bounce and shaved his off stump. Then he took one on the gloves in front of his face and it fell just short of Haynes in a close catching position on the off side. Haynes was back on his heels at the time; had he been better balanced it might have made a crucial difference.

Gooch has wearied of Croft's over-use of the short stuff and determined to have a go at anything pitched wide of the off stump. He did it well, too, except that he started to waft a bit dangerously and I cautioned him to be selective. A couple of half-volleys were despatched for four, and Gooch was on his way.

He came down the pitch and warned me that I wasn't getting far enough across against Holding, bowling over the wicket. One or two had bounced and I'd con-centrated on staying away from the line a little; Gooch told me he could see too much of my stumps, just as in Barbados when Holding bowled me out. That's what partners are for....

I felt I was going very well, in fact the only sign of a chance was early on when one from Marshall got big, hit the handle and looped over short-square-leg's head. Gooch had one let-off when he'd made 27 and tried to sway back to cut a short one from Croft over the slips. It followed him as he leaned away, took the edge and whistled between Murray and Lloyd at first slip. Gooch escaped only because Murray had anticipated the ball going down the leg side and moved across; had he stood still it would have been a simple catch straight to him and Lloyd left him in no doubt about the fact.

There were more good shots than scares, and at lunch we were 92 for no wicket. We could hardly have hoped for anything better, or even as good. It was a very satisfactory morning's work and we were entitled to be pleased with ourselves – for the time being.

Richards bowled a maiden to me straight after lunch, then Garner's first delivery lifted, just touched my right thumb and went through comfortably to Murray.

Gooch rattles the score along in England's first innings on his way to a fine century.

England 93 for one, and the arrival of Athey triggered the expected return of Croft.

In a way, the situation became ideal for a player like Athey who has not scored runs and needs a bit of time to build runs and confidence. Gooch launched into a marvellous attacking spell, and was particularly severe on Croft. Suddenly the match revolved round him, and Athey had the chance to make his runs practically unnoticed. Certainly, England's situation did not put him under pressure, and the fact that Gooch was commanding the spotlight can only have helped. But Athey did not look comfortable, and I never really felt he was going to do himself justice.

Gooch was rattling along. Croft no-balled and Gooch cut him over the slips for six to reach his 50; the next over from Croft included three fours – cut, drive and slash over slip – the field spread and Holding was called back into the attack. His first ball was whipped high and hard off Gooch's body for four. Garner was driven straight and through mid-off for boundaries, and when Marshall at silly-mid-off made a brave attempt at a catch, the ball brushed aside his hands and went for another four. Gooch doubled his lunch score in no time, took another couple of fours off Holding and had reached 99 when he lost his sleeping partner....

Athey shaped to play Holding on the leg side, got much too far over and lost his leg stump after batting fifty minutes for three. He had done a job – the partnership with Gooch was worth 55 – but he never really looked like asserting himself. Gooch paused for drinks, then drove hard past Holding's outflung right hand for four to reach his century in ten minutes over three hours. England were then 155 for two.

Croft replaced Garner but looked laboured and tired. He had put a lot into his confrontation with Gooch and me earlier in the day, and that long run of his suddenly looked very, very long; he was flogging himself before he got half-way through it. He was still awkward and still lively, but much of the venom of his early bowling was missing. He went round the wicket to Gower, who flipped him high off his legs for four and pushed him away for twos without much trouble.

Gower played very well and produced one memorable stroke off Richards, a drive through the covers for four which was exquisitely timed. But he had one escape – when he cut Croft, and Greenidge, at deepish gulley, got two hands to it but put it down. Greenidge had swayed to his left anticipating the edge and was off balance when the ball flew to his right. It looked as though Gower might be set for a big score when he misjudged Croft's angle, got too far over trying to work him on the leg side and had his leg stump plucked out of the ground; England were 196 for three and some of the gloss of the morning had already disappeared.

Marshall did not bowl between lunch and tea, which was inexplicable considering first that West Indies had struggled to capture wickets and second that Croft looked increasingly jaded. But he was on immediately afterwards, and with his fifth delivery almost dismissed Gooch, who was on 125, when a relatively easy return catch slipped out of his right hand.

Richards gave the ball plenty of air, flighting it and teasing Gooch as though he was prepared to buy his wicket, as in the second innings in Antigua. Gooch moved inside the line and lifted Richards over extra cover for four, both batsmen took singles and kept a weather eye on Marshall who was bowling very accurately to two slips and a gulley. Willey had cause to be especially wary; every time they have met, Marshall has taken Willey's wicket – and it wasn't too long before he made it six out of six!

Marshall bowled off his short run, a short delivery going wide down the leg side, and Willey tried to work it off his hip; he gets quite a lot of runs that way. But he got a very fine edge through to the wicket-keeper – strangled out, as we say – and England were in trouble again. After a 90-plus partnership for the first wicket we were 210 for four, which is no great score in a Test match; instead of building from that early position we had let it slip again and given away three wickets without too much help from the bowlers.

Butcher played well and for the first time looked like a solid, compact Test-match batsman. He played his shots, not least the hook which brought him a couple of boundaries against Marshall, but he looked altogether more sound than he often has – no longer playing and missing or edging his shots. It was good to see.

Richards kept tantalizing Gooch, and we had visions of him holing out, but he sensibly took singles to deep mid-on and mid-off. We simply could not afford to lose another wicket at this stage – certainly not by slogging – and it made sense to 'milk' Richards rather than try to belt him out of the ground.

Not that Gooch was afraid to play his shots. When Garner replaced Marshall and bowled a full-toss, Gooch promptly hit it straight for four; the next delivery was dug in hard and he thick-edged that down to third-man. He had batted for five and a half hours and played many shots of real quality, including two sixes and twenty fours, when he fell to Holding for 153. He got an inside edge, driving, and Murray had to throw himself to his left to take a very good catch; Gooch was not sure it had been taken, but Murray rolled over and then threw the ball up to dispel any doubt and England were 249 for five.

Botham went in and the innings took an odd turn. He whacked Holding through gulley for four; got an inside edge trying to drive Garner; cut at Holding and missed; tried to hook a bouncer from Garner and was hit on the helmet. 'Blimey,' said Willey, 'is this a one-day match?' Old went out with a drink and carried a message to 'get your head down', but Botham made no noticeable reply.

Butcher had played several violent shots but straight off the middle of the bat. He survived a catch at second slip off a no-ball, hooked Holding for four and drove Croft confidently off front and back foot. But when he had made 32 with easily his most impressive innings on tour he hit across a delivery of full length from Garner and got an inside edge on to his leg stump.

England finished the day on 275 for six, which did not represent our worst day's work of the tour but was certainly less commanding than it might have been. In fact we had wasted a very good chance to run up a big score without losing too many wickets; early in the day it had looked as though we might do just that, but again it was too good to last.

Second Day

'Pace like fire, man ...' – we heard the phrase often enough and Michael Holding put it in grim perspective, as far as we were concerned, in an horrendous first half-hour. England lost four wickets for seven runs in thirty minutes, and four of those were byes! Holding took three wickets for two runs in twelve deliveries ... statistics like those really don't need a lot of enlargement: we were annihilated by sheer pace and a bit of bounce.

The pitch was probably a bit quicker than on the first day, which is not usual in Test matches. What moisture there is at the start dries out and the pitch is likely to gain a little pace, a little being a lot too much for our late-order batsmen.

Holding took the new ball immediately and announced that he meant business with a couple of short deliveries, one of which sailed high and wide beyond Murray for four byes. Marshall accounted for Botham, who played that wide drive which he attempts so often and was caught at third slip by Greenidge; then Holding polished off the tail. Fast.

Downton could do no more than fend off a rising delivery towards backward short-leg, where Croft back-pedalled slowly and took an easy catch. Jackman was beaten and arrowed a catch to fourth slip where Mattis floundered to his left and pushed the ball upwards; Richards tried to grab it but Jackman was reprieved, for a moment. . . .

A delivery from Marshall sat Emburey on his backside, and Croft lunged forward from backward short-leg clapping and urging Marshall on. Haynes, embarrassed at short-square-leg, had the good grace to tell him to shut up. Holding bowled murderously quick again and Emburey, shuffling away, lost his middle stump. 'That's the first time in my life I've backed away,' said Emburey, and I reckon it was too.

Poor Jackman went painfully. A delivery from Holding seared on to his left glove, the bat flew out of his hand one way and the ball lobbed the other to the waiting Haynes. Jackman trailed off wringing a painful bruise on the knuckle of his little finger and England were all out for 285. Whatever happened to 196 for three. . . .

We needed a lot from Dilley and the pacey pitch should have encouraged him to put everything in. He flared and then faded, which is still a disquieting feature of his game, a reminder that he is still very young in his ways. He was quick at first: quick enough to dig one in at Greenidge which took off and flew off an inadvertent nick high over Downton's head. And he was aggressive enough to swap heated remarks with Greenidge, though I'm bound to say I don't go along with that sort of behaviour: if players must swear they should swear at themselves.

But after only two overs he announced to Botham that he was tired, which was extraordinary, coming from a young man who had not bowled in a match for the last twelve days. In his second spell of the morning he was cut for four over cover by Greenidge and driven through mid-on and mid-off by Haynes; his head went down and I remembered the words of Viv Richards: 'When you hit some bowlers their heads go down and they don't come back.' The fire and the aggression seemed to have burned out very quickly.

Dilley also ran into trouble over a simple matter which no professional should have overlooked. His first spell was cut short because a heel came off his boot and he had to go off; then it was discovered that he had only one pair of bowling boots at the ground. We had to put out an SOS over the public address system for a bootmaker, and the crowd loved that. Botham and Alan Smith left Dilley in no doubt about their annoyance, for a young man who has had trouble with his footwear in the past really should know better than to arrive at a Test match without a pair of boots in reserve.

At lunch West Indies were 53 without loss, and Botham and I discussed our broad tactical plan for the afternoon. We agreed that Emburey should bowl at one end while we alternated the seamers at the other, bowling to two slips and a gulley only, making them work hard for every run. We had to tie the game down.

Greenidge fretted quite a bit against Emburey but was the more forceful batsman against the seamers, giving himself room to hit them off the back foot square and through the covers. Emburey crowded him, with five men round the bat, and Greenidge suddenly launched into a huge straight six to force mid-off and mid-on back; then he could take his singles.

Haynes picked up the odd run off the seamers but Emburey tied him down expertly with four men round the bat. Haynes took some deliveries on his pad, he got a few bat-pads which, fortunately for him, dropped short of the close fielders; the only runs he was able to get came from a push off his hip to square-leg.

When Dilley came on for his first spell of the afternoon I was fielding at mid-off and went to have a word with him. He gets a bit miffed because he reckons everyone who advises him tells him something different, and he's usually not short of advisers. I always tell him the same two things, and this time was no different: bowl rhythm and length at a fairly rapid pace and if the batsman hits you, keep your head up and run in. Remember, it only takes one delivery to get any batsman out.

Bowling rhythmically gives Dilley pace. And at his pace, bowling length means the batsman always has to make a decision: does he play forward, back, duck or what? The more difficult decisions a batsman has to make, the more likely he is to come up with the wrong answer and get out.

I reckon that's fairly simple, and it's meant to be. Remember Dilley is a youngster in cricket terms: he hasn't played all that much cricket either at county or Test level. And being inexperienced he's bound to find it hard to assimilate a lot of advice, especially if some of it conflicts; I don't think he can handle a lot of theory about where to bowl.

Dilley ran in well, bowled intelligently and took the wickets of Greenidge and Richards – which can't be a bad job of work in any spell. Greenidge got a great delivery which flicked off his bat at chest height to first slip, and Richards was well caught down the leg side by Downton. Richards has never scored a century in

Jamaica, and a couple of characteristically explosive shots suggested that he might be in the mood; for a fielding side it's always good to see the back of him.

Emburey was still bowling splendidly, tight and accurate, and although Haynes still gathered the odd run off his hip he had a new responsibility now that Greenidge and Richards had gone. They had scored fairly smartly; Mattis is no player of spin and it was obviously a good time to put pressure on Haynes now that he was looking to take the lead.

I offered Emburey my advice at tea and we took out backward short-leg and put him behind square-leg saving one, the one which Haynes had kept pinching with that shot off his hip. We put the sweep man finer to cut off the three or four, and we put two men in front of the wicket where Haynes could see them and worry about them. Now Haynes would have to do something different, and for several overs he couldn't get a run off Emburey, which was just what we wanted.

Suddenly, Emburey went round the wicket to Haynes and broke the spell. Haynes banged him straight back over his head – almost through his head in fact – for four; then he cut him delicately for another. The over cost nine runs, and I thought that perhaps Emburey had been smitten with a touch of the sun ... in six deliveries he had undone the hard, sensible work of half an hour. Variety may be a good thing, but not when you are obviously on top and the batsman is fretting; that's the time to stick to the pattern of bowling that works and let him do all the worrying. Emburey soon went back to tying Haynes down, and he had to revert to picking up his ones and twos off the seamers.

Haynes is not a particularly good player against a spinner bowling well. He has a sound defence but he's nowhere near as fluent as against the seamers; no matter how long he faced Emburey he still could not avoid the occasional undignified jab or bat-pad. He tried hard to compensate by attacking Jackman, and I thought he was going to get out; there were several loud lbw appeals, and when he did connect, Athey increased his frustration with a couple of magnificent stops in the field at mid-on.

Haynes finally fell to the off-spinner and it was ironic, perhaps, in view of his long tussle with Emburey that it should be Willey who took his wicket. Unlikely, too, since Haynes got himself in a terrible tangle and Willey yorked him leg stump! His 84, hard earned every inch of the way, took him four and a half hours.

Mattis was mesmerized. With Emburey on we mounted our familiar field against him: sweep man saving one, mid-on and mid-off back a bit to prevent him hitting over the top, very straight silly-mid-on almost standing on the pitch at the bowler's end. He just did not know where his next run was coming from, and at one stage laboured for an hour for a single. Haynes kept talking to him, trying to jolly him through, and took the strike whenever he could because Mattis was obviously in limbo.

He was dropped on two by Botham at second slip off Dilley – a good-length delivery which drew him a bit wide and was edged downwards. Botham mistakenly thought it would not carry and tried to scoop the ball; it arrived early and bounced

An edge too far ... Bill Athey gets too far across and loses his leg stump to Holding after batting for fifty minutes.

Desmond Haynes in the driving seat. Graham Dilley is the bowler.

out of his hands. And after that Mattis barely scored a run until he played a sweep-slog for four off Willey and off drove him for four a couple of deliveries later. The confrontation between Emburey, in particular, and Mattis and Haynes was a fine piece of cricket, and I think the crowd appreciated and enjoyed it.

Lloyd came in to split Mattis and Gomes, which was obviously a sound move since he is a better player and in good form. He cut and swept Willey for boundaries but looked decidedly less happy against Emburey, who bowled very straight at him and gave him no room. Lloyd was crowded with a slip, a backward short-leg and a man in front catching on the off side. He got a couple of bat-pads but neither went to hand.

West Indies were 193 for three when Emburey finished his marathon four-hour spell at the close. A fine, professional performance from him, one he could be proud of – and yet he did not have a single wicket to show for all his efforts. It just goes to show that figures aren't everything; when you are assessing a man's performance in the context of a match, they can be inadequate or even misleading.

Third Day

The throat infection which troubled me during the match against Jamaica was back, only worse. It felt as though somebody was strumming my Adam's apple with a hacksaw. I saw a doctor at the ground before play started and he prescribed some tablets for pharyngitis; they hadn't arrived when we went out to field.

The new ball was available and we took it straight away because although Mattis is better organized against the seamers he is no great shakes against the new ball. Lloyd clattered Dilley and Botham; it was soon obvious that he was in that mood where he has no intention of blocking, and if we didn't get him out he would get runs.

Dilley unleashed a magnificent bouncer and Mattis, jerking his head out of the way, lost his cap as well as his dignity. He sent for a floppy hat – presumably on the assumption that he could jam it on his head to stay – but before it arrived he should already have been out. The next ball, just short of a length, was the perfect tester for jangled nerves, and Mattis edged it towards Gooch at first slip – a straightforward enough catch until Botham sailed across and punched it away. For half a minute the air was full of anger and frustration.

Mattis rode his luck for another 21 runs until he leaned back to try and drive Dilley and spooned a mis-hit to Gatting, the substitute fielder, at cover. West Indies 227 for four, but Lloyd, wearing a crash helmet for the first time, had picked up runs pretty freely against the seamers and Emburey was needed to slow him down. Emburey bowled straight so that Lloyd's only real shot against him was the sweep, and there were a couple of promising moments. Lloyd almost got a bat-pad to Gatting, catching close in on the off side, he drove uppishly just short of extra cover and was beaten by Emburey's arm ball from round the wicket, but it did too much before hitting the pad. Lloyd and Gomes eventually got on to the back foot to hit through cover, which relieved the pressure a bit. So did the arrival of Willey who, good a bowler as he is, does not command Emburey's pinpoint accuracy. Lloyd hit him off the back foot for one four and swept him for another.

By lunch, West Indies had put on 96 in the session and were 289 for four, looking ominously ready to go in search of a big lead. The tablets which had been prescribed for my throat had arrived so I took a couple, ate a little food and within fifteen minutes I was sweating and sick. There was no alternative, I had to go back to the hotel and get to bed; I spent the rest of the day sleeping fitfully and catching up on the latest score on the radio. Gatting was already on for Butcher, who had strained a groin muscle, so Bairstow did my stint in the field.

Lloyd was in trouble again against the pace of Dilley, but seemed determined to carve and slash his way out. He played and missed a fair bit which annoyed Dilley; the faster Dilley bowled the harder Lloyd tried to whack him. Lloyd was hit a glancing blow on the helmet, and Dilley glared; he lifted Dilley through cover for four, and the glare became an expletive; he launched into a savage square slash for four more, and Dilley applauded ironically. The pair were rubbing sparks off each other and Lloyd was getting the better of it, luckily or otherwise – when he had made 91 he was hit on the glove, and Dilley seemed quite frantic when the ball fell short of Botham at slip. Lloyd had brief repairs but did not last much longer.

Jackman came on and got one to bounce – off a ridge, says Lloyd, though nobody else can find it – and Downton took the catch behind which left Lloyd stranded five from a century. Murray joined Gomes with West Indies 345 for five, and although they had a bit of trouble between the wickets they put on 27 with Gomes playing with increasing confidence. Gower was close with a couple of attempted run-outs and Athey almost beat Murray with an intelligent throw from cover. Murray, backing up, would have been out had it hit the stumps.

Willey and Emburey were brought together soon after tea, Emburey bowling to a backward short-leg, forward short-leg, slip and man catching close on the off side. Gooch took a brilliant catch to dismiss Murray, anticipating the shot as Murray played the ball off his thigh and plucking the ball out of the air at backward short-leg: West Indies 372 for six.

Marshall had not scored when Gower flung himself at silly mid-off and clutched a bat-pad off Emburey but the umpire was not satisfied it had been taken cleanly; Marshall lifted Emburey over mid-on for four, and when he played a similar shot rather squarer soon afterwards, Botham jogged out of the slips and closed the gap at mid-wicket.

Gomes had played well in his unpretentious way, hitting the loose delivery hard, looking for his ones and twos and playing very few rash shots. It looked as though he only needed to find a sound partner to be sure of making a hundred, but that was easier said than done: Marshall did not look too permanent, and when Botham came on he slogged artlessly and was bowled. The new ball was taken and Gomes, 82 when Marshall fell, could only watch his support withering away at the other end.

Garner, awkward and angular as ever, took a fair bit of shifting – new ball or not.

He off-drove Botham stylishly for four and three, cut Dilley for four and then flipped him off his hip through mid-wicket for another boundary. He'd made 19 in no time when he holed out to Bairstow at extra cover and left the field, looking very annoyed with himself; Gomes, on 89, did not look too impressed either.

Holding and Croft lasted less than ten minutes between them, and poor Gomes was left high and dry on 90. Holding hooked violently at a bouncer from Botham and was caught behind off his glove; Croft pushed forward and Gatting took a smart, left-handed catch at forward short-leg. West Indies finished on 442, with a lead of 157, which was a fairly formidable advantage considering our batting so far in the series; we had a rest day to ponder on it.

Fourth Day

It was a humid, overcast day with the threat of rain from clouds shrouding the Blue Mountains behind the ground. 'Do we play to save the game right from the start, or just play normally and look for runs where we can,' I asked Botham. 'Just play normally until we get in front,' he said. The pitch was good now, though it was criss-crossed with cracks and the odd delivery was liable to keep low; Holding and Marshall ran in as though their lives depended on it.

They obviously reckoned the first hour or so could be decisive and we certainly felt it was important not to lose a wicket – easier said than done when Holding and Marshall are firing round the wicket, as they did to me; when the bowlers are fresh and the batsmen are perhaps a bit jaded because they've faced the situation so many times before. In a little under an hour we were three down and in obvious trouble.

Gooch went in the fourth over. He was looking to force a delivery from Marshall away off the back foot with a straight bat, but it bounced a bit and was too close to his body for that shot. The ball slid off the edge and Lloyd took a comfortable catch at first slip.

Athey did not last long either, though in fairness to him it was a very unfortunate way to get out, and particularly for a young batsman who had been badly out of runs. Holding bowled over the wicket and short of a length, Athey dropped his hands and swayed his head and chest out of the way of the expected flight of the ball – and it bounced only enough to flick his gloves and carry through to Murray. Not long afterwards a delivery from Holding to me pitched about the same length and went through throat high. . . .

What happened next was uncannily familiar: a throwback to Trinidad, Barbados, Antigua; a frustrating action replay. Croft replaced Marshall, so there was bound to be a fair bit of short stuff flying about. As before, I determined to let the short deliveries pass in front of my body and get across and over the line of anything pitched up. Croft dug one in short, I shaped to let it pass but it followed me and I was forced to play it awkwardly at throat height; I got myself turned round in the process and the ball lobbed away to gulley and Garner. England were 32 for three and the locals, understandably enough, were licking their lips in anticipation of the rout.

It never came, partly because the weather helped us out, but chiefly because Gower and Willey got their heads down and played with splendid professional determination through the rest of the day. Gower had been threatening to put together a really impressive score: making fluent twenties or thirties, looking set for a genuinely big innings, and then getting out – sometimes getting himself out – to relatively innocuous deliveries. But the form was there and the attitude had matured to a very marked degree; Gower simply needed to put it all together, and the opportunity was certainly there now.

Willey is easily underestimated because he is not the greatest stylist in the world, but the West Indies have the greatest respect for him because they recognize a born fighter when they see one. Willey gets everything behind the ball and battles it out inch by inch, minute by minute.

He stands over six feet, and the ball isn't usually bouncing quite so high by the time he gets in, which of course helps. But there have been taller players with less grit and determination against the quick stuff; Willey's character is the key.

Gower battled sensibly, but played his shots whenever he could do so with reasonable safety. He thumped Marshall square off the back foot for four, cut and hooked Croft for four and even cut Holding over the slips for a six, high into the stand on the short boundary edge. Holding bowled a few deliveries at him round the wicket and Gower obviously found difficulty with the angle; the ball speared into his body and he gloved a couple to fine-leg. But Holding was rebuked for running on the pitch and had to revert to bowling over the wicket.

When Gower had made 29 he was dropped by Lloyd at first slip. Richards had just come on and Gower cut at his second delivery, edging it fast into Lloyd's chest. It bounced out and Gower survived, thank goodness. It's an ironic thought but if the catch had stuck we would have been left with just another Gower innings – a well-constructed 30 and then out. He deserved his slice of luck and made the best of it.

At lunch England were 91 for three, with Gower 46 and Willey 25. They had done a great job in shoring up the innings so far and as they walked off for lunch a steady drizzle set in. We lost over an hour and started again at 2.20 p.m.

West Indies' effectiveness was reduced by one-quarter because Marshall was off the field with strained rib muscles, a legacy of the effort he had put in with the new ball early in the morning. But they were still a very formidable attacking force and Gower and Willey did marvellously well to hold them off. They attacked, too – forcefully enough to raise a century partnership in 112 minutes.

Willey had his slice of good fortune when he had made 25 – an edge off a bouncer from Croft which whistled between Murray and Lloyd at first slip. They glared at each other but I reckon Murray was the more blameworthy – he had anticipated the ball going down the leg side again and moved across; when the edge came he dived back and under it. Willey played a sparkling off-drive for four against Croft, a shot full of power, took more boundaries off him and Garner, and off-drove Holding for three when his direction strayed uncharacteristically.

Gower played a superlative shot to reach his 50, steering Croft past gulley with the deft elegance of a d'Artagnan. Richards fancies getting him out and taunted him with some well-flighted deliveries; Gower went down the wicket to drive him for four, took a couple of quicker deliveries on the pad and tickled a single to bring up the hundred stand.

Rain from the Blue Mountains had been advancing steadily down the valley all afternoon; by tea the ground was ringed by heavy clouds and the light began to fail. A clammy, misty drizzle enveloped the ground, the light went and no further play was possible. England were 134 for three and, thanks to Gower and Willey, still in the match.

Fifth Day

Clive Lloyd has been around long enough to make life difficult for any opposition. England were only 23 behind and bound to create a lead of some sort; Lloyd knew that every run was worth double because of the time factor involved. So he compromised with his usual, aggressive field placings and determined to cut off the flow of runs, to deny Gower and Willey any momentum. Gower gets many of his runs with a firm push towards mid-off, so Lloyd put a man there; Willey is adept at running the ball down off his hip, so Holding stationed a man behind square saving the single. The batsmen were obviously going to have to work hard.

For an hour they battled through and did nothing extravagant, little rash. Willey chased Holding outside the off stump and missed, Gower tried to hit Mattis square off the back foot and edged, fortunately, just wide of slip for four – but they generally looked composed and more or less in command of the situation.

Then Richards came on and Willey fell for the temptation. It should not happen, of course – we all know that and tell ourselves not to do anything silly. But after playing the quicker bowlers Richards represents a release – and more than that you feel you will look foolish if you play him as circumspectly as the faster bowlers. It is surprising how daft you can look trying not to look daft....

Willey tried to hit a flighted delivery over the top, got too far under it and lofted a catch to Greenidge at mid-wicket. It is not a shot Willey attempts too often, and this was not the time to start; Willey knew he had made a bad error of judgement and nobody had to tell him, he was furious with himself when he got back to the dressing-room. England 168 for four – only just nosing in front – and as so often happens, the loss of one wicket quickly became the loss of two.

Butcher padded up to Croft, the ball hit his back leg and he was very lbw. Botham padded up a couple of deliveries later and survived a tantrum from Croft when another big lbw appeal was turned down; Richards even had to run from slip and tell Croft to calm down. At least it reminded us, if any reminder were needed, that West Indies only needed a couple of successes to be right on top.

Botham clearly appreciated that and played very sensibly, refusing to be tempted even when Richards threw the ball high and grinned at his straight bat. Botham is a good sweeper and likes to play the shot when he can but even deliveries which

Left: No escape: Gordon Greenidge is caught by Ian Botham off Graham Dilley for 62.

In England's second innings Roland Butcher padded up outside the off stump without offering a shot – and fell lbw, another victim for Colin Croft.

strayed on to the leg stump were treated with respect; he blocked, padded away, kicked the ball away when he had to – but no risk shots. It was good to see.

Gower's attitude was summed up by seven careful runs in the first hour, which is not exactly the style on which he built his reputation! Richards teased him and momentarily got through; Gower went down the pitch and hit him in the air towards mid-off, Richards almost caught it himself, and Greenidge only just failed to get to the ball as he dived. Gower cursed himself quietly and got his head down again; he swept Gomes for four to reach a hard-earned century.

The new ball has brought something extra out of the West Indies bowlers throughout the series – aggression, optimism, sheer destructive pace. It was available straight after lunch, when England's lead was only 52; our prospects of saving the match depended on how we managed to see it off. Holding and Garner knew that, too; they raced in with fierce determination and the match moved into its crucial stage.

It began badly for us, when Botham fell to the second delivery from Holding. He pushed firmly towards cover but the ball bounced a little and sped off the handle – and Botham's finger end – to Garner at gulley. It only just carried but Garner took it as easily as if he were picking a flower; Downton walked into a situation fraught with danger – and he was on a pair. . . .

It would be difficult to imagine a more searching test of his ability or attitude, and yet he came through with flying colours. Lots of guts, lots of fight, even when the ball was flying round his ears or, rather less classically, hitting him on the backside as he took evasive action. Holding knew that one wicket would expose the tail and the first innings had shown what might happen then; he really tore in, and even Garner whistled down a bouncer or two.

I told Downton to forget about playing shots, just to play in the V between mid-off and mid-on. He would get runs that way because the ball would come off the bat fast and most of West Indies' fielders would be catching . . . just put bat to ball and make them work to get you out. That's how Alan Knott started, and he developed into a very fine batsman in his own right; Downton had a real taste of life in the fast lane and came through it admirably.

He ducked and weaved and skipped about a fair bit, which was only to be expected. One delivery flicked off his shoulder and he was credited with four runs, another bounced wickedly and hit him under the armpit – but it was noticeable that the nearest thing to a chance was given by Gower.

Holding, bowling round the wicket, tucked him up with a delivery just short of a length and the ball bounced off his glove wide of Haynes at short-leg. He leaped and got a hand to the ball when it seemed to have gone past him – it would have been a marvellous catch – but luckily for Gower and us he could not hang on. Gower was attacked again from round the wicket by Holding and Croft, but he battled through splendidly; Croft went over the wicket and made him drive and miss: I wondered if Gower was getting tired.

Marshall was off the field all day with his rib injury, and that meant Lloyd could not

No praise is too high for David Gower's performance in the last Test. He grew in stature as the tour progressed, and for him at least the series ended with an unqualified success.

rotate his bowlers as frequently as he would like. He prefers to bowl them in short spells, letting Croft do the donkey-work, to keep them fresh and endlessly competitive. Croft had bowled long spells and was looking a bit frayed; Lloyd now turned to Richards and Gomes, and the battle was slowly being won by the batsmen.

Richards lobbed the ball high to Gower inviting him to do something rash, Gower drove him uppishly for four and swept him for four, but refused to swallow the bait; Richards unleashed a bouncer at Gower and another at Downton. He grinned, but the frustration was plain to see.

At tea Gower was 132 and Downton 14. They had done a great job but I warned them that it wasn't quite finished yet. We were only 105 ahead, and if West Indies broke through quickly they were quite capable of scoring at five or six an over off the last twenty overs to win the match. It was imperative that they stayed there for another hour: don't relax - concentrate on staying around.

They did, too, until West Indies had to concede defeat of a sort and the match finished in a draw. Holding finally went off his short run, but even then he was able to surprise Gower with a bouncer and clang him on the helmet - Holding really is the most magnificent bowler to watch, especially when you are sitting beyond the boundary. . . .

Downton's performance will stand him in good stead for the future, not just in terms of impressing selectors but in proving to himself what he is capable of. And no praise is too high for Gower's performance; he disciplined himself perfectly to the situation and I was pleased that he finished with a big total which reflected how well he had played. The two do not always go together.

By the time he walked off, 154 not out, Gower had batted the whole day for 84 runs, and that can be infinitely harder than smashing the same score in a couple of hours. A draw, even against West Indies, isn't exactly a flag day for English cricket but for David Gower at least the series ended with an unmitigated success.

20

Conclusion

Heathrow was a profound relief to us all, especially a Heathrow bathed in April sunshine – we usually seem to get home to six inches of snow. It had been a long, wearing tour, dogged by misfortunes: the loss of Willis and then Rose, the Jackman business and, of course, the tragic death of Kenny Barrington. The series was lost, no great surprise in itself, but few could look back with complete satisfaction at their own performances. That may sound carping and perhaps I will be accused of being over-critical, but there is no point in glossing over the facts just because they are embarrassing; if we are honest we may learn.

Apart from one spell on the greentop in Barbados we never looked like winning a Test match; apart from the pace of Dilley and the skill of Emburey our attack looked very ordinary and lacking in penetration. Young batsmen were given the opportunity to establish a claim for a regular place, especially after Rose went home, and they blew it – though certainly not for want of trying. The circumstances and playing conditions for the Australia series will no doubt be very different, and players may redeem themselves; I hope so. But when we were pitted against the best in the world we had some pretty chastening experiences, and the fact that they are the best is not an excuse in itself.

Disregarding the results for a moment, I did not think we gave a very good account of ourselves. Losing is always a disappointment but you can give a good account of yourself, even in defeat. You can lose with character and some credit, you can even lift your reputation because the people who follow cricket aren't fools: they see more in a performance than just who wins and loses. How you lose matters, and on that score I thought we did not do ourselves justice as a team.

There were consolations and I have already charted the progress made by Dilley, the development of Emburey as an off-spinner who must already be the best in the world. Gooch played well; the power game suits him, and I enjoy batting with him because I reckon we are good foils for each other; and Gower had a lot to be satisfied with even before that marvellous 150 in the last Test.

I never really had many doubts that Gooch would do well, because his strength of stroke puts him in good stead against fast bowling, but I confess I had my reservations about Gower. Not in terms of ability, there is no doubting that, but in terms of mental make-up. I do not have those reservations any more.

Throughout the tour, Gower made a conscious effort to bring his game forward, to add new dimensions to his game by applying himself. He did it quietly, like slipping away for a net on a concrete strip during the Jamaica Test when there might have been an excuse for not bothering, but he did it conscientiously nevertheless. I am not saying he's the finished product as an established Test player but he showed on tour that he has the mental capacity to apply himself and once he has mastered that there is no end to his potential. One of the tour's successes and it was good to see.

So was Willey. It is staggering to me how people patronize him by saying that he is playing above himself at Test level – 'limited ability' is the favourite phrase. This is a backhanded compliment which obviously suggests he gets more out of himself than they think he is capable of.

But there was no sign of limited ability in Antigua; that was as fine a Test innings as I have seen, and I've seen quite a few. Willey is a Test batsman in his own right, a good down-to-earth professional who should clearly have been batted higher in the order from the start. He has tremendous courage, which is the first requirement against genuinely fast bowling, and I hope that after two good series against West Indies he gets the recognition he deserves as a very fine player, because that is what he is.

There were those who said I should not have accepted the tour, that at forty I would only be cannon-fodder for the likes of Holding and Roberts. They meant well, I suppose, but cricket is my profession after all, and as my own sternest critic – in a professional sense – I feel I played consistently well. I felt better than my scores all through the tour. Luck does not really come into it, because I have always felt you make your own luck to a great extent, but there was a fair amount of brutal stuff flying about and I got more than my share of unplayable deliveries. They did not get me out bowling round the wicket, which pleased me a lot; it was obviously a tactic they had decided on before the tour started and used frequently, but I took steps to combat it, successfully as it turned out. Ironically, perhaps, the answer was forged during a short pre-tour trip to South Africa for a quiet holiday and a bit of practice in the sun, when my Yorkshire team-mate Arnie Sidebottom bowled a lot at me round the wicket off twenty-one yards....

I played in all the matches and stood up to it physically, apart from a couple of throat infections – so one can forget the notion that Test life ends at forty. My one regret is that I made only one century; there should have been more.

The media made gloomy forecasts before the tour started about the Bouncer War waiting for us. Well, I'm bound to say that although there was a fair bit of flak flying, it never got out of proportion. Bowlers of the calibre of Holding, Roberts and Garner used the bouncer sparingly, as a weapon rather than as a battering-ram, which is fair enough.

Having said that, it is important to understand the difference between a bouncer

Richards the dominator.

and a delivery pitched just short of a length which rears at a batsman somewhere between chest and throat. The better West Indies bowlers have mastered the art of that sort of delivery and they used it unceasingly. A batsman facing that sort of bowling at around 90 mph has a split second in time to decide whether to attempt to get over the ball and try to play it down, to hook or to take some sort of evasive action. So although there weren't too many bouncers, there was rarely a respite from deliveries attacking the body … bouncers usually whizz spectacularly over a batsman's head, which excites the crowd but is nowhere near as testing as the constant short stuff.

Croft overdid both the bouncer and the short stuff, I thought, and was always allowed to get away with it; I do not recall one occasion when the umpires stepped it to enforce the law on intimidation. But I am more concerned about what the authorities are going to do about his persistent bowling from wide of the return crease. Croft is difficult enough to play at the best of times, because of his angled delivery into the body from over the stumps. But when he bowls from so wide that his left foot is outside the return crease, then I feel that the law as it stands allows him an unfair advantage, and that the ICC should examine the rule before more bowlers start to emulate him. The whole idea of the return crease is that the bowler should deliver from within it. This is fundamental to the game. If there were no return crease, bowlers could be firing in at you from mid-off or wherever they wished. In Antigua Crofty was bowling from so wide of the stumps that he was actually disappearing off the sight screen. The ball was appearing out of the crowd, and at least two England players were bowled with balls they never 'picked up'. Croft seems to fancy himself as a mean, moody individual, something of a caricature of the fast bowler who rarely talks to anyone and loves to hate. I happen to think it's all a bit of a show, but in any case it's a sad image that he can do without.

Chris Old has a history of injuries and had more than his fair share again. It's a genuine problem for him but there comes a time when you simply have to cut your losses and go for the man who is reliably fit; I fear it could be the last time he is picked for an overseas tour, which would be a waste of a very fine bowler. Miller didn't fare a great deal better in terms of playing days; he was ill later in the tour but he played only four days' cricket after being named as vice-captain, which was obviously distressing for him and slightly ludicrous as far as the needs of the team were concerned. A vice-captain, surely, should do more than organize the nets and act as a selector! I am not knocking Miller, but where was the sense in making him vice-captain without the assurance that he was an automatic choice, injuries apart, for the side?

I am a strong supporter of Bairstow, but it was a soul-destroying tour for him. He went out as England's number one wicket-keeper and returned knowing that his career at the highest level could be finished; he was very disappointed, very downhearted and it was to his great credit that he kept his spirits up. Having lost his place to Downton, Bairstow will find it terribly hard to fight back, harder than getting there in the first place. But he is a fighter by nature, capable of putting together the sort of performances which will force the selectors to keep him in mind; he must at least aim to demand a place on next winter's tour of India.

Politics and sport never seem to be far apart these days, and there's no need for me to rake over the details of the Robin Jackman business. But one thing is certain: Jackman will be remembered as long as cricket is played, as long as politicians and sportsmen continue to bounce off one another – which promises to be some time yet. It's ironic really that Jackman had to wait so long for the opportunity to become famous, or some might say infamous; I'm sure he would have preferred to be remembered as the man whose wickets helped England to victory in a Caribbean series . . . still, that's the way it goes.

I have played and coached in South Africa myself and I know some people consider that to be wrong, a form of support for apartheid, even if only by implication. It's a complicated issue and I don't claim to be able to sort it out or even give my own position in a few well-chosen words. The critics always seem to have their arguments off pat. But let me say quite clearly that I hate apartheid as much as I love South Africa. I detest the system just as I detest Communism; yet I confess I would love to go to Russia or China for a visit.

If that is illogical, it's no more illogical than the stand taken by governments who trade with communist countries, or have diplomatic relations with regimes they publicly frown upon. Governments who are supposed to be expert in these matters don't seem to be able to agree that isolation is the answer, so why should sportsmen carry the can?

There is some evidence that sporting contacts with South Africa have helped, even in a small way, to break down the racial barriers there. West Indians play with and against South Africans in English county cricket, and I don't suppose for a moment that they consider that by doing so they are suggesting approval of apartheid. Croft, Lloyd and Kallicharran come from Guyana, whose political attitude towards South Africa is pretty plain – but are they racists? It's nonsense to suggest it.

The Gleneagles Accord leaves a great deal of room for personal decision, as you would expect in a democratic system. If a British government actually bans sporting contacts with South Africa – and I guess they would have to include the communist bloc if they were consistent – then I would accept that ban and follow the instructions of the elected government. I imagine at the same time they would extend the ban to any form of contact with those regimes, including trade and foreign relations; that would only be consistent.

And it is a bad joke that the political pot should be stirred by Guyana of all places. Their track record in human rights is laughable; talk about the pot and the kettle. . . .

The West Indies Cricket Board has an unusually difficult task because it deals with several governments, and who knows what politicians will do next? But it must be in a position to make some guarantees, otherwise no tour will be safe from interference once it has got under way. I'm inclined to think we should have come home as soon as Guyana refused to accept our choice of players; that might at least have brought matters to a head. On the other hand two wrongs probably do not make a right, and we were looking for cricket, not confrontation.

Ian Botham's captaincy attracted a great deal of publicity and even controversy, partly because England have developed something of a fixation regarding their captains and partly because Botham is the kind of character who will always be hard to ignore.

The more I read and hear about the England captaincy, the more I am convinced that we have our priorities wrong. There is a great deal of talk about leadership quality, popularity, the ability to pull the team together – and I am not suggesting that they are unimportant. But captaining England against seasoned, capable Test countries is also a matter of experience and technical know-how, and I believe we simply do not put enough emphasis on that. Ian Botham suffered in West Indies – and England suffered as a result – from his lack of experience and technical skill as a captain on the field.

It was inevitable when you consider Botham's experience at Test level – and I am not speaking with the advantages of hindsight. I said before he became England's captain that he needed more time as a player or we would waste the best of him; I still believe that, and Botham knows it because I have discussed it with him.

Nobody – not even a player as highly talented as Botham – can expect to cram into three Test years the experience and worldliness which most county captains take ten years or more to sharpen into a fine edge. It is illogical to expect it, inevitable to criticize his mistakes and equally inevitable that Botham will become defensive and attempt to justify himself.

When he returned from West Indies, for example, Botham replied to criticisms of his personal performances by pointing out that he had taken most wickets on tour. He insisted that he had led England twice against the best team in the world and that he was learning all the time as a captain.

Fair enough, but facts are facts. Botham's haul of Test wickets on tour was fifteen; given enough time and enough overs I would take fifteen wickets – anybody would. He did not strike out West Indies' major batsmen; more often than not he cleaned up the tail. Quite simply we lost him as a player – and he is far too good a player, in a team not bursting with world-class performers, for that to be an acceptable state of affairs. No one disputes the fact that West Indies are the best in the world, but as I have already said there was little real evidence that England ran them close or lost with a great deal of distinction. And the fact that Botham is learning is little consolation in the intensely competitive and demanding atmosphere of a Test match. Hard as he tries – and let nobody doubt his commitment – I do not believe that England can afford a captain with L-plates.

None of this is Botham's fault except that, like all young men, he wants things to happen too quickly. He should have been encouraged to take a longer view and I believe he should have been groomed for three or four years longer; that would have been in his best interests and in the best interests of English cricket.

Beach cricket at Bathsheba, Barbados.

Had Botham been given, say, four years without the responsibility of captaincy, he would undoubtedly have made a tremendous impression in terms of personal achievement.

I think he would have scored a mountain of runs and gone a long way towards becoming the record-holder for Test wickets; and at the same time he would have matured as a player and a person to the point where the captaincy was his as a natural progression. By his late twenties he would have been experienced and weathered enough to have taken it in his stride and done it without attracting the controversy which sometimes dogged him on this tour. He would have been in command of his game and of himself, and ready, as Richie Benaud was, to fulfil himself as a player and as a captain, and to be remembered as one of the all-time greats.

That is my view of how Ian Botham should have been allowed to develop, for his own good and for the good of England. Instead his lack of tactical expertise was exposed and English cricket was plunged into another captaincy controversy – not entirely of his making but imposed by the system which seems to have developed a preconceived idea of what a captain should be.

A personality, preferably but not necessarily a good player, a man for the media with bags of flair and charisma. Experience and hard-headed professionalism seem to drop lower and lower in importance; the identikit picture is entitled The Great Leader, and that is what England now expect their captains to be.

But when England hit a low ebb in the past they turned for salvation to two men whose tactical appreciation of the game was second to none – to Brian Close and Ray Illingworth. Both had success because they were respected as shrewd students of the game, and that is all; they were not Great Leaders bred in some fanciful academy in the sky. Each was a disciplinarian, firm enough to command the respect of the side and probably to inspire fear in many members of it. Above all they knew cricket, and their success against good Test opposition was a direct result of that.

Botham is too valuable a player to be spoiled by bitterness. The Caribbean tour was not a great success for him, but there are other battles to be fought, other tours to be undertaken. Not long ago Botham was being hailed as the greatest all-rounder since Keith Miller; I should hate him to lose the substance in search of a dream he may not yet be ready to achieve.

Tour Record and Statistics

PRESIDENT'S YOUNG WEST INDIES XI v. ENGLAND XI
Played at Guaracara Park, Pointe-a-Pierre, 23, 24, 25 and 26 January 1981.

England XI won by 190 runs.

ENGLAND XI

Batsman	Dismissal	Runs	2nd innings	Runs
B. C. Rose	c Payne b Marshall	0	b Marshall	43
G. Boycott	b Harper	87	b Harper	87
D. I. Gower	c Mattis b Harper	187		
M. W. Gatting	b Harper	94		
R. O. Butcher	c & b Harper	42	(6) not out	20
†I. T. Botham	b Harper	11	(5) c Payne b Alleyne	33
P. Willey	not out	16	(4) c Williams b Marshall	10
G. Miller	not out	12	(7) not out	4
‡D. L. Bairstow			(3) lbw b Marshall	0
C. M. Old	did not bat			
G. R. Dilley				
Extras	(B7 LB7 W2 NB18)	34	(LB5 W3 NB3)	11
Total	(6 wkts dec)	483	(5 wkts dec)	208

BOWLING

	O	M	R	W	O	M	R	W
Marshall	25	9	54	1	18	4	48	3
Alleyne	27	5	62	0	19	1	46	1
Harper	43	6	142	5	23	5	58	1
Daniel	21	6	58	0	16	5	36	0
Austin	39	8	133	0	6	2	9	0

FALL OF WICKETS

1–0, 2–198, 3–396, 4–404, 5 446, 6–457

1–114, 2–114, 3–134, 4–179, 5–187

PRESIDENT'S XI

Batsman	Dismissal	Runs	2nd innings	Runs
R. A. Austin	c Miller b Botham	25	b Miller	19
R. S. Gabriel	run out	22	c Bairstow b Miller	22
†T. Mohammed	b Miller	37	b Willey	35
E. H. Mattis	c Miller b Dilley	41	b Miller	46
T. R. O. Payne	st Bairstow b Miller	1	b Miller	1
H. L. Alleyne	b Willey	33	(10) lbw b Miller	6
J. Dujon	not out	105	(6) c Botham b Willey	1
‡S. I. Williams	c Old b Miller	13	c Gatting b Willey	4
M. D. Marshall	c Old b Botham	27	(7) run out	31
R. A. Harper	lbw b Botham	0	(9) lbw b Miller	0
A. E. Daniel	c Gower b Old	0	not out	0
Extras	(B7 LB4 NB5)	16	(B8 LB4 NB4)	16
Total		320		181

BOWLING

	O	M	R	W	O	M	R	W
Dilley	22	1	104	1	10	3	18	0
Old	13.3	4	34	1	4	0	27	0
Botham	12	0	43	3	4	0	21	0
Miller	26	8	69	3	26.2	9	70	6
Willey	16	3	54	1	17	6	29	3

FALL OF WICKETS

1–38, 2–68, 3–123, 4–127, 5–133, 6–193, 7–230, 8–319, 9–319, 10–320

1–37, 2–56, 3–93, 4–94, 5–95, 6–159, 7–170, 8–171, 9–175, 10–181

President's XI won the toss.

Umpires: C. Cumberbatch and S. E. Parris.

WINDWARD ISLANDS v. ENGLAND XI (40-over match)
Played at Arnos Vale, St Vincent, 1 February 1981.

England XI won by 16 runs.

ENGLAND XI

G. A. Gooch	c & b Kentish	13
B. C. Rose	c Cadette b Davis	1
R. O. Butcher	c Hinds b Kentish	44
†I. T. Botham	st Cadette b Hinds	31
D. I. Gower	b Jack	14
M. W. Gatting	c Browne b Hinds	16
G. B. Stevenson	c Cadette b Jack	0
‡P. R. Downton	not out	23
J. E. Emburey	c Shillingford b Davis	3
G. R. Dilley	c Sebastien b Hinds	7
R. G. D. Willis	not out	0
Extras	(B5 W1 NB8)	14
Total	(9 wkts, 40 overs)	166

BOWLING

	O	M	R	W
Davis	8	0	17	2
Jack	8	1	23	2
Warner	8	1	32	0
Kentish	8	1	21	2
Hinds	8	0	59	3

FALL OF WICKETS
1–6, 2–43, 3–76, 4–111, 5–116, 6–116, 7–138, 8–152, 9–161

WINDWARD ISLANDS

L. C. Sebastien	c Botham b Willis	9
L. D. John	c Botham b Dilley	17
M. Warner	c Botham b Gooch	24
†I. T. Shillingford	c Gower b Stevenson	26
C. Browne	lbw b Botham	16
S. J. Hinds	c sub (Miller) b Dilley	7
J. Guiste	c Rose b Botham	3
‡I. Cadette	not out	17
W. W. Davis	c Gooch b Dilley	7
T. Kentish	lbw b Botham	0
J. Jack	not out	4
Extras	(B1 LB8 W1 NB10)	20
Total	(9 wkts, 40 overs)	150

BOWLING

	O	M	R	W
Willis	7	0	30	1
Dilley	8	0	28	3
Stevenson	8	1	22	1
Emburey	8	1	18	0
Botham	8	0	30	3
Gooch	1	0	2	1

FALL OF WICKETS
1–31, 2–31, 3–76, 4–107, 5–111, 6–118, 7–118, 8–136, 9–136

England XI won the toss.
Umpires: P. Alleyne and M. Hippolyte.

WINDWARD ISLANDS v. ENGLAND XI (40-over match)

Played at Arnos Vale, St Vincent, 2 February 1981.

England XI won by 6 wickets.

WINDWARD ISLANDS

L. C. Sebastien	lbw b Botham	9
L. D. John	lbw b Gooch	58
†I. T. Shillingford	c Gooch b Willey	31
M. Warner	c & b Gooch	3
C. Browne	b Old	20
H. Williams	st Bairstow b Gooch	9
‡I. Cadette	run out	10
S. J. Hinds	not out	18
W. W. Davis	lbw b Old	0
K. Hobson	b Stevenson	4
J. Jack	run out	5
Extras	(B3 LB8 NB5)	16
Total	(53.2 overs)	183

BOWLING

	O	M	R	W
Old	9	0	34	2
Botham	7	1	21	1
Stevenson	9.2	0	25	1
Willey	11	1	23	1
Emburey	11	0	41	0
Gooch	6	1	23	3

FALL OF WICKETS
1–33, 2–90, 3–109, 4–116, 5–130, 6–151, 7–156, 8–157, 9–174, 10–183.

ENGLAND XI

G. A. Gooch	c sub (Guiste) b Warner	50
G. Boycott	not out	85
B. C. Rose	b Jack	3
D. I. Gower	st Cadette b Hobson	6
P. Willey	c sub (Guiste) b Hobson	11
G. B. Stevenson	not out	20
R. O. Butcher		
†I. T. Botham		
‡D. L. Bairstow	did not bat	
J. E. Emburey		
C. M. Old		
Extras	(B1 LB2 W1 NB6)	10
Total	(4 wkts, 52.5 overs)	185

BOWLING

	O	M	R	W
Davis	10	3	27	0
Jack	9.5	3	26	1
Hobson	11	1	46	2
Warner	11	0	46	1
Hinds	11	0	30	0

FALL OF WICKETS
1–89, 2–118, 3–132, 4–152

Windward Islands won the toss.
Umpires: P. Alleyne and M. Hippolyte.

WEST INDIES v. ENGLAND (One-day International)
Played at Arnos Vale, St Vincent, 4 February 1981.

West Indies won by 2 runs.

WEST INDIES

D. L. Haynes	c Emburey b Stevenson	34
S. F. A. Bacchus	c Stevenson b Old	1
E. H. Mattis	run out	62
A. I. Kallicharran	b Emburey	2
†C. H. Lloyd	c Willey b Stevenson	2
H. A. Gomes	b Willey	8
‡D. A. Murray	b Gooch	1
A. M. E. Roberts	st Bairstow b Gooch	2
J. Garner	run out	4
M. A. Holding	b Botham	1
C. E. H. Croft	not out	2
Extras	(B4 W1 NB3)	8
Total	(47.2 overs)	127

BOWLING

	O	M	R	W
Old	5	4	8	1
Botham	8	1	32	1
Stevenson	8.2	2	18	2
Emburey	10	4	20	1
Willey	10	1	29	1
Gooch	6	1	12	2

FALL OF WICKETS
1–5, 2–48, 3–51, 4–58, 5–89, 6–90, 7–102, 8–110, 9–120, 10–127

ENGLAND

G. A. Gooch	c Lloyd b Roberts	11
G. Boycott	c Mattis b Croft	2
P. Willey	c Murray b Croft	0
D. I. Gower	c Haynes b Kallicharran	23
R. O. Butcher	c Murray b Croft	1
†I. T. Botham	c Murray b Croft	60
M. W. Gatting	b Croft	3
‡D. L. Bairstow	b Croft	5
J. E. Emburey	b Holding	5
G. B. Stevenson	not out	6
C. M. Old	b Holding	1
Extras	(LB8)	8
Total		125

BOWLING

	O	M	R	W
Roberts	10	1	30	1
Holding	9.2	0	30	2
Croft	9	4	15	6
Garner	10	2	17	0
Kallicharran	10	2	25	1

FALL OF WICKETS
1–14, 2–14, 3–14, 4–15, 5–80, 6–88, 7–111, 8–114, 9–123, 10–125

England won the toss.
Umpires: D. M. Archer and S. Mohammed.

TRINIDAD AND TOBAGO v. ENGLAND XI
Played at Queen's Park Oval, Port-of-Spain, 7, 8, 9–10 February 1981.
Match drawn.

ENGLAND XI

G. A. Gooch	b Nanan	117
G. Boycott	b Joseph	70
B. C. Rose	c Murray b Joseph	11
D. I. Gower	c Nanan b Daniel	77
G. Miller	run out	19
†I. T. Botham	c Murray b Daniel	0
P. Willey	b Joseph	28
‡P. R. Downton	lbw b Joseph	10
J. E. Emburey	c Gabriel b Joseph	1
G. B. Stevenson	b Nanan	0
G. R. Dilley	not out	15
Extras	(B4 LB2 W1)	7
Total		355

BOWLING

	O	M	R	W
Burns	16	5	33	0
Gomes	7	4	3	0
Nanan	43	9	116	2
Daniel	23.3	5	79	2
Joseph	51	11	116	5
Logie	1	0	1	0

FALL OF WICKETS
1–173, 2–201, 3–201, 4–243, 5–243, 6 292, 7–320, 8–324, 9–325, 10–355

TRINIDAD AND TOBAGO

R. S. Gabriel	lbw b Botham	38
K. R. Bainey	b Botham	0
H. A. Gomes	st Downton b Miller	75
A. L. Logie	c Downton b Gooch	30
A. Rajah	lbw b Dilley	19
T. Cliffy	b Stevenson	61
†‡D. L. Murray	c Emburey b Willey	75
R. Nanan	not out	66
A. G. Burns	b Willey	1
A. E. Daniel	not out	0
H. Joseph	did not bat	
Extras	(B2 LB13 NB12)	27
Total	(8 wkts dec)	392

BOWLING

	O	M	R	W
Dilley	21	8	63	1
Botham	16	4	44	2
Emburey	32	11	72	0
Stevenson	16	3	46	1
Miller	25	6	65	1
Willey	20	3	61	2
Gooch	12	6	14	1

FALL OF WICKETS
1–1, 2–101, 3–148, 4–170, 5–205, 6–266, 7–388, 8–392

Trinidad and Tobago won the toss.
Umpires: C. Cumberbatch and C. Shaffrali.

FIRST TEST
WEST INDIES v. ENGLAND
Played at Queen's Park Oval, Port-of-Spain, 13, 14, 16, 17 February 1981.

West Indies won by an innings and 79 runs.

WEST INDIES

C. G. Greenidge	c Botham b Emburey	84
D. L. Haynes	c & b Emburey	96
I. V. A. Richards	c Gower b Miller	29
E. H. Mattis	c Miller b Emburey	0
H. A. Gomes	c Downton b Old	5
†C. H. Lloyd	b Emburey	64
‡D. A. Murray	c Botham b Emburey	46
A. M. E. Roberts	not out	50
M. A. Holding	lbw b Botham	26
J. Garner	lbw b Botham	4
C. E. H. Croft	not out	4
Extras	(LB15 NB3)	18
Total	(9 wkts dec)	426

BOWLING

	O	M	R	W
Dilley	28	4	73	0
Botham	28	6	113	2
Old	16	4	49	1
Emburey	52	16	124	5
Miller	18	4	42	1
Gooch	2	0	3	0
Willey	3	1	4	0

FALL OF WICKETS

1–168, 2–203, 3–203, 4–215, 5–257, 6–332, 7–348, 8–383, 9–393

ENGLAND

G. A. Gooch	b Roberts	41	lbw b Holding	5
G. Boycott	c Richards b Croft	30	c Haynes b Holding	70
B. C. Rose	c Haynes b Garner	10	c Murray b Holding	5
D. I. Gower	lbw b Croft	48	c Murray b Roberts	27
G. Miller	c Murray b Croft	3	c Greenidge b Croft	8
†I. T. Botham	lbw b Croft	0	c Holding b Richards	16
P. Willey	lbw b Garner	13	c Lloyd b Garner	21
‡P. R. Downton	b Gomes	4	c Lloyd b Roberts	5
J. E. Emburey	not out	17	b Roberts	1
G. R. Dilley	b Croft	0	not out	1
C. M. Old	b Roberts	1	c sub (Bacchus) b Garner	0
Extras	(B4 LB4 NB3)	11	(B1 LB3 NB6)	10
Total		178		169

BOWLING

	O	M	R	W	O	M	R	W
Roberts	13	3	41	2	21	7	41	3
Holding	11	3	29	0	18	6	38	3
Croft	22	6	40	5	16	5	26	1
Garner	23	8	37	2	25	10	31	2
Richards	7	2	16	0	10	6	9	1
Gomes	2	1	4	1	9	4	14	0

FALL OF WICKETS

1–45, 2–63, 3–110, 4–121, 5–127, 6–143, 7–151, 8–163, 9–167, 10–178

1–19, 2–25, 3–86, 4–103, 5–134, 6–142, 7–163, 8–167, 9–169, 10–169

England won the toss.
Umpires: C. Cumberbatch and D. Sang Hue.

WEST INDIES v. ENGLAND (One-day International)
Played at Albion Sports Complex, Berbice, 26 February 1981.

West Indies won by 6 wickets.

ENGLAND

G. A. Gooch	c Murray b Roberts	11
G. Boycott	b Richards	7
M. W. Gatting	c Mattis b Gomes	29
D. I. Gower	b Gomes	3
R. O. Butcher	c Haynes b Gomes	5
†I. T. Botham	b Roberts	27
P. Willey	b Croft	21
‡D. L. Bairstow	b Croft	16
J. E. Emburey	c Croft b Holding	0
G. B. Stevenson	not out	8
G. R. Dilley	b Croft	3
Extras	(B4 LB2 NB1)	7
Total	(47.2 overs)	137

BOWLING

	O	M	R	W
Roberts	7	0	17	2
Holding	7	1	13	1
Richards	10	0	26	1
Croft	6.2	1	9	3
Gomes	10	2	30	3
Garner	7	2	35	0

FALL OF WICKETS
1–16, 2–27, 3–34, 4–59, 5–62, 6–108, 7 112, 8 119, 9 132, 10 137

WEST INDIES

C. G. Greenidge	run out	2
D. L. Haynes	c Gooch b Emburey	48
I. V. A. Richards	c Stevenson b Dilley	3
E. H. Mattis	b Emburey	24
H. A. Gomes	not out	22
†C. H. Lloyd	not out	25
‡D. A. Murray		
A. M. E. Roberts		
J. Garner	} did not bat	
M. A. Holding		
C. E. H. Croft		
Extras	(B4 LB8 NB2)	14
Total	(4 wkts, 39.3 overs)	138

BOWLING

	O	M	R	W
Dilley	5	0	21	1
Botham	7	1	24	0
Stevenson	6	0	21	0
Emburey	10	4	22	2
Gooch	2	0	8	0
Willey	9	0	23	0
Gower	0.3	0	5	0

FALL OF WICKETS
1–6, 2–11, 3–85, 4–90

West Indies won the toss.
Umpires: D. Narine and C. F. Vyfhuis.
Men of the Match: H. A. Gomes (W.I.), J. E. Emburey (E.).

BARBADOS v. ENGLAND XI
Played at Kensington Oval, Bridgetown, 5 March 1981.
England XI won by 11 runs.

ENGLAND XI

G. A. Gooch	hit wkt b Garner	84
G. Boycott	c Murray b King	14
M. W. Gatting	b King	25
D. I. Gower	c Murray b Garner	39
R. O. Butcher	b Daniel	9
†I. T. Botham	b Daniel	12
P. Willey	not out	1
‡D. L. Bairstow	not out	6
G. B. Stevenson		
J. E. Emburey	} did not bat	
C. M. Old		
Extras	(B5 LB11 NB1)	17
Total	(6 wkts, 50 overs)	207

BOWLING

	O	M	R	W
Clarke	10	4	14	0
Daniel	10	1	34	2
Garner	10	0	38	2
King	10	2	37	2
Padmore	9	1	58	0
L. N. Reifer	1	0	9	0

FALL OF WICKETS
1–30, 2–97, 3–161, 4–178, 5–200, 6–201

BARBADOS

C. G. Greenidge	c Old b Stevenson	1
A. T. Greenidge	lbw b Botham	9
E. N. Trotman	c Gatting b Stevenson	9
G. N. Reifer	c Willey b Botham	55
C. L. King	b Willey	43
L. N. Reifer	c Emburey b Botham	38
S. T. Clarke	b Botham	4
J. Garner	c Botham b Stevenson	9
‡D. A. Murray	b Stevenson	8
†A. L. Padmore	b Old	13
W. W. Daniel	not out	2
Extras	(LB3 NB2)	5
Total	(49.3 overs)	196

BOWLING

	O	M	R	W
Botham	10	2	30	4
Stevenson	10	2	38	4
Gooch	6	0	31	0
Old	5.3	0	29	1
Emburey	9	2	40	0
Willey	9	3	23	1

FALL OF WICKETS
1–1, 2–15, 3–25, 4–92, 5–158, 6–158, 7–169, 8–177, 9–185, 10–196

Barbados won the toss.
Umpires: L. Barker and S. E. Parris.

BARBADOS v. ENGLAND XI
Played at Kensington Oval, Bridgetown, 7, 8, 9, 10 March 1981.
Match drawn.

ENGLAND XI

G. A. Gooch	b Clarke	18	c Murray b Daniel		29
G. Boycott	c Trotman b Padmore	77	c King b Clarke		13
M. W. Gatting	c Murray b Marshall	11	b Marshall		22
D. I. Gower	run out	18	c Clarke b Padmore		44
R. O. Butcher	c Greenidge b Padmore	43	lbw b Marshall		32
†I. T. Botham	c Murray b Padmore	40	c Murray b Marshall		0
P. Willey	c Murray b Clarke	51	not out		34
‡D. L. Bairstow	run out	22	not out		26
G. B. Stevenson	b Clarke	2			
R. D. Jackman	b Padmore	5			
J. E. Emburey	not out	0			
Extras	(B2 LB2 NB7)	11	(B9 LB9 NB1)		19
Total		298	(6 wkts dec)		219

BOWLING

	O	M	R	W	O	M	R	W
Clarke	35	9	67	3	23	6	55	1
Daniel	27	4	82	0	22	5	51	1
Marshall	19	6	42	1	18	7	25	3
King	13	2	25	0	7	3	9	0
Padmore	58.4	10	71	4	22	5	51	1
G. N. Reifer					1	0	7	0
Haynes					1	0	2	0

FALL OF WICKETS
1–24, 2–47, 3–92, 4–168, 5–179, 6–252, 7–282, 8–284, 9–294, 10 298
1–35, 2–63, 3–83, 4–144, 5–144, 6–168

BARBADOS

C. G. Greenidge	c Botham b Emburey	45
D. L. Haynes	c Bairstow b Jackman	44
G. N. Reifer	c Gower b Jackman	71
E. N. Trotman	c Botham b Emburey	10
C. L. King	lbw b Botham	76
L. N. Reifer	c Bairstow b Jackman	4
‡D. A. Murray	c Butcher b Emburey	19
M. D. Marshall	not out	29
†A. L. Padmore	c Butcher b Emburey	0
S. T. Clarke	b Jackman	0
W. W. Daniel	b Emburey	21
Extras	(B2 LB8 W1 NB4)	15
Total		334

BOWLING

	O	M	R	W
Botham	24	6	79	1
Stevenson	13	2	66	0
Emburey	49.4	13	92	5
Jackman	25	6	68	4
Willey	10	4	14	0

FALL OF WICKETS
1–83, 2–100, 3–124, 4–254, 5–262, 6–269, 7–296, 8–296, 9 296, 10–334

Barbados won the toss.
Umpires: D. M. Archer and S. E. Parris.

THIRD TEST
WEST INDIES v. ENGLAND
Played at Kensington Oval, Bridgetown, 13, 14, 15, 17 and 18 March 1981.
West Indies won by 298 runs.

WEST INDIES

C. G. Greenidge	c Gooch b Jackman	14	lbw b Dilley	0
D. L. Haynes	c Bairstow b Jackman	25	lbw b Botham	25
I. V. A. Richards	c Botham b Dilley	0	(4) not out	182
E. H. Mattis	lbw b Botham	16	(5) c Butcher b Jackman	24
†C. H. Lloyd	c Gooch b Jackman	100	(7) lbw b Botham	66
H. A. Gomes	c Botham b Dilley	58	run out	34
‡D. A. Murray	c Bairstow b Dilley	9	(9) not out	5
A. M. E. Roberts	c Bairstow b Botham	14	c Bairstow b Botham	0
J. Garner	c Bairstow b Botham	15		
M. A. Holding	c Gatting b Botham	0		
C. E. H. Croft	not out	0	(3) c Boycott b Jackman	33
Extras	(B4 LB6 W2 NB2)	14	(B3 LB7)	10
Total		265	(7 wkts dec)	379

BOWLING

	O	M	R	W	O	M	R	W
Dilley	23	7	51	3	25	3	111	1
Botham	25.1	5	77	4	29	5	102	3
Jackman	22	4	65	3	25	5	76	2
Emburey	18	4	45	0	24	7	57	0
Gooch	2	0	13	0				
Willey					6	0	23	0

FALL OF WICKETS

1–24, 2–25, 3–47, 4–65, 5–219, 6–224, 7–236, 8–258, 9–258, 10–265

1–0, 2–57, 3–71, 4–130, 5–212, 6–365, 7–365

ENGLAND

G. A. Gooch	b Garner	26	c Garner b Croft	116
G. Boycott	b Holding	0	c Garner b Holding	1
M. W. Gatting	c Greenidge b Roberts	2	b Holding	0
D. I. Gower	c Mattis b Croft	17	b Richards	54
R. O. Butcher	c Richards b Croft	17	lbw b Richards	2
†I. T. Botham	c Murray b Holding	26	c Lloyd b Roberts	1
P. Willey	not out	19	lbw c Croft	17
‡D. L. Bairstow	c Mattis b Holding	0	c Murray b Croft	2
J. E. Emburey	c Lloyd b Roberts	0	b Garner	9
R. D. Jackman	c Roberts b Croft	7	b Garner	7
G. R. Dilley	c Gomes b Croft	0	not out	7
Extras	(B1 LB1 NB6)	8	(B1 LB3 NB4)	8
Total		122	...	224

BOWLING

	O	M	R	W	O	M	R	W
Roberts	11	3	29	2	20	6	42	1
Holding	11	7	16	3	19	6	46	2
Croft	13.5	2	39	4	19	1	65	3
Garner	12	5	30	1	16.2	6	39	2
Richards					17	6	24	2

FALL OF WICKETS

1–6, 2–11, 3–40, 4–55, 5–72, 6–94, 7–94, 8–97, 9–122, 10–122

1–2, 2–2, 3–122, 4–134, 5–139, 6–196, 7–198, 8–201, 9–213, 10–224

England won the toss.
Umpires: D. M. Archer and D. Sang Hue.

LEEWARD ISLANDS v. ENGLAND XI
Played at Sturge Park, Plymouth, Montserrat, 21, 22, 23 and 24 March 1981.
England XI won by 5 wickets.

LEEWARD ISLANDS

A. L. Kelly	c Old b Stevenson	72	c Downton b Old	17
†V. Amory	c Gatting b Stevenson	37	b Miller	56
E. E. Lewis	c Downton b Dilley	1	lbw b Miller	36
‡S. I. Williams	b Stevenson	5	b Dilley	62
H. E. Ryan	b Dilley	0	lbw b Jackman	0
D. R. Parry	c Butcher b Dilley	1	c Miller b Old	21
J. E. Archibald	c Downton b Stevenson	7	lbw b Dilley	2
N. C. Guishard	not out	8	not out	42
A. C. M. White	c Bairstow b Stevenson	18	c & b Old	4
J. B. Harris	c Old b Dilley	0	b Miller	5
J. C. Newton	b Dilley	0	c Downton b Dilley	6
Extras	(B2 LB4 NB6)	12	(LB6 NB6)	12
Total		161		263

BOWLING

	O	M	R	W	O	M	R	W
Dilley	13.4	2	48	5	16	5	50	3
Old	5	2	18	0	18	3	60	3
Jackman	5	0	22	0	12	2	35	1
Stevenson	15	5	50	5	11	1	64	0
Miller	2	0	11	0	12	2	42	3

FALL OF WICKETS
1–102, 2–111, 3–124, 4–125, 5–128, 6–125, 7–135, 8–157, 9–161, 10–161

1–35, 2–106, 3–123, 4–124, 5–190, 6–198, 7–202, 8–216, 9–235, 10–263

ENGLAND XI

G. Boycott	run out	72	lbw b Guishard	15
†P. R. Downton	c Williams b Harris	0	c Guishard b Ryan	9
C. W. J. Athey	c Parry b White	41	c Kelly b Parry	37
M. W. Gatting	c Archibald b Guishard	4	c Kelly b Guishard	0
R. O. Butcher	b Guishard	5	not out	77
†G. Miller	not out	91	lbw b Newton	14
D. L. Bairstow	c Amory b Harris	0	not out	14
G. B. Stevenson	b Guishard	3		
R. D. Jackman	b White	17		
C. M. Old	b Harris	4		
G. R. Dilley	c Williams b Guishard	0		
Extras	(B6 LB3 W1 NB4)	14	(B5 LB1 NB2)	8
Total		251	(5 wkts)	174

BOWLING

	O	M	R	W	O	M	R	W
Harris	23	6	56	3	12	3	39	0
White	20	6	63	2	5	1	16	0
Parry	22	6	53	0	14	3	48	1
Newton	9	2	18	0	6	1	23	1
Guishard	21.3	5	34	4	15	4	23	2
Archibald	4	0	13	0				
Ryan					6	3	16	1
Amory					0.1	0	1	0

FALL OF WICKETS
1–3, 2–113, 3–120, 4–126, 5–128, 6–143, 7–154, 8–222, 9–227, 10–251

1–14, 2–45, 3–45, 4–73, 5–109

England won the toss.
Umpires: T. Brambell and P. White.

FOURTH TEST
WEST INDIES v. ENGLAND
Played at the Antigua Recreation Grounds, St John's, Antigua, 27, 28, 29 and 31 March and 1 April 1981.
Match drawn.

ENGLAND

G. A. Gooch	run out	33	c Greenidge b Richards	83
G. Boycott	c Murray b Croft	38	not out	104
C. W. J. Athey	c Lloyd b Croft	2	c Richards b Croft	1
D. I. Gower	c Mattis b Holding	32	c Murray b Croft	22
R. O. Butcher	c Greenidge b Croft	20		
†I. T. Botham	c Lloyd b Croft	1		
P. Willey	not out	102	(5) not out	1
‡P. R. Downton	c Murray b Garner	13		
J. E. Emburey	b Croft	10		
G. B. Stevenson	b Croft	1		
G. R. Dilley	c Murray b Holding	2		
Extras	(B6 LB7 W1 NB3)	17	(B11 LB3 NB9)	23
Total		271	(3 wkts)	234

BOWLING

	O	M	R	W	O	M	R	W
Roberts	22	4	59	0	17	5	39	0
Holding	18.2	4	51	2	9	2	21	0
Garner	16	5	44	1	15	3	33	0
Croft	25	5	74	6	16	4	39	2
Richards	9	4	26	0	22	7	54	1
Gomes					13	5	21	0
Mattis					1	0	4	0

FALL OF WICKETS
1–60, 2–70, 3–95, 4–135, 5–138, 6–138, 7–176, 8–233, 9–235, 10–271
1–144, 2–146, 3–217

WEST INDIES

C. G. Greenidge	c Athey b Stevenson	63
D. L. Haynes	c Downton b Botham	4
I. V. A. Richards	c Emburey b Dilley	114
E. H. Mattis	c Butcher b Botham	71
H. A. Gomes	c Gower b Botham	12
†C. H. Lloyd	c Downton b Stevenson	58
‡D. A. Murray	c Boycott b Botham	1
A. M. E. Roberts	b Stevenson	13
J. Garner	c Butcher b Dilley	46
M. A. Holding	not out	58
C. E. H. Croft	not out	17
Extras	(B1 LB7 W1 NB2)	11
Total	(9 wkts dec)	468

BOWLING

	O	M	R	W
Dilley	25	5	99	2
Botham	37	6	127	4
Stevenson	33	5	111	3
Emburey	35	12	85	0
Willey	20	8	30	0
Gooch	2	2	0	0
Boycott	3	2	5	0

FALL OF WICKETS
1–12, 2–133, 3–241, 4–268, 5–269, 6–271, 7–296, 8–379, 9–401

England won the toss.
Umpires: D. M. Archer and S. Mohammed.

.

JAMAICA v. ENGLAND XI
Played at Sabina Park, Kingston, 4, 5, 6 and 7 April 1981.

Match drawn.

ENGLAND XI

Batsman	Dismissal	Score	2nd Innings	Score
G. A. Gooch	st Dujon b Austin	31	c A. B. Williams b Austin	122
G. Boycott	c Mattis b Malcolm	98	(10) not out	4
C. W. J. Athey	lbw b J. A. Williams	11	lbw b Tucker	25
D. I. Gower	run out	24	c Austin b Malcolm	0
R. O. Butcher	c Tomlinson b Tucker	44	st Dujon b Mattis	51
M. W. Gatting	c Dujon b Tucker	93	c Dujon b Mattis	42
†I. T. Botham	c Austin b Tomlinson	26	c Malcolm b Mattis	14
C. M. Old	c Malcolm b Tomlinson	8		
J. E. Emburey	c Austin b Malcolm	34	(8) c & b Mattis	1
R. D. Jackman	not out	0	(9) not out	11
‡P. R. Downton	absent ill	—	(2) lbw b J. A. Williams	0
Extras	(B8 LB21 W1 NB 14)	44	(B16 LB4 NB4)	24
Total		413	(8 wkts)	294

BOWLING

	O	M	R	W	O	M	R	W
J. A. Williams	22	2	77	1	16	7	28	1
Tomlinson	23	5	60	2	16	2	45	0
Austin	26	2	95	1	19	2	50	1
Malcolm	28.2	6	77	2	20	5	51	1
Tucker	21	4	60	2	25	4	69	1
Mattis					13.5	6	22	4
Neita					2	2	0	0
A. B. Williams					2	0	5	0

FALL OF WICKETS
1–55, 2–95, 3–134, 4–194, 5–278, 6–312, 7–330, 8–413, 9–413
1–1, 2–77, 3–78, 4–196, 5–257, 6–264, 7–272, 8–285

JAMAICA

Batsman	Dismissal	Score
R. A. Austin	c Butcher b Emburey	62
A. B. Williams	c Gooch b Botham	10
E. H. Mattis	b Jackman	15
†L. G. Rowe	lbw b Botham	116
‡J. Dujon	b Emburey	6
H. S. Chang	run out	12
M. C. Neita	st Downton b Emburey	67
M. A. Tucker	lbw b Emburey	36
D. O. Malcolm	c sub (Bairstow) b Emburey	6
J. A. Williams	not out	11
P. U. Tomlinson	st Downton b Emburey	7
Extras	(B1 LB3 NB16)	20
Total		368

BOWLING

	O	M	R	W
Old	6	1	20	0
Botham	23	2	111	2
Emburey	34	9	92	6
Jackman	21	6	57	1
Gooch	16	3	58	0
Gatting	3	1	10	0

FALL OF WICKETS
1–17, 2–39, 3–141, 4–153, 5–181, 6–295, 7–327, 8–335, 9–356, 10–368

England XI won the toss.
Umpires: L. Bell and J. Gayle.

FIFTH TEST
WEST INDIES v. ENGLAND
Played at Sabina Park, Kingston, 10, 11, 12, 14 and 15 April 1981.
Match drawn.

ENGLAND

G. A. Gooch	c Murray b Holding	153	c Lloyd b Marshall	3
G. Boycott	c Murray b Garner	40	c Garner b Croft	12
C. W. J. Athey	b Holding	3	c Murray b Holding	1
D. I. Gower	b Croft	22	not out	154
P. Willey	c Murray b Marshall	4	c Greenidge b Richards	67
R. O. Butcher	b Garner	32	lbw b Croft	0
†I. T. Botham	c Greenidge b Marshall	13	Garner b Holding	16
‡P. R. Downton	c Croft b Holding	0	not out	26
J. E. Emburey	b Holding	1		
R. D. Jackman	c Haynes b Holding	0		
G. R. Dilley	not out	0		
Extras	(B9 NB8)	17	(B6 LB13 NB4)	23
Total		285	(6 wkts dec)	302

BOWLING

	O	M	R	W	O	M	R	W
Holding	18	3	56	5	28	7	58	2
Marshall	16	2	49	2	5	0	15	1
Croft	17	4	92	1	29	7	80	2
Garner	20	4	43	2	24	7	46	0
Richards	12	2	29	0	23	8	48	1
Gomes					13	3	18	0
Mattis					5	1	10	0
Haynes					1	0	4	0

FALL OF WICKETS
1–93, 2–148, 3–196, 4–210, 5–249, 6–275, 7–283, 8–283, 9–284, 10–285
1–5, 2–10, 3–32, 4–168, 5–168, 6–215

WEST INDIES

C. G. Greenidge	c Botham b Dilley	62
D. L. Haynes	b Willey	84
I. V. A. Richards	c Downton b Dilley	15
E. H. Mattis	c sub·(M. W. Gatting) b Dilley	34
†C. H. Lloyd	c Downton b Jackman	95
H. A. Gomes	not out	90
‡D. A. Murray	c Gooch b Emburey	14
M. D. Marshall	b Emburey	15
J. Garner	c sub (D. L. Bairstow) b Dilley	19
M. A. Holding	c Downton b Botham	0
C. E. H. Croft	c sub (M. W. Gatting) b Botham	0
Extras	(LB8 W1 NB5)	14
Total		442

BOWLING

	O	M	R	W
Dilley	29.4	6	116	4
Botham	26.1	9	73	2
Jackman	26.2	6	57	1
Gooch	8	3	20	0
Emburey	56	23	108	2
Willey	18	3	54	1

FALL OF WICKETS
1–116, 2–136, 3–179, 4–227, 5–345, 6–372, 7–415, 8–441, 9–442, 10–442

West Indies won the toss.
Umpires: G. Cumberbatch and D. Sang Hue.

TEST AVERAGES

ENGLAND – BATTING AND FIELDING

	M	I	NO	RUNS	HIGHEST	AVGE	100	50	C	ST
G. A. Gooch	4	8	0	460	153	57.50	2	1	3	–
D. I. Gower	4	8	1	376	154	53.71	1	1	2	–
P. Willey	4	8	3	244	102	48.80	1	1	–	–
G. Boycott	4	8	1	295	104	42.14	1	1	2	–
R. O. Butcher	3	5	0	71	32	14.20	–	–	3	–
P. R. Downton	3	5	1	48	26	12.00	–	–	6	–
I. T. Botham	4	7	0	73	26	10.42	–	–	5	–
J. E. Emburey	4	6	1	38	17	7.60	–	–	2	–
R. D. Jackman	2	3	0	14	7	4.66	–	–	–	–
G. R. Dilley	4	6	3	11	7	3.66	–	–	–	–
C. W. J. Athey	2	4	0	7	3	1.75	–	–	1	–

Played in one Test: D. L. Bairstow 0, 2 (5 ct); M. W. Gatting 2, 0 (1 ct); G. Miller 3, 8 (1 ct); C. M. Old 1, 0; B. C. Rose 10, 5; G. B. Stevenson 1

ENGLAND – BOWLING

	OVERS	MDNS	RUNS	WKTS	AVERAGE	BALLS PER WICKET
I. T. Botham	145.2	31	492	15	32.80	58
R. D. Jackman	73.2	15	198	6	33.00	73
G. B. Stevenson	33	5	111	3	37.00	66
G. Miller	18	4	42	1	42.00	108
G. R. Dilley	129.4	25	450	10	45.00	77
C. M. Old	16	4	49	1	49.00	96
J. E. Emburey	185	62	419	7	59.85	158
P. Willey	47	12	111	1	111.00	282
G. A. Gooch	14	5	36	0	–	–

Also bowled: G. Boycott 3–2–5–0

WEST INDIES – BATTING AND FIELDING

	M	I	NO	RUNS	HIGHEST	AVGE	100	50	C	ST
I. V. A. Richards	4	5	1	340	182	85.00	2	–	3	–
C. H. Lloyd	4	5	0	383	100	76.60	1	4	7	–
H. A. Gomes	4	5	1	199	90	49.75	–	2	1	–
D. L. Haynes	4	5	0	234	96	46.80	–	2	3	–
C. G. Greenidge	4	5	0	223	84	44.60	–	3	6	–
E. H. Mattis	4	5	0	145	71	29.00	–	1	3	–
M. A. Holding	4	4	1	84	58	28.00	–	1	1	–
C. E. H. Croft	4	5	3	54	33	27.00	–	–	1	–
A. M. E. Roberts	3	4	1	77	50	25.66	–	1	1	–
J. Garner	4	4	0	84	46	21.00	–	–	4	–
D. A. Murray	4	5	1	75	46	18.75	–	–	13	–

Played in one Test: M. D. Marshall 15

WEST INDIES – BOWLING

	OVERS	MDNS	RUNS	WKTS	AVERAGE	BALLS PER WICKET
M. A. Holding	132.2	38	315	17	18.52	46
C. E. H. Croft	157.5	34	455	24	18.95	39
M. D. Marshall	21	2	64	3	21.33	42
J. Garner	151.2	48	303	10	30.30	90
A. M. E. Roberts	104	27	251	8	31.37	78
I. V. A. Richards	100	35	206	5	41.20	120
H. A. Gomes	37	13	57	1	57.00	222

Also bowled: D. L. Haynes 1–0–4–0; E. H. Mattis 6–1–14–0

TOUR AVERAGES

BATTING AND FIELDING

	M	I	NO	RUNS	HIGHEST	AVGE	100	50	CT	ST
G. A. Gooch	7	13	0	777	153	59.76	4	1	4	–
D. I. Gower	8	14	1	726	187	55.84	2	2	4	–
G. Boycott	9	17	2	818	104	54.53	1	7	2	–
P. Willey	7	13	5	383	102	47.87	1	2	–	–
G. Miller	4	7	3	151	91	37.75	–	1	4	–
R. O. Butcher	7	13	2	385	77	35.00	–	2	7	–
M. W. Gatting	5	9	0	268	94	29.77	–	2	3	–
C. W. J. Athey	4	8	0	121	41	15.12	–	–	1	–
I. T. Botham	8	14	0	197	40	14.07	–	–	8	–
B. C. Rose	3	5	0	69	43	13.80	–	–	–	–
D. L. Bairstow	4	7	2	64	26	12.80	–	–	9	1
R. D. Jackman	5	7	2	47	17	9.40	–	–	–	–
J. E. Emburey	7	10	2	74	34	9.25	–	–	3	–
P. R. Downton	6	9	1	67	26	8.37	–	–	11	3
G. R. Dilley	7	8	4	26	15	6.50	–	–	–	–
C. M. Old	4	4	0	13	3	3.25	–	–	5	–
G. B. Stevenson	4	4	0	6	3	1.50	–	–	–	–

BOWLING

	OVERS	MDNS	RUNS	WKTS	AVERAGE
G. Miller	109.2	29	299	14	21.35
R. D. Jackman	136.2	29	380	12	31.66
I. T. Botham	224.2	43	790	23	34.34
G. R. Dilley	212.2	44	733	20	36.65
G. B. Stevenson	88	16	337	9	37.44
J. E. Emburey	300.4	95	675	18	37.50
P. Willey	110	28	269	7	38.42
C. M. Old	62.3	14	208	5	41.60
G. A. Gooch	42	14	108	1	108.00

Also bowled: G. Boycott 3–2–5–0; M. W. Gatting 3–1–10–0

THE GLENEAGLES ACCORD

The member countries of the Commonwealth, embracing peoples of diverse races, colours, languages and faiths, have long recognized racial prejudice and discrimination as a dangerous sickness and an unmitigated evil and are pledged to use all their efforts to foster human dignity everywhere. At their London Meeting, the Heads of Government reaffirmed that apartheid in sports, as in other fields, is an abomination and runs directly counter to the Declaration of Commonwealth Principles which they made at Singapore on January 22, 1971.

They were conscious that sport is an important means of fostering understanding between the people, and especially between the young people, of all countries. But, they were also aware that, quite apart from other factors, sporting contacts between their nationals and the nationals of countries practising apartheid in sport tend to encourage the belief [however unwarranted] that they are prepared to condone this abhorrent policy or are less than totally committed to the Principles embodied in their Singapore Declaration.

Regretting past misunderstandings and difficulties and recognizing that these were partly the result of inadequate intergovernmental consultations, they agreed that they would seek to remedy this situation in the context of the increased level of understanding now achieved.

They reaffirmed their full support for the international campaign against apartheid and welcomed the efforts of the United Nations to reach universally accepted approaches to the question of sporting contacts with the framework of that campaign.

Mindful of these and other considerations, they accepted it as the urgent duty of each of their Governments to vigorously combat the evil of apartheid by withholding any form of support for, and by taking every practical step to discourage contact or competition by their nationals with sporting organizations, teams or sportsmen from South Africa or from any other country where sports are organized on the basis of race, colour or ethnic origin.

They fully acknowledged that it was for each Government to determine in accordance with its laws the methods by which it might best discharge these commitments. But they recognized that the effective fulfilment of their commitments was essential to the harmonious development of Commonwealth sport hereafter.

They acknowledged also that the full realization of their objectives involved the understanding, support and active participation of the nationals of their countries and of their national sporting organizations and authorities. As they drew a curtain across the past they issued a collective call for the understanding, support and participation with a view to ensuring that in this matter the peoples and Government of the Commonwealth might help to give a lead to the world.

Heads of Government specially welcomed the belief, unanimously expressed at their Meeting, that in the light of their consultations and accord there were unlikely to be future sporting contacts of any significance between Commonwealth countries or their nationals and South Africa while that country continues to pursue the detestable policy of apartheid. On that basis, and having regard to their commitments, they looked forward with satisfaction to the holding of the Commonwealth Games in Edmonton and to the continued strengthening of Commonwealth sport generally.

GLENEAGLES June 12, 1977

REVOCATION OF PERMIT

Under

Section 21(4)(b) of the Immigration Act

(Cap. 14:02)

TAKE NOTICE that on the direction of the President the

permit granted to you on 23rd February, 1981, to enter and

remain in Guyana for a period of two weeks is hereby revoked

with immediate effect.

....

J. Thome, Deputy Supt.
Immigration   Officer
26th February, 1981

To: Mr. Robin David Jackman,
     Pegasus Hotel,
     Georgetown.

Notice to quit: the deportation order which led to the cancellation of the second Test. Reproduced by kind permission of Robin Jackman.